INTRODUCTION TO MARKETING, ADVERTISING AND
PUBLIC RELATIONS

Macmillan International College Editions will bring to university, college, school and professional students, authoritative paperback books covering the history and cultures of the developing world, and the special aspects of its scientific, medical, technical, social and economic development. The International College programme contains many distinguished series in a wide range of disciplines, some titles being regionally biassed, others being more international. Library editions will usually be published simultaneously with the paperback editions. For full details of this list, please contact the publishers.

Other Related Titles

N.G. Nwokoye: *Modern Marketing for Nigeria*
S.Y. Lee and Y.C. Jao: *Financial Structures and Monetary Policies in Southeast Asia*
G.O. Nwankwo: *The Nigerian Financial System*

Introduction to Marketing, Advertising and Public Relations

FRANK JEFKINS

BSC(Econ), BA(Hons), FIPR, MCAM, MInstM, MAIE

M

First published 1982 by
THE MACMILLAN PRESS LTD
London and Basingstoke
Companies and representatives throughout the world.

Reprinted 1983

Typeset in IBM Press Roman by Thames Typesetting, Abingdon
Printed in Hong Kong

ISBN 0-333-32400-5
ISBN 0-333-32401-3 (pbk)

This book is dedicated to my wife Frances, my son John, and my daughter Valerie

Contents

PART THREE
PUBLIC RELATIONS

Part One

Marketing

1 What is Marketing?

EVOLUTION OF MARKETING

Marketing is a term which has been misused so you should be clear about its meaning right from the start. An American housewife will say she is going marketing when she is going shopping. In Britain, people who sold advertisement space for newspapers were once called space representatives: now it is fashionable to call them marketing executives.

In developing countries it is said by people such as Gordon Draper of the University of the West Indies that marketing does not exist; only selling and advertising exist in these countries. What Draper means is that imported or assembled goods are not *marketed*. However, the situation can be very different in Nigeria if imports are restricted, and indigenous production is encouraged, or if locally produced goods make it unnecessary to import. In Nigeria shoes can be made entirely of Nigerian raw materials by Nigerian workers and they have to be marketed.

But in an apparently sophisticated trade centre like Hong Kong there is little concept of marketing, partly because labour is cheap; partly because with so many shops and so many goods there is a buyer's market; and largely because the astute Chinese businessman thinks he does not need marketing techniques!

Marketing began with the industrial revolution in Europe, and Britain and France led this revolution. The German and Italian states were not then unified; America was colonised. With American independence and German unification, the USA and Germany adopted industrialisation. Associated with this development was population growth, urbanisation and the development of transportation and communication networks. Together they formed a social and economic pattern which made marketing possible. Before that there was only selling. All this happened in the eighteenth and nineteenth centuries. Marketing situations did not occur in developing countries until they gained independence in the latter half of the twentieth century.

MARKETING DEFINED

The first definition of marketing comes from Adam Smith who wrote in *The Wealth of Nations* — published in 1776 —

> Consumption is the sole end and purpose of all production and the interest of the producer ought to be attended to, only so far as it may be necessary for promoting that of the customer.

More recent definitions are:

> Marketing is producing and selling at a profit goods that satisfy customers (David Malbert, late City Editor, *Evening Standard*, London).

> Marketing is the management process responsible for identifying, anticipating and satisfying customer requirements profitably (Institute of Marketing, UK).

> Marketing is the set of human activities directed at facilitating and consummating exchanges (Philip Kotler, *Marketing Management*, USA).

With slightly different wording, these definitions confirm that marketing is concerned with what people want or need, and that it is a top management responsibility. A criticism of British management during the recession years of the late 1970s and early 1980s was that it failed to be marketing conscious. If that has been true of comparatively sophisticated management with a tradition of experience, what must be the situation in the underdeveloped nations?

Let us see how and why marketing has been adopted in industrial nations, and why it may have been less accepted or practised in other parts of the world. Perhaps there are special reasons for these contrasts?

WHY MARKETING REPLACED SELLING

The market-place and the shop are the familiar places for buying and selling goods. In some parts of Nigeria the days of the week used to be named as market days. In Europe, centuries ago, the old cities of what is now Holland and Belgium were the Marts to which English wool and later woollen cloth was taken to be sold. Markets tended to deal with products brought in from the countryside, shops with goods made by tradesmen such as shoemakers, hatters and clothiers.

The revolution came with machinery and water, steam and other power to drive it. Production capacity increased beyond possible sales to people living close by. At the same time the population was growing and the towns and cities were expanding. They were becoming linked by canals, roads and then railways. There were also improvements in communications such as postal services and newspapers, and eventually the telegraph, the telephone and the typewriter came about. All this took 500 years! The developing world is trying to do all this in mere decades, borrowing from the old world.

The new circumstances of *capacity to mass-produce* and *mass markets to consume,* of buyers *remote* from manufacturers, created the situation in which marketing became the opposite to face-to-face selling between producers and their customers. Marketing meant finding out what people wanted or needed and then, if this could be done profitably, producing, distributing and selling.

DIFFERENCE BETWEEN WANTS AND NEEDS

There is a difference between a *want* and a *need.* Wants are basically the economic ones of food, clothes and shelter. As society becomes more sophisticated, so do the wants. Needs, however, may be goods and services which can only be demanded once they are available, such as many of the new goods of today – colour television, hi-fi, convenience foods, and even air-conditioning.

CREATION OF NEW MARKETING TECHNIQUES

As mass-production, new products, and higher standards of living developed in the West, new marketing techniques were created. In the late 1930s in both Britain and the USA market research emerged. However, the Second World War put an end to marketing in Britain from 1939 until controls and rationing were withdrawn in the early 1950s. Thus, during those 10 years America made advances in marketing, and market research, which were impossible in Britain, but Britain quickly borrowed these techniques from 1950 on.

FROM COLONIALISM TO INDEPENDENCE

Most of the overseas trade between the West and its colonies was to do with the primary products — palm products, cocoa, sugar, cotton, tea, coffee, fruits, spices, minerals and so on. The ports and railway systems, even the roads and towns, were mostly created for the production, transit and export of these goods. Little thought was given to the internal infrastructure for the nationals.

Independence brought great changes, as has been seen in the reconstruction of cities like Accra, Nairobi and Lusaka. New ports like Tema were built. In Nigeria, port congestion has led to new port, dock and warehouse developments such as the 'instant harbour' at Tin Can Island, and other projects at Calabar, Warri, Sapele and Onne, plus a ₦360 million port development budget in the Fourth National Development Plan.

In the last two decades Nigeria especially has seen an economic reversal to the inflow of manufactured goods. However, payment for this inflow has required a new primary export; namely oil.

RELEVANCE OF MARKETING IN THE DEVELOPING WORLD

We begin to see the relevance of advertising, marketing and public relations in the new independencies. The emphasis on production and distribution has changed. As in the West, 100 or more years ago, popular mass media have emerged to provide communications. People have moved from the countryside to the towns. The supermarket has arrived. Roads, motor cars, lorries, domestic airlines and improved railway systems have been created. The fabric of a new social and economic order has been woven. This has been going on during the past 25 years — a very short time!

Where does marketing fit in?

In many independent developing countries marketing has hardly fitted in at all. Generally, it is confused with selling. Why is this?

Gordon Draper was right to a large extent. If marketing means producing and selling at a profit what people want, it excludes all those products which are imported, made under licence or assembled and then *sold* without any market research to discover whether anyone wants them! They are not marketed, only advertised and sold. Too often, products which have succeeded in the West are thrust upon developing countries as if they are bound to satisfy wants or needs. Buyers have to accept what they can get.

How many foreign motor cars really satisfy the drivers or the driving conditions in developing countries? There may be too little road clearance, inadequate suspension, poor cooling systems. A manufacturer may assume Africa is a hot country and think a heater unnecessary, yet the nights can be bitterly cold in central Africa. If marketing techniques were applied motor cars would be designed for markets, and production would not be difficult when there was local assembly. On the whole, the French and the Germans have done their overseas marketing better than the British, while the reliability of Japanese cars has been the supreme marketing exercise.

On the other hand, if an indigenous company plans to put a new product on the market it is most likely to succeed if it has first investigated the market to find out what is most likely to satisfy demand and to sell.

MARKETING PROBLEMS IN DEVELOPING COUNTRIES

Let us look at some of the complications and problems of marketing in developing countries.

1. *Elitist minorities*

In many countries there is a minority of well-to-do and middle-class people who form the educated, well-off, urban minority who are often 'Westernised'. In a country like India, with its vast millions, even this elitist minority can be reckoned in millions. In most developing countries elitists may not represent more than 20 per cent of the population.

The proportion of elitists depends on how densely populated the country is. The proportion could be higher in a Caribbean island like Trinidad or Barbados where the populations are small. But in a country like Kenya which, while not heavily populated, has many remotely located tribes; in Tanzania which is largely agricultural; or in Zambia which is a large country rather dependent on one mineral, copper, and urbanised along 'the line of rail' and in the copper belt, the proportion of intellectuals may not exceed 20 per cent.

Because they have enjoyed Western education, perhaps in Europe or the USA, speak a Western language such as English, French or Portuguese, and may still relate to the original colonial power, elitist minorities adopt Western living standards and culture. This may include foods, clothes, housing, motor cars and Western attitudes generally.

But as these countries become better educated, more people without Western experience will enter the cash economy, and they will tend to want more of the traditional things to which they are accustomed mingled with foreign goods which do enhance their living standards. Thus, in a country like Nigeria there could be an increased demand for beautiful and colourful national dress and less demand for London-made suits, coupled with a big demand for modern transport and household appliances. Strong beer, yes; French wines, no. Thus, the wants of people can be very mixed.

But going back to the general situation of an urban literate minority with Western tastes, there are the marketing problems that the vast majority of the people are poor and can buy only in very small quantitites, calling for somewhat uneconomic distribution, while the poorest people are subsistence farmers who seldom have any spending money.

2. *The population triangle*

The next major marketing problem is that the population triangle — that is, the number of people in different age groups from birth to death — is very different from that in the West. Western societies have ageing populations with more old people of increasingly greater age and fewer young people. In developing countries it is often true that 50 per cent of the population are under 15 years of age. That means that half the people have no income and are outside the market for most advertised goods.

So, between the poor rural dwellers and the young, there are millions of people who are outside the market and beyond the reach of advertising. The mass market does not exist as it does in the West where, for instance, the three-quarters of the population who read the popular press, watch TV and buy mass consumer goods are the *working class*. Whereas TV is an elitist medium in many developing countries (although battery sets and community viewing are popularising TV), it

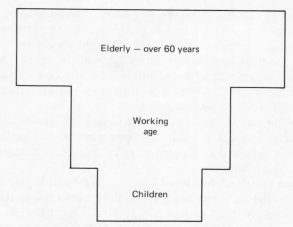

Fig. 1.1. Population triangle of Western country

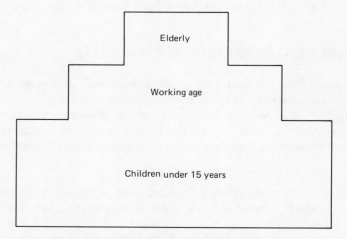

Fig. 1.2. Population triangle of developing country

is a mass medium in the West where it may be despised by the intelligentsia. The everyday purchases of the British, French, German, American, Canadian or Australian working class and lower middle class are the treasures of the elitist urban minority in cities like Lagos, Accra, Lusaka, Nairobi, Freetown, Port-of-Spain, Kuala Lumpur and Jakarta.

Few people in the West have ever heard a cigarette called a 'stick' because cigarettes are not sold singly. Even five-cigarette packs disappeared many years ago. Packets of detergent are giant or economy size, not the little packets seen on village stalls in Africa. The whole concept of buying and selling is different because cash values are different. Marketing in the West is typified by the magic letters FMCG, meaning fast-moving consumer goods.

One of the largest shops in Nigeria is Kingsway Stores in Lagos. You would hardly notice it in a British shopping centre. But neither would you find in Britain the shopping plaza complexes of Singapore. The scale of selling is different.

In Lagos there are streets and streets of shabby little market shops, and far into the night vendors squat on the pavements with their spluttering candles. A street market is a novelty in most English towns, a traffic-free shopping precinct the norm. Not for an Englishman the privilege of having a suit run up on the spot while you wait: he would have to wait six weeks and might never meet the tailor personally.

WHERE WESTERN MARKETING TECHNIQUES DO APPLY

Accepting that the marketing situation, experience and usage differs very much between the Western industrialised societies of Europe, North America, Australia and Japan and the developing countries of Africa, Asia, the Gulf, the Caribbean and South America, there are certain areas where Western-style marketing does apply. Some of these are:

1. The *export* of primary products such as foodstuffs, extractive products, timber and raw materials like cotton, silk, furs and skins.
2. The *export* of products which are traditional to particular countries such as textiles, jewellery, brass, copperware and silverware.
3. *Tourism*, provided there are good climatic, hotel, food and transport facilities. In this respect countries like Kenya and Zambia will score over Nigeria and Ghana, while the Caribbean will be blessed with many natural attractions; as will the East. In spite of its size, Nigeria has little to attract the tourist. With one or two exceptions – the Durbah in Kaduna – most Nigerian hotels are bad. Is this because the good hotels in other countries are run by

international experts with international standards?
4. *International airline services* which can compete with Western airlines, to quote only Thai International, Malaysian Airlines, Nigeria Airways, Singapore Airlines, Kenya Airlines, Air Zimbabwe, Air Jamaica and British West Indian Airways.

In some cases, e.g. India and Korea, new industries have been developed and machinery, watches, steel and ships may be sold abroad. In all these cases marketing techniques have to be applied in the overseas countries, for both promotional and competitive purposes. In these cases marketing is required on a world scale, using all the skills of public relations, advertising, government services, overseas trading agencies, trade fairs and other aids.

MARKETING APPLIED TO DEVELOPING COUNTRIES

However, while the same principles may apply we shall concentrate in this book on marketing, advertising and public relations as applied in developing countries where established techniques can be blended with the special needs, situations and conditions of these countries. They are becoming urbanised and industrialised but retain characteristics which seldom apply in the West such as multi-ethnic and multi-language circumstances together with problems of distance, poor communications, poverty and illiteracy.

A serious marketing problem in many parts of the developing world is lack of concern for the customer; in fact there is almost a basic contempt for people. Too much emphasis is placed on making money, too little on satisfying customers. On the other hand it is noticeable in the thousands of shops and restaurants in Hong Kong, where it is said you can see the dollars glittering in the eyes of the Chinese, the customer may expect courtesy and service. The 'service with a smile' and 'satisfaction guaranteed' aspects of British retailing could well be borrowed in some parts of the world. There is more to marketing than maximising profits.

PROBLEMS MET BY THE STUDENT

Three problems will be met by the student in a developing country, whether studying at home or overseas.

1. Marketing, advertising and public relations have their own special *jargon*. Many of the words used may even sound familiar, yet they will have special meanings when applied to these three subjects. Unless they are understood the examination student is liable to misread questions, as happened when an African candidate confused the blanket on his bed with the blanket used in offset-litho printing to offset the printing matter from the plate to the paper. The simple word 'plate' in the previous sentence is yet another word with an everyday meaning and one special to printing. This book will introduce readers to many words with special meanings.

2. English-speaking students may read both British and American textbooks, or study abroad in either Britain or America or, again, study under British or American lecturers in their home countries. There are many differences between British and American 'English'.

   Different words may be used for the same thing, e.g. movies and films, while the same word may have different meanings in the two countries. In America, 'billboard' is a *large* poster but in Britain it refers to a *small* poster displayed on a board as seen outside a shop. If the student is preparing for a British examination such as that of the Institute of Marketing; the Communication, Advertising and Marketing Education Foundation (CAM); or the London Chamber of Commerce and Industry (LCCI), it would be safer for him to read only British textbooks.

3. British examinations (with the exception of the LCCI) are biased towards British practice which is likely to be foreign to the experience of the student outside Britain. An advantage of the LCCI examinations in Marketing, Advertising and Public Relations is that questions are set which can be answered on the basis of local conditions.

The chapters in this book will discuss the principles and practice of the three subjects as they apply in Britain and then consider their relevance and application in developing countries, with examples from many parts of the developing world. Since Nigeria is the largest country in Africa, it will feature strongly, but as already shown in this introductory chapter, Africa is a continent of 50 countries, all of which are very different, and examples will be quoted from other African countries.

We shall also look at marketing, advertising and public relations in the Caribbean, the Gulf and Asia where the situations also vary tremendously. But, generally, we shall try to help the student outside the Western world to come to terms with these Western subjects in his own national situation. He may find that some Western techniques are relevant or irrelevant to his needs and situation, or that they have to be adapted rather than adopted, or that purely local techniques operate better. And if he is taking a British examination, this book will aim to help him if he is limited by his national experience and local conditions.

2 The Role of Marketing Management

Organisations tend to become more marketing-orientated as two situations arise:

1. Selling becomes more competitive.
2. Customers become more distanced from the producer.

In the first case more sophisticated promotional and communication methods are required, and in the second more information is required about the consumer, and a sales and distribution network is necessary. We have now moved beyond the more simple organisational situation of a sales manager and his sales staff. We have arrived at the point when marketing management is required which will act in conjunction with the production and financial functions of the business, all of which will be co-ordinated by the chief executive. This can be expressed as shown in Figure 2.1.

Fig. 2.1. Overall management relationships

Thus, the chief executive (managing director) will direct the activities of the production director (who plans and controls what is made), the marketing director (who advises on what should be made and how it shall be distributed), and the financial director (who is responsible for financial control). The marketing director will be seen as the vital link between production and finance. He has to maintain an information or intelligence system (based on research, sales reports and market intelligence) which will enable research and development and production to produce the right products at the right price at the right time. His information will also enable the financial director to raise funds and invest in the production, and anticipate a satisfactory return.

To explain this in further detail, bearing in mind that every company will have its own special variations, marketing management is responsible for:

1. Forecasting market wants or needs.
2. Discussing with production departments whether these wants or needs can be satisfied at a profit.
3. Planning the communication, promotional and distribution strategies which will best satisfy the market, and company policy, economically and profitably.

The marketing department is likely to consist of the sections shown in Figure 2.2, each headed by its own manager.

Fig. 2.2. Marketing department organisation

In the figure, public relations (PR) is positioned within the marketing department, but this is because this is so in some organisations, not that it is desirable, as will be discussed more fully in Part Three. What is more important here is to consider the role of PR in marketing. Marketing and PR have much in common, although in many marketing books PR is scarcely recognised while in America authors sometimes confuse it with 'publicity'. Yet marketing and PR are both to do with human relations and communication with people.

Whether or not a company's public relations officer (PRO) is located in the marketing department — ideally he should be independent, servicing all functions of a business and being answerable to the chief executive – the modern view is that the marketing director himself should be *PR-minded*. He can then apply PR philosophy so that all his actions and decisions are enhanced, as will be seen when we look at the marketing mix in the next chapter. The same can be said of top management, where the managing director should be the first PRO. This is, of course, to recognise that PR concerns the total communications of any organisation.

However, it has to be accepted that in many organisations only marketing has recognised the value of PR techniques, even if they are applied only in a limited way to the marketing operation. It also depends on the nature of the organisation: industrial companies which need to educate the market about technical products may rely more heavily on a PR department than a consumer company which makes greater use of advertising. These are matters we shall deal with more thoroughly in Parts Two and Three.

The three major sections of the marketing department are therefore *market research* to provide information about the market, *sales* to secure distribution through wholesalers and retailers, and *advertising* to promote products and services to consumers.

RANGE OF RESPONSIBILITIES

However, the marketing director and his team, in collaboration with those parts of the organisation which buy raw materials, produce the goods, pack them, and despatch or deliver them, have many responsibilities. As we shall see in the next chapter, the marketing mix (or strategy) begins with product planning and goes right through to the after-market of after-sales service and maintaining customer interest. Because of the need to take these activities in logical time sequence, that is from start to finish, we shall ignore the misleading four P's (Product, Place, Price, Promotion) concept. It is a timeless hotch-potch which has confused many students in the past by its oversimplification.

Before analysing the marketing mix, let us look briefly at the marketing director's links with other departments.

He will be concerned with the design of products to the extent of planning a product which will sell, and this will include the use or purchase of components, ingredients or raw materials. For instance, shall the case of, say, a clock be made of wood, metal, glass or plastic?

The question of costs, availability, attractiveness or customer preference will produce discussions between the marketing director and those
responsible for design, production and purchasing.

The question of production may lead to discussions on when the
product can be made, and when it will be available to the market. Products with seasonal demand may have long intervals between design,
selling, production and delivery, but all these stages must be co-
ordinated. A Christmas gift product could be designed 18 months
before it was bought by the final purchaser, samples would be available
a few months later, orders would be taken, products would be made,
delivery to shops would take place, and they would be on sale in time
for the Christmas market. This sort of planning is a good example of
the time-scheduling which is essential to good marketing. The pattern
might be as follows:

Market research	– July
Product design	– September
Samples ready	– January
Trade exhibition	– February
Selling to trade	– February–March
Production	– April–July
Delivery	– August
On sale	– September–December

In the motor-car industry two or three years might be spent on designing and testing the new model, then the factory would be set up for
production, and the date for introduction of the new model would be
chosen to replace the old model when its sales had fallen below an unprofitable level. This follows the leapfrog effect product life cycle
which will be discussed in the next chapter with other forms of product
life cycle.

Packaging is very much the marketing director's concern. It is not
only a means of containing and protecting the product but it is the first
form of advertising. This will call for liaison with those in production
who are responsible for filling, packing and preparing goods for despatch. From this will follow liaison with those responsible for warehousing, despatch and delivery.

Transportation could affect the efficiency of marketing. In Western
countries blessed with networks of canals, rivers, roads, tunnels, railways, airways, postal and parcel delivery services, there are no transport

problems. But in countries with poor transport the marketing director is badly handicapped.

A country with no coast, like Zambia, relies on railways but wars in neighbouring countries have made it difficult to ship copper and cobalt or to receive imports. The Chinese-built Tanzara Railway has proved disappointing. Breakdowns on the 1860 km line, and congestion in the Tanzanian part of Dar-es-Salaam, have made this outlet a disappointment.

In the Sudan a very different problem was that the railways could not carry enough bales of cotton to port before the rains came and the boll weevil attacked. A solution was to treat the untransported bales of cotton with insecticidal gas.

Nigeria has problems of more goods, increasing traffic but bad roads made dangerous by storms, floods, rutted and holed surfaces. The side of the highway north to Kano is littered with burnt-out vehicles, mostly tankers. In 1980 the railway was washed away at Ibadan during a storm. However, improved railways, and the transit of containers from the ports to the north, have brought modern transport to Nigeria.

From all this it will be clear that the marketing director has to work closely with all sections of a business and be a sound businessman himself. He will also need the support of the financial director, to justify investment in his projects, and be accountable for the financial results of the marketing operation.

3 Introduction to the Marketing Mix

The marketing mix, or strategy, provides a logical way of understanding the range of marketing activities. The marketing mix will be different for different products or services, so here we shall look at all the elements from which a selection could be made for a particular mix. Sometimes the whole range of elements may be used. Each will be described in this chapter, and most of them will be discussed in greater detail in succeeding chapters. Advertising and public relations (PR) have their separate parts.

However, PR – being a bigger subject than either advertising or marketing – should be considered in two ways. Since PR concerns the total communications of any organisation, commercial or non-commercial, and whether or not the organisation engages in marketing or advertising, it follows that PR is not *part* of the marketing mix. It is involved in every aspect of the marketing mix. Since the marketing director is constantly involved in human relations and communications he needs to be PR-minded. That is the first way in which PR should be considered. The second way has to do with the special communications activities and techniques of the PR specialist, whether he be a PRO employed by the company, or an outside PR consultant who advises the company and carries out PR work for it.

ELEMENTS OF THE MARKETING MIX

The easiest way to analyse the marketing mix is to adopt a step-by-step method of discussing the elements as they happen. This is more logical than the '4 P's' division of the marketing mix into Product, Place, Price and Promotion which does not suggest any time sequence. We begin with the creation of the product and go through all the stages until the product is sold. After that, we look at the marketing director's responsibilities *after* the product has been sold.

Instead of looking at PR as a single element like advertising, or merely as 'publicity', we recognise four aspects of PR throughout the mix. First, there is feedback or information flowing in or obtained about consumer wishes, complaints or attitudes. Second, there are many forms of marketing communications such as the product name, labelling, instructions and advertising. Third, there is education of the market so that advertising will work. Fourth, there is the need to avoid creating bad feeling because the product is faulty, advertising is exaggerated, or distribution and after-sales services are poor. These are all aspects of public relations philosophy which apply to the marketing director's handling of many parts of the total marketing strategy.

The marketing mix can be analysed under the following 20 headings:

1. Conception, innovation or modification of new products.
2. The place of the product in the product life cycle.
3. Marketing research.
4. Naming and branding.
5. Product image.
6. Market segment.
7. Pricing.
8. Product mix, rationalisation and standardisation.
9. Packaging.
10. Distribution.
11. Sales force.
12. Market education.
13. Corporate and financial PR.
14. Industrial relations.
15. Test marketing.
16. Advertising.
17. Advertising research.
18. Sales promotion and merchandising.
19. The after market: after-sales service, spares, guarantees, instructions.
20. Maintaining customer interest and loyalty.

In this chapter we will concentrate on the first element which involves two important preliminary steps in planning the marketing strategy. First we have to consider customer behaviour, and second we have to decide on the product or service which can be marketed most successfully.

ENVIRONMENT AND THE MIX

There is always the danger that the marketing strategy may fail because it is planned to suit ideal circumstances; but recognition is necessary of outside forces which may interfere with an ideal marketing situation.

What are the *political* or *legal* constraints? Is there government policy or legislation which may affect the marketing plan? There may be import quotas, or proposed export markets may be restricted by Government decree. There may be a policy to produce only certain goods. Some products may not be permitted on commercial TV when this would be the ideal medium, e.g. cigarettes in Britain. The product may contain a certain ingredient which is banned, or which requires that the product is sold only through certain outlets such as chemists. At one time, starch products were banned from foods in Europe, simply because they were wrongly listed as chemicals instead of as foods, and new legislation had to be passed to change this so that the ingredient could be used in soups, sauces and salad cream.

There may be Government Commissions which are carrying out investigations (e.g. Monopolies Commission in Britain), or Government White Papers which make recommendations which have to be observed. For instance, certain poisons may not be used in insecticides in certain countries, the tar content of cigarettes may have to be declared, breakfast cereals may have to possess a certain nutritional value, motor-cars may have to possess certain safety standards, and some clothes may have to be made of non-inflammable material.

Are there any *economic* constraints such as unemployment; low or high wages; trade union activities; housing shortages or housing booms; high or low interest rates; restrictions on loans, overdrafts or mortgages which may depress or encourage the market?

What about the *psychological* influences? Are people prejudiced about the product, fearful of it, or misled by misconceptions? Nuclear power worries some people. Others fear that gas is an explosive and dangerous fuel. Some foods are feared as being fattening and likely to lead to heart disease. There are still millions of people in developing countries who are as scared of flying as Europeans were of travelling by train a century-and-a-half ago. Foreign multi-nationals arouse fears in the Third World, especially American ones. In some South East and Far East countries Japanese cars evoked war-time hatreds, and they were actually burned in the streets of Jakarta.

Ethnic attitudes can arouse further constraints, as the beer industry has found in Moslem countries. While Pakistan has banned brewing and drink advertisements have been banned in Egypt, beer sales have boomed in Northern Nigeria, so Moslem attitudes can vary from country to country. Questions of product names and colours may also be the subject of ethnic considerations. Ethnic attitudes to dress are important too. Immodest dress may be frowned upon, and offence may be caused if one used the sort of advertising seen in Britain for ladies' tights, which reveals not just the legs but the thighs and buttocks.

It is necessary, therefore, to consider what is known as the 'negotiated environment', that is the environment in which it is possible to market successfully.

CONSUMER BEHAVIOUR

Why do people buy? In a developing country the basic economic needs of food, clothing and shelter will dominate. As a society develops, as people earn more money and have greater spending power, they will buy for pleasure and also to impress other people. In Nigeria the growth of breweries in recent decades has shown the shift from drinking palm wine to beer as a sign of growing prosperity. This is one way of satisfying pleasure. Purchase of a motor-car symbolises status.

Money in excess of that required for the necessities of life is called *'disposable income'*. Since this may be the smallest part of a person's income he has to choose carefully and there is great competition for his choice. 'Opportunity cost' occurs here: one can choose between buying, perhaps, either a camera or a holiday but not both.

Maslow's hierarchy of needs is worth quoting. He has set out three primary and two secondary needs which influence buying behaviour, these being:

(*a*) basic physiological needs – the ones which affect bodily comfort and are close to the basic economic needs mentioned above;

(*b*) safety needs –man's instinctive desire to protect himself from danger;

(*c*) the need for recognition –to be loved and to be accepted by society;

(d) ego-satisfying needs – which produce self-esteem;

(e) self-fulfilment needs – satisfying ambitions and personal development.

Thus we have a combination of needs which satisfy the *physical* needs of maintaining life, the *psychological* needs which are to do with pleasure, and the *sociological* needs which concern relations with other people.

In planning and marketing a product or service it is necessary to decide whether, to be successful, it should satisfy one or more of these essential human needs.

A food may satisfy (a) above, a mosquito killer (b), a gift (c), a charitable contribution (d), and a correspondence course (e).

Two services which are being marketed increasingly in developing countries are banking and insurance. Both can be shown to provide safety and also, to some extent, self-esteem. It is not only the wealthy who need banking services and insurance policies. A marketing problem, requiring marketing education, is how does the marketing director convince farmers that a bank is honest and reliable, and that if money is hidden in the mattress it could all be lost in a fire? This is a typical marketing exercise in West Africa and elsewhere.

Similarly, there can be great suspicion of insurance services, yet as people acquire personal possessions and family responsibilities they need such protection. Marketing can be seen as a means of resolving conflicts between fear of loss and fear of untrustworthy services. To millions of people in developing countries, banking and insurance are new and sometimes frightening concepts.

PRODUCT PLANNING

Some products or services are totally new, as air-conditioning, air travel, hi-fi, computers and calculators have been in recent decades. Others are innovations – that is, improvements upon older ones. Most things today are innovations, and the planning of a product may be to offer something more efficient such as a small car which is easier to drive and park in congested cities, and which uses less petrol since the cost of petrol keeps rising.

In a developing country an innovation may be to make a Western-style product more acceptable in a different market. For instance,

Nigerian Guinness is much stronger than British or Irish Guinness. In some parts of Asia, television sets operate from 6-volt car batteries which overcome the lack of electricity.

Product planning will require decisions on:

1. economical products;
2. market segments;
3. the product mix.

Economical products are those which can be made with existing resources of production, staff, sales force and distribution network, or are made with the economical uses of new investment in production, staff and an extended sales network, if possible using the same distributors. The latter point can be critical. A new food product can be introduced because it can be sold by the same or a larger sales force to the same wholesalers and retailers and sold to the same consumers. An example is the Coca-Cola Company introducing Fanta and Sprite, using the same bottlers. But if such a company diversified into selling shirts or toothbrushes it would need different salesmen selling to different distributors, which could be uneconomical.

Market segments are the sections of the market for which the product is aimed. Thus Mercedes-Benz and Datsun aim at different segments; say, company directors and taxi-drivers. The same thing could apply to everyday products. For instance, Bata shoes serve a fairly popular segment. Newspapers serve different market segments or readerships, to name only *The Financial Times*, *The Punch* and *National Concord* in Nigeria.

One way of planning a new product is to design one which will satisfy a group of customers (a market segment) which is not already satisfied. For instance, the Japanese succeeded in popularising the motor-cycle by producing lower-powered machines than those usually built by British firms. Ready markets were found not only in Britain but in developing countries such as Nigeria.

The product mix means the range of products or services offered. There may be different models (as with motor-cars) or flavours (as with food-stuffs) or colours (as with paints). Or there could be a range of prices or qualities to suit people with more or less money. Again, there could be a mix of complementary products as with hi-fi, sports equipment, clothing, cameras and accessories, or computers and software.

Rationalisation and standardisation are two important aspects of the product mix. There is said to be *proliferation* when there are too many choices available, and this may lead to *rationalisation.*

By *rationalisation* we mean producing the smallest number of profitable lines. The consumer may prefer a large variety of, say, flavours, colours, sizes or weights. Usually some of these choices are more popular than others and it will be an economic decision to produce and sell only those which promise to make the most profit. Or, because of the goodwill involved, it may pay to offer as wide a range of choices as possible.

Some products may sell simply because there are many varieties to choose from, many food products falling into this category. A restaurant may be popular because of its extensive menu. A market stall may attract customers because it displays so many fruits, designs of cloth, or classes of leather goods. A supermarket is an obvious example of a shop which succeeds because of its wide variety of goods. But an industrial company may find that it is more profitable to concentrate on a limited range of machines which sell well.

Standardisation means the use of uniform products which can be used in many ways or to fit various makes of goods. The most common example is the nut and bolt made in standard sizes which can be tightened with a standard spanner. Other examples are electric-light bulbs of any make which fit any lamp-holder, batteries which fit any battery-operated equipment, tyres for every make of car, or films which fit every camera. A product is more easily sold if standard refills or replacements can be bought. Some ball-point pens can be disappointing if refills are not obtainable.

Product planning may have less significance in developing countries, and the marketing mix may seem rather theoretical, but these concepts are necessary as the trend towards indigenous products gains pace. Where the policy is merely to assemble the parts of a foreign product, import ready-packed products, or import foreign products to pack for re-sale, the development of new products is non-existent.

Consequently, the colour, package, name and other foreign characteristics come with the product or licence to make it locally, and there is no original product philosophy based on the actual local market. Moreover, there is probably no test marketing to perceive what the market really needs and prefers. Much of the so-called marketing is therefore imposed from abroad. As a result, product orientation prevails, not market orientation, and the product is sold instead of the market being supplied. There is a conceit that because a product is successful in the West it must be equally desirable in the Third World.

PRODUCT IMAGE

The word 'image' will appear several times in this book, especially in
the section on PR, where the basic definition is 'a clear idea or impression' of a subject. This cannot be invented.

In marketing, however, and particularly in advertising, we speak of
the *product image,* and this has its own special meaning. The product
image is the idea people have of a product, and it may be one created
by advertising. For example, a pen may be a very good one but not
necessarily any better than any other good pen. However, if the pen can
be established as a rather special gift it can be sold at a higher price.
People will give it because it is expensive, and people will be proud to
receive it because it is known to be expensive. Yet all it does is write,
and perhaps no better than something much cheaper.

Similarly, some products have an image of being cheap or economical, reliable, safe, well-finished, rust-proof, backed up by good after-
sales service, or guaranteed. The *product image* is therefore its character, and it can be a vital part of the marketing strategy to establish a
worthwhile product image which will both distinguish and help to sell
the product.

FINDING NEW PRODUCTS

The task of finding new products is a big responsibility of a marketing
director. He has to avoid the mistake of continuing to market the same
products which may become unpopular or unfashionable. Sometimes
it is necessary to give an old product a 'facelift' to maintain sales.

This may be a simple change in the outward appearance although
the basic product remains unchanged. But it could be better to bring in
new lines and drop old ones. There are, of course, products such as
matches which do not change; but razors and razor blades have seen
many changes in recent years, mainly because of competition between
wet shaving and electric razors and between rival manufacturers like
Gillette and Wilkinson. Similarly, brewers bring out new beers, and in
recent years the different brewers in Nigeria have produced many new
beers.

Marketers in developing countries should learn from the experiences
of Western marketers who have found that 80 per cent of new products
have failed to sell. Test marketing – which is used very little in develop-

ing countries — could prevent losses on new products. It may be difficult to test-market, for reasons which will be dealt with in the chapter on marketing research. Even so, it is usually possible to get opinions on a new product before investing money in production and marketing programmes. Samples can be given to people to try out, or demonstrations can be given at exhibitions, and those taking part can be asked to state their opinions. There is nothing worse than believing a product will succeed, only to find out to one's cost that no-one will buy it.

However, if the product is entirely new it may be necessary to apply the *innovator* or diffusion method. This requires acceptance of a new product by an imaginative and influential person who will encourage others to adopt his advice. This method is an old one which has been used the world over and has been applied particularly in farming. One farmer will adopt a new machine and other farmers will be invited to see a demonstration on the innovator's farm.

The method can be applied to many other products, and has even been applied to family planning. In rural communities the innovator may be the king, oba, emir, headman or other social leader upon whose recommendation the local community will rely. The system is explained by the Everett Rogers model shown in Figure 3.1, which demonstrates the average percentage of people who may fill the succeeding categories of adopters.

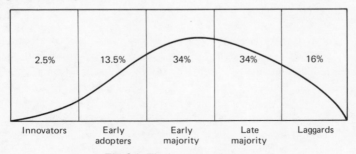

Fig. 3.1. The innovator theory

The value of this model is that it indicates the rate at which people may adopt a new idea or product, the laggards being the more reluctant or conservative people who are slow to become convinced and persuaded. This could be represented over a time scale to show how sales and promotional efforts have to be spread over a period of time to achieve penetration of the market, break-even and profit. *Penetration of the market* means reaching a target number of customers or a target volume of sales.

New products may be found by a variety of means such as:

1. *Research and development* into new product ideas, improved products, use of new materials and new production methods.
2. *Ideas from the trade or customer* which may be submitted to the company.
3. *Marketing research* to discover people's preferences and market needs.
4. *Salesmen's reports* on market needs.
5. *Study of foreign products* to see whether something similar can be designed or adapted to suit the local market.
6. *Study of literature* such as international trade and technical journals and research reports which may suggest ideas for products that can be developed locally. Perhaps they can be imported under an agency agreement or produced under license.
7. *Study of rival products* to see whether other companies have types of products which the company should also make, perhaps in different or improved forms.

4 The Product Life Cycle

Many products and services come and go over a period of time, and this may also apply to product groups, that is, a number of similar products. It is helpful to the marketing director to know (*a*) the point in the product life cycle (PLC) reached by an existing product; (*b*) the likely time span of a proposed new product; and, very important, the type of PLC which applies to his product.

The standard product life cycle is represented by the model shown in Figure 4.1. In this model there are six stages. After *development*, the

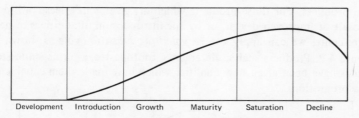

Fig. 4.1. The standard product life cycle

product will be launched on the market, and at the *introductory* stage investment will be necessary in production, selling, distribution and advertising. It may be necessary to buy one's way into the market, that is making no profit – probably a loss – for the time being until the product is established. For a product requiring much research, such as a medicine, it may take a long time to recover research costs. For this reason the product may be high-priced at first, or money may have to be spent on heavy promotion, on very good trade terms to dealers, or on special offers to customers.

The *growth* or take-off stage is when the product succeeds and there is a rapid build-up of sales. *Maturity* occurs when target sales have been achieved, and *saturation* takes place when no further sales are possible. After that — possibly because the product has lost its appeal or has been superseded by a rival and better product, sales fall and the product enters the decline stage. Eventually, because it is unprofitable to go on, production ceases and the product is withdrawn.

For different products there will be different time scales. A motor-car may last 10 years, a fashion or novelty product may survive for only a year or a few months. There are certain products which do not comply exactly to this standard PLC. They may never decline, and they may have ups and downs over a very long period of time. Coal is a typical example with a PLC extending over some 2000 years, with a revival in recent years as the energy crisis has necessitated the sinking of new pits, while China has become a coal-exporting country. Copper has a very long history going back to the Palestine of Biblical times; but skateboards, mini-skirts, certain ladies' hairstyles and some brands of cigarettes have suffered comparatively brief life cycles.

However, the standard PLC does not apply to all products or life cycles and the following three variations may be better models for certain products. For those products which are given a new lease of life as a result of improved design, or by the introduction of additives or new ingredients, we can apply the *recycled product life cycle* as shown in Figure 4.2. Products such as detergents, toothpastes, aspirins, and razor blades have been given new qualities which have made them capable of new promotion.

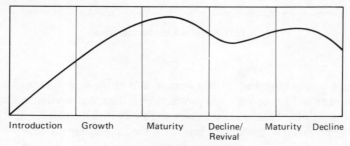

Fig. 4.2. Recycled product life cycle

The *leapfrog effect PLC* applies to products which are replaced by new models such as motor-cars, motor-cycles, domestic appliances, cameras and hi-fi equipment. The model is depicted in Figure 4.3.

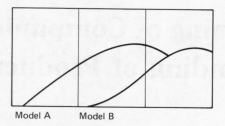

Model A   Model B

Fig. 4.3. Leapfrog effect product life cycle

Then there is the *staircase effect PLC*, one which provides the marketing director with the need to develop a series of marketing programmes for each step of a life cycle which never suffers a decline. This model can be applied to products and services whose life is extended by new uses or changes. A good example is shipping, which has progressed through many stages such as passenger ship, mail ship, cruise ship, container ship, bulk carrier and car ferry. The model is shown in Figure 4.4. Market use in this model could mean that new market uses are found for a product. Nylon is a good example with its uses for ladies' stockings, textiles, parachutes, fishing nets, rope and more recently wheels for motor-cycles.

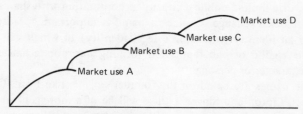

Fig. 4.4. Staircase effect product life cycle

5 Naming of Companies and Branding of Products

The careful naming of a company, or a brand of product, or a line of products bearing the same brand, is one of the most important forms of marketing communication. Three kinds of naming are mentioned and each is different and should be clearly understood.

COMPANY NAME

This is the name of the trading organisation, whether it be an individual using a business name, a partnership, a private company with share-holders, or a limited public company or corporation with shares quoted on the stock exchange. Choice of name is important because it will become an identity (including a legal identity) to which will become attached a good or bad reputation forming a corporate image. It will have a character or personality.

Some names are based on the founder's name, like Ford, Cadbury, Guinness, Lipton and Singer. Others will be of a more general but per-haps imposing nature such as Premier, National, Nigerian, Honest, Perfect or Marvellous. And others may be based on the product as in the case of Coca-Cola, or mention the service such as China Bus Company. Banks and insurance companies combine a significant name with service, for example First Bank of Nigeria or Hong Kong and Shanghai Banking Corporation. And already, company names have been quoted which have geographical place names.

A modern tendency has been to use either the initials of a full name, like IBM, NEPA and UAC, or to form words or acronyms based on the initials of the company, such as Esso, Fiat and Sabena. Long and diffi-cult names such as Tokyo Shibaura Electrical Company are reduced to the more manageable name of Toshiba. The Royal Dutch Airlines have

a long name in the Dutch language, but the airline has been readily recognised as KLM for more than 50 years.

The names of long-established organisations may have been chosen
haphazardly or for personal reasons, long before marketing considerations demanded more careful choice of names. Also, today, one is
less able to choose any name because it may already exist. In most
countries business names have to be registered under company law.
Some names may not be accepted or, if it is a common name, it will
have to be made more distinctive by including the name of the place
where the company has its registered or head office.

BRAND NAMES

These are the specially devised names used to distinguish products.
They may also be company names, like Heinz, Guinness, Star or Sanyo
but they can be quite different names of which Daz, Omo, Ultrabrite,
Lux, Marlboro, Sprite, Elephant or Lion are good examples. Such
names are usually registered, and if designed in a distinctive way brand
names of all types can be registered as trade marks.

Both names designed in a distinctive way, and original symbols, can
be registered as trade marks, and this is the case of both the name of
Guinness in a type face resembling Bodoni and the Irish harp symbol
being drawn in a special way to qualify for registration. These examples
may be observed on a Guinness bottle label, although in Indonesia a cat
symbol is used.

TRADE NAMES

Unregistered names are usually called *trade names,* and this term should
not be confused with business names. Trade names consist of names
given to types or ranges of products. The Ford Motor Company Ltd is a
registered name, and the written name in an oval shape is a trade mark,
but the names given to Ford cars such as Escort, Fiesta, Cortina and
Granada are trade names. It is interesting that Granada Television in
Britain failed at law to prevent Ford from using the name Granada.

Confusion can be caused if there is too great a variety of names.
Sometimes the proprietary name is not emphasised, and the brand is
allowed to sell on its own merits and reputation. On the other hand

some companies will exploit the reputation of the company name when promoting products, especially new ones. The 'halo effect' operates, the new product benefiting from the already established good name of the manufacturer or his earlier or other products. Cadbury's will do this, but sometimes you have to look at the small print on a package to see who is the maker.

An example of the presence of three names is the British product Gold (a spread which competes with butter and margarine) whose pack carried the St Ivel badge, long established among dairy products, plus the manufacturer's name, Unigate (a vast dairy and food products company). However, Unigate has been dropped in favour of St. Ivel Ltd.

Obviously, company policies will differ and the marketing director will have to make naming decisions accordingly, but he should endeavour to influence company policy in the interests of good market communication.

In the above analysis, reference has been made to company name (singular), but brands, trade marks and trade names (plural).

LOGOTYPES AND CORPORATE IDENTITY

Associated with company names and brand names are also *logotypes* — symbols or badges of distinctive design — which help to create easy recognition. This may be the sort of special typography used by ITT, or a written name like Coca-Cola, or a distinguishing form like the maple leaf on the tail of an Air Canada airliner. Such designs may form part of a complete house style or corporate identity which is used on company vehicles, uniforms, stationery and print, packaging, advertising, and on many other items such as ashtrays, ties, cuff-links and so forth.

From these opening remarks on forms of business naming it will be seen that this is not only a valuable part of the marketing mix but, since it is to do with communication and the creation of knowledge and understanding, it has distinct PR implications.

ESSENTIALS OF GOOD NAMES

When deciding on a name, and sometimes it may be desirable to change a name, the following essentials should be considered:

1. *Is it distinctive?* Does it have individuality? Is it sufficiently different from others in the same field?
2. *Does it lend itself easily to display* and use in advertising? Short names can be printed larger than long ones.
3. *Is it easy to say?* Names which can be said in different ways or are difficult to pronounce can be misleading. The German car Audi should be pronounced *Owdy* but people outside Europe tend to call it *Ordy*. The German composer Wagner is pronounced *Vargner* but the American actor Robert Wagner is known as *Wagner.*

   In countries like Nigeria vowels are soft whereas in Europe they are hard, and Ife would be pronounced as in knife, Kano would be pronounced as in cane, and Ibadan would be given a long or hard middle 'a' as in hard. Consequently, in naming a product one needs to be careful about possible mispronunciations. The examples from Nigeria could be important when marketing tourist, airline or freight services. It cannot be assumed that strangers will pronounce words in the same way.

   An amusing example of mispronunciation which the author has noticed when listening to Nigerian broadcasters is the word *corps*. The word is pronounced 'core', but Nigerian newsreaders refer to 'corpse', which is a dead body.
4. *Is it easy to remember?* Even more important is whether the name sticks in the memory so that customers remember to ask for the right company or brand. Easily remembered names are often ones which contain the vowels 'a', 'e', 'i', 'o' in two or three syllables. Well-known examples are Omo, Oxo, Coca-Cola (a pair of twin syllables), Rentokil, Yamaha and Heineken.

PERMANENCY OF A NAME

When conceiving a name it has to be one which will last. It takes time and money to establish a name, and it is therefore foolish to change it except for a very good reason. However, a change may be necessary. There may be an amalgamation of companies, or a name may have outlived its usefulness or no longer be meaningful. There could be political reasons for change. This could be a good thing, but it may confuse people, and they may have less faith in the new name, thinking it represents something inferior.

Let us consider some difficult and some successful changes of name.

When colonialism ceased and independent countries adopted new names these may have satisfied national pride, but the rest of the world often had difficulty in identifying them geographically. Some countries reverted to old names or based them on, say, local rivers. Over the years, Ghana, Malawi, Lesotho, Tanzania and Zimbabwe have emerged. In other parts of the globe we now have Gabon, Kampuchea, Kiribati, Namibia, Tuvalo, and Vanuato. All these new names have taken time, or are taking time, to establish themselves in the outside world. Name-changing can be very perplexing for outsiders.

The motor company of Hillman became Rootes, then Chrysler, and finally Talbot, with inevitable marketing problems of identity. Morris (and other motor companies) went through the changes of BMC, British Leyland and now BL, a somewhat unhappy procession of names.

On the other hand, when the two banks National Provincial and Westminster combined to be known briefly as Nat-West, this was a happy innovation.

When a company name gains a popular version, e.g. Marks and Sparks for Marks and Spencer, Bee-wee for British West India Airways, or Black Cat (in Indonesia where the Guinness label carries a black cat instead of an Irish harp), this can provide helpful and often friendly recognition. In Nigeria, Guinness is better known as *odeku* after the fat man in Guinness advertisements.

Some twenty companies with difficult names existed under the holding company of the founder business, British Ratin, until the best known name (because it sold retail products while the others were servicing companies) was adopted, and Rentokil became the single name for the group.

When the interests of the United Africa Company became more international it became sensible to re-name this large organisation UAC International without losing its identity in West Africa.

S. Smith & Son (London) Ltd, originally the name of a firm of watchmakers, became more meaningful as Smiths Industries Ltd, since the company had developed into many product areas. But the basic name was not lost.

In Nigeria the Standard Bank became the First Bank of Nigeria, an attractive change of name since Standard was in fact the first bank to be set up in Nigeria. However, when Barclays Bank in Trinidad became the Republic Bank there was a less easy transformation because it sounded like an entirely new bank.

The marketing (and public relations) implication of a name is therefore very important. In developing countries there may be special reasons for choosing a name. Importance may be attached to using the name of the country in the business name, perhaps to disassociate it from any foreign involvement. But in some developing countries there may be the dilemma that people may have so little faith in local products or services that Western names are deliberately adopted to create confidence!

In countries where there are different ethnic groups it will be necessary to avoid names which cause offence. Victory cigarettes was not a tactful name in Nigeria after the civil war of the 1960s. The Japanese car names Cherry and Laurel sound odd in the West where car names usually suggest power or prestige.

The meanings or inferences of names may vary over time. Rentokil, some 50 years ago, was conceived by an entomologist for a product designed to kill wood-boring insects. Thus to 'ento' was added 'kil', and for purposes of registration the 'R' was placed in front. Today, there are many names like Rent-a-car and people interpret the name Rentokil to mean rent a killing service for pest control.

6 Packaging, Labelling, Containers and Materials

A good package or container is a major aid to successful marketing. The essentials of a good package are:

1. That it *distinguishes* the product, especially when there are many rival brands, making it easily identifiable.
2. That it *protects* the product. This is important in countries where there may be conditions of heat, damp or dust which could quickly harm the contents. Cans may be necessary instead of paper or cardboard wrappings.
3. That it is *convenient* to the customer, that is, easy to use and perhaps re-use, or to carry or handle. Pails of detergents are popular in the Third World. It should also be convenient for transporting and warehousing, and stocking by wholesalers and retailers.
4. That it is *cheap to transport,* and lightness could be a big factor as when press-out pharmaceuticals are produced in tablet rather than liquid form and are packed in blister packs instead of bottles.
5. That it contributes to good *display* and *advertising* purposes.
6. That it is *characteristic* of the product, the sort of package people will expect, although this does not rule out original packages which satisfy other essentials.
7. That it is *quickly associated* with other products made by the same company, having a family resemblance, and maintaining corporate identity.

FACTORS AFFECTING PACKAGING

In addition to the above considerations, there may be special features which the marketing director may have to study when adopting a packaging policy, these being: costs, materials, forms, colours, and instructions.

Costs

Packaging is a distributive cost, and the costs will need to be controlled. It is obviously cheaper to pack tobacco in a foil pouch than in a metal tin. But whereas milk can be packed in a waxed paper container, wine cannot, although when it was proposed to put milk in disposable plastic bottles there were such protests from conservationists that the idea was dropped. Schweppes did use non-returnable plastic bottles for soft drinks, but protests led to a return to glass bottles. The use of non-returnable bottles saves the cost of collection, return and washing for re-use.

However, use of an expensive pack may be psychologically good for a product which is bought as a gift, the package impressing and pleasing the receiver. Examples of this can be seen with items like the better ball-point pens which are packed in presentation cases, perfumes, cutlery, chocolate and other things which are primarily gifts.

Costly packaging may be necessary because the product is fragile and needs protection — biscuits for example — while shirts are often placed in boxes with plastic windows which not only keep the product clean but enhance its display value. Japanese motor-car manufacturers have been commended on the way they pack even simple things like nuts and bolts in plastic bags. The use of expanded polystyrene to protect breakable products, whether electronic goods or china ornaments, is a means of making it possible to send such sensitive products by post. Packaging therefore calls for considerable thoughtfulness. It may be made possible to market some products because they are packed in a certain way.

Materials

Already we have touched on the materials in which goods are packaged. We have to remember that the package may consist of one or more elements, the container itself, a label on the container, and sometimes an outer container such as a box or carton. Among the materials which may be used for different products are:

1. Glass, as with beer bottles.
2. Plastics, as with cosmetics bottles.

3. Wood, as with boxes or chests.
4. Paper, as with biscuits.
5. Cardboard, as with chocolate boxes.
6. Metal foil, as with individual sweets.
7. Metal, as with tinned foodstuffs.
8. Cellophane, as with protective outer wrappings.

Forms

Packages may take many forms and part of the marketing strategy may be to present the product in an attractive or convenient package. We have already mentioned the advantage of medicine marketed in small tablet form, instead of being in a liquid state, so that it can be packed conveniently in a lightweight press-out blister pack. Here are some different forms of package:

1. Cardboard boxes, as used for matches, chocolates, shirts.
2. Cardboard tubs with metal or plastic lids, as used for aspirins.
3. Metal cans as used for drinks, butter, fish, vegetables and many foodstuffs, but also for liquids such as oil and paint.
4. Sachets (usually containing a measured quantity for single use) as with shampoos, soups, garden insecticides.
5. Paper packets as used for seeds.
6. Plastic bubble packs in which products such as screws are visible.
7. Bottles and jars as used for drinks and foodstuffs.
8. Plastic bottles for liquids including perfumes, shampoos, drinks.
9. Tubes – metal or plastic – as used for toothpaste, shaving cream, lotions and convenience foods such as prepared mustard and ketchup.
10. Aerosols which either eject shaving cream or spray insecticides for mosquitoes or cockroach control, polishes, hair lacquer or other materials.
11. Paper wrappings as used for confectionery, flour bags, and for those food products which can be kept under refrigeration.
12. Waxed cartons for milk and soft drinks.
13. Ejector and pull-out packs as used for saccharin sweetener tablets, razor blades, tissues, and toilet-paper, which both protect products and avoid waste.
14. Plastic trays on which products such as meat or fish are laid, the whole covered by stretched plastic film.

15. With consumer durables and industrial goods the product may be created around the package. The outer casing of the sewing machine or the vacuum cleaner forms a kind of packaging, as does the bodywork of a motor-car.

Great ingenuity has been shown by some manufacturers in devising packs which are extremely convenient for the consumer who may buy the product because of the way it is packed. He may be prepared to pay extra for a product that is well-packed.

Some products can be wasted or used wrongly if the pack does not encourage proper usage. Disappointed customers may complain or at least refrain from making a repeat purchase. In contrast, the thoughtfully designed pack may lead not only to repeat purchase, but to recommendation. Here we see another instance of marketing PR, of the danger of provoking ill-will and the ability to create good-will.

A good instance is the product which produces the best results if the correct quantity or dosage is used. Such a pack is the simple tea bag.

In developing countries, and especially among the majority of the people who may be poor and illiterate, people are unlikely to have forms of measurement such as scales, weights and measures, or tea-spoons, dessert-spoons or table-spoons – all common forms of household measurement in the West. They may be unfamiliar with ounces or grammes, pounds or kilos, pints or litres, inches or centimetres, feet and yards or metres. They may measure by more simple methods such as a handful, an arm's-length or some other natural measurement. Perhaps they will consider whether, a piece of meat, a fish, a hand of bananas or a bowl of fruit is large enough for the family. After all, a yard is basically the length of a stride or three human feet!

If the package can in some way remove all doubt or fear about how its contents should be properly used, that product is likely to be successful.

Colours

The colour of the container, package or label can be significant for the following reasons:

1. It may be *distinctive,* either a colour for which the product is known and recognised such as the yellow Kodak film box, or because it is *different* from that of rival products. Brands of most

fast-moving consumer goods have distinctively or differently coloured packs as may be seen on the shelves of a supermarket. Toblerone chocolate has its triangular pack, German wines have their long bottles, and American cigarettes are packed differently from British ones.

2. It is an *inoffensive, appropriate* or *flattering* colour. Africans like bright colours, Nigeria tends to favour green (e.g. Nigeria Airways), but in Asian countries or where Chinese are represented in the population there is a language of colours which has to be observed. Red is a popular colour because it stands for health and happiness. Green — and not forgetting jade — represents a long life. Yellow or gold means money and prosperity. But blue is for sadness and white represents death. A wrongly coloured package or product could be disastrous when selling to the Chinese, as the Japanese discovered with blue sewing machines.

   In Nigeria, a white car is common, and especially among Peugeots and Mercedes-Benz, but in Hong Kong the streets are full of red Datsun taxis, although those plying in the New Territories beyond Kowloon are green. The bright colours of Japanese motor-cycles have been popular in Africa.

3. It may be a *house colour* and part of a *corporate identity* scheme, so that the colour is symbolic of the manufacturer. In 1980, Rentokil introduced a special shade of red in its new corporate identity scheme.

4. It will help *colour advertising* in the press, on posters and on TV to create easy pack recognition so that customers, having seen the advertising, will quickly recognise the product in the shops.

Instructions

How to use the product may be explained on the label, container, outer package or in a leaflet or small booklet inserted in the outer package (called a 'stuffer'). If very detailed instructions are necessary, a separate manual will have to be supplied.

The preparation of instructions, and their clear presentation, is one of the most important marketing responsibilities because it means communication between manufacturer and consumer which should be successful but can be disastrous.

If the customer cannot understand the instructions the product may be used with unexpected, disappointing and possibly tragic results. This could lead to complaints, a bad reputation for the manufacturer, and rejection by both distributors and customers. The products could be banned if proved to be dangerous.

The world's worst case has been the marketing of milk powder, known internationally as the baby milk scandal. Public authorities have sought to educate mothers that breast-feeding is best. How do you instruct a woman in a rural area who speaks no English, has no knowledge of sterilisation, possesses no refrigerator, regards the product as expensive and uses so little milk powder that her baby dies of malnutrition? You cannot, and the product is in the wrong hands. But for many years multi-national milk companies exploited developing countries without scruple, and although public outcry has meant the banning of the worst practices, such as dressing-up sales girls as fake nurses, the situation remains unsatisfactory.

However, where the product can be beneficial provided the instructions can be understood, the simplest way to overcome language and literary problems is to draw pictures demonstrating how to use it. Told in cartoon form, instructions can be made intelligible.

The pictures must be credible. There have been unfortunate experiences in Kenya and Uganda where people have refused to use pesticides because the picture of the insect (e.g. tsetse fly or mosquito) on the container has been larger than normal. The product was rejected because the people had never seen such a giant insect. Of course, marketing and advertising people often use big pictures for dramatic effect, but to the African farmers it seemed that the insecticide was intended for protection against creatures which did not exist in their district.

In countries where the majority of the people are poor, illiterate and mostly rural, and where there may be several languages, it is insufficient to rely on printed instructions in, say, English and another written language. Not all languages are written. The picture or diagram can portray the message effectively.

Two examples can be taken from planned parenthood campaigns. In Asia posters pictured the parents and two children as a happy family while a third child looked miserable. An East African leaflet, with Swahili wording, also demonstrated the message with drawings of a row of corn sown haphazardly and another row of corn spaced out so that each plant grew healthily. Similar devices can be applied to the instructions which accompany products.

But even pictures can be misleading if not used sensibly. Mistakes are often made by expatriates whose marketing is planned in Europe or the USA, generally with no overseas knowledge (and probably little interest). Indigenous marketing directors can learn much from the mistakes of foreigners!

One of the best remembered ill-fated expatriate marketing ventures was the attempt to launch a meat substitute in Nigeria, a product called Metex. This has become a classic case study of how not to do it. It was a German product made by an international multi-national company noted for bungled marketing operations in Africa. The product was contained in a box which carried a splendid picture of appetising-looking meat. The flaw lay in the instructions that when prepared the housewife would have one pound of meat, a meaningless weight and a misleading expression for Nigerian housewives who did not buy by weight but by visible size.

7 Pricing Theory and Practice

The pricing of products is vital to marketing strategy for two reasons. First, the price must recover costs and return a profit, unless there is a deliberate policy of subsidising the price when the product is launched; second, the price must be such that people will be willing to pay it. But it is not as simple as that. There are many reasons leading to pricing decisions. Many factors influence them.

There may be a good reason why a product is sold at an unprofitable price, even though this seems to be bad business. It is usually easy to reduce a price but difficult to raise one. Company policy and marketing strategy will need to work together very carefully. For example, in order to establish a foreign market for a motor-car it may be good policy to sell the vehicle at a loss-making price in order to establish it in the market. In succeeding years, when owners wish to replace old models with new ones, the normal price can be charged.

FOUR KINDS OF PRICE

There are four kinds of price: economic, opportunity, psychological and market, and they will be discussed first.

The economic price

This is the price at which it is profitable to produce or supply a product or service. If that price cannot be charged it is uneconomic to market the product or service.

This is not to be confused with the economist's supply and demand view of price, meaning that when prices go up demand falls and that when prices fall demand rises. This depends on the products. Staple, everyday products are not affected by price movements; and, as politicians have learned, interest rates have to rise or fall very substantially before there is any effect on demand. The economist's view can therefore be an over-simplification, a theory not always proved by practice.

The opportunity price

This resembles opportunity cost, and concerns decisions to spend discretionary income in excess of that which satisfies basic needs. Price may determine on which product, usually a luxury, the consumer will sacrifice money. For people with different incomes, luxury can mean different things. A luxury to a poor person could be a new suit or dress, but to a wealthier person it could be more new clothes. As standards of living increase, luxuries become necessities.

But, generally speaking, opportunity price concerns competition between relatively expensive purchases. One has to sacrifice buying, say, a motor-car in order to have a holiday abroad of similar cost. So the motor-car manufacturers and the holiday tour operators will offer competitive prices to capture discretionary income. But for poorer people, the choice could be between beer and cigarettes.

The psychological price

This can be expressed in two ways. A price may be charged which seems to be cheaper than it really is, 99 sounding a lot less than 100. Or people will pay a high price because this implies high value, whereas a low price suggests poor value. The value-for-money suggestion of price can be important. A product may sell because it is known to be expensive, like a Rolls-Royce car, or may fail to sell because it has too low a price. Smiths failed to sell British watches, which were often better quality than imported ones, because they were under-priced. The higher price may have a status value: few people like to receive a prize or gift if its price is known to be small! The lady is thrilled by the gift of an 'expensive' perfume.

The market price

This is the standard price one expects to pay for a good. If a higher price is charged it will look like over-charging, if a lower price prevails it could be regarded with suspicion. It may be essential to charge the price which people expect to pay. This is when a seemingly unjustified increase in price could cause a fall in demand. This has happened with price increases for newspapers, sales falling off until the new price has become accepted as the market price, and demand has returned.

PRICING STRATEGY

Some prices are affected by conditions and special costs such as delivery and there are five forms of pricing strategy.

1. *Non-discriminatory price,* as in the cases of products with a basic ex-works price to which is added a delivery charge according to the distance or carriage charge between the factory and the customer. This could also be based on home and overseas postal charges.
2. *Uniform delivery price,* transport or delivery prices being averaged out so that there is a standard price everywhere.
3. *Special price discrimination* which happens when different prices are charged in different places, as when a monopoly situation occurs in contrast to the competitive situation on a street with rival traders. One may have to pay more for cigarettes in a big hotel than in a main street shop.
4. *Basic point pricing,* the price differing in various places according to the transport costs from the source of supply. This is similar to No. 1 except that, as in the case of a motor-car, the customer knows the ex-works price and the delivery charge but with basic point pricing the final price is calculated and charged so that the customer is aware only of the price at the point of purchase. Fuels such as oil, petrol and coal are priced like this.
5. *Multiple basing point pricing* means that the price changes and increases as it passes through many hands or middlemen before it reaches the customer. Fresh foods come into this category, the producer being paid very little compared with the price charged by the final retailer.

From the above it will be seen that the cost of distributing, and that includes both transport and handling by distributors, adds considerably to price. The customer has to pay for the privilege of having goods carried, stored and placed where he can conveniently buy them. Meanwhile, many people earn a living, perhaps on a commission basis, in getting the goods from their place of origin to the person who wants them.

Before examining some models on which to base pricing decisions let us consider some factors and aspects of pricing.

Price elasticity

This has to do with customer relations to price changes. A price is said to be elastic when it responds to demand; inelastic when it does not. It is important, therefore, to understand what effect demand is likely to have on your price. Something rare like an antique or some form of art will have an elastic demand according to its rarity. A good example is a painting since only one original exists. If the artist is unknown the price will be low but if he becomes famous the price will be high. If you produce a lot of paintings, as did Picasso, you do not put them all on the market because the reduced rarity would depress the price. Something that is in constant demand, like yams or fish, may have an inelastic price because demand, is steady. At one time it was thought in Britain that a cheap and popular drink like beer would have an inelastic demand, but beer has been taxed so heavily that breweries have been closed down.

Price distortion

This happens when the producer has little control over price because the real price is obscured by other influences such as taxes which increase price, devaluation which changes the buying power of money, or subsidies which create falsely low prices. In these circumstances it may be difficult for the producer to demonstrate value for money. When gin costs more than £4 in Britain and less than £1 at Dubai Airport, how can one decide what is a fair value-for-money price for it?

Price plateaux

Rather like the market price, this is a ceiling or maximum price higher than which customers do not expect to pay. If a newcomer to the market tries to sell at a price higher than that usually paid, the product may well fail. It will have priced itself out of the market. This has been the case with Concorde flights.

Price stability

This means that prices remain the same — difficult in times of inflation — but the sort of thing that creates goodwill and regular customers.

Price-bashing and double-pricing

This has arisen as a result of a change in attitudes towards the control of prices of manufacturers. Two systems can exist.

First, the manufacturer can lay down a *minimum* retail price and advertise it so that customers know that the price will be the same whereever they shop. This can lead to the abuse of the *price ring* which fixes prices which may be considered too high. This happened in the radio and tyre industries. But it can also lead to the setting up of pirate cut-price shops which the manufacturer may try to close down by refusing supplies. The minimum price maintenance system is useful to makers of expensive goods who need a certain retail price to cover the cost of training the service staff of distributors, as in the motor-car trade. It is less important with low-priced, fast-moving, repeat purchase goods like matches, razor blades, confectionery which require no servicing and have a small profit margin because of the large volume of sales.

Second, as is common in many countries today, the price differs from shop to shop, the supermarket selling more cheaply than the neighbourhood shop or village stall. This takes into account the advantages of bulk buying which are passed on to the customer in competitive prices. Even so, many manufacturers need to indicate some idea of price — and prices continue to be a dominant feature of much advertising. So, advertisers state 'recommended' or 'list' prices or even go so far as to meet the trend by saying 'at so much or less'. The customer can then shop around for the best buy. Retail advertising then offers competitive prices for the same goods.

But this second method — often a political sop by Governments pretending to help the consumer! — leads to the common abuse of *double-pricing* and *price-bashing*. Manufacturers may publish deliberately high list prices so that retailers may appear to be offering discounts by cutting list prices. The real price becomes the lowest the customer can find. We have seen many examples of this with cameras, radios, calculators, hi-fi and electronic equipment, and domestic appliances. This has become a pricing racket.

Geographic pricing

This occurs when the manufacturer, and also some retailers with branch stores, adopt different prices according to the purchasing ability of people in different areas, regions or even countries. For example, an Italian washing-machine manufacturer sells his products at various prices through Europe. But it could also happen between the high-class and the low-class parts of a city.

Controlled prices

These occur when a Government endeavours to keep prices down, but it is often a bad policy leading to a black market where people can buy scarce commodities at inflated prices.

Penetration pricing

This describes the method of buying one's way into the market by starting with a low, competitive price, sometimes described as an introductory offer.

Premium price

A premium price offer means offering goods (which may be unrelated to the original product) at a special low price if labels, packet tops and so on are sent in with payment of the premium price. For instance, a coffee firm may offer a coffee table for so many labels and a money payment which is less than the retail price of the table.

Premium

This is another use of the word premium meaning that something additional to the stated price has to be paid to obtain possession. It applies to things in short supply, and in the real estate business it is known as 'key' money which will secure purchase or rent of property.

Loss leader

This is a device used by retailers whereby a popular product is offered at a cut price in order to attract customers into the shop. Manufacturers dislike loss leaders because they cheapen the product image.

Competitive pricing

This is an economic theory concerning prices which are standard for all competing products so that the only way to make sales more profitable is to cut costs in some way.

Skimming

Skimming takes place when the manufacturer introduces a product at a high price which will attract sufficient sales to repay his costs of development and production, after which he will introduce cheaper versions. Two examples are books — which are first published as hardbacks, and when this market has been skimmed paperbacks are issued — and motor-cars, where the expensive model is introduced first and more popular versions are introduced later.

Mark-up

Mark-up is the profit added by the retailer to the wholesale price. Different shops may have different mark-ups such as 33½ per cent or 50 per cent. Different prices will attract different classes of buyers, or market segments.

PRICING MODELS AND POLICIES

There are many such formulae, and the following are four which are frequently used:

1. *Break-even model.* This indicates the point which sales at a given price must reach to cover fixed and variable costs but without making a profit. The unit price has to be adjusted accordingly.
2. *Full-cost model.* Here the method seeks to determine the price by working out direct costs and adding percentages for anticipated overheads and profits.
3. *Marginal-cost pricing.* The price is determined by calculating all contributions of variable costs to the price which must be recovered, including profit, on the basis of selling a fixed volume of goods according to production capacity. It ignores fixed costs. It is a method which can be applied to extra sales such as night flights, out-of-season hotel guests, or off-peak rates for gas and electricity.

4. *Marginal cost–marginal revenue model.* Will marginal revenue exceed marginal cost? This method aims at maximising profits by observing changes in production costs and charges in prices as sales increase.

In reality pricing calls for a study of prevailing market conditions, the control and recovery of costs, and the need to produce a profit which will repay investment and result in a satisfactory net profit. Profit is usually a tiny proportion of price. As a society's standards of living increase and wages increase correspondingly, the cost of labour becomes an increasingly larger proportion of price.

In the West, labour costs amount to some 70 per cent of price. Raw material and energy costs also affect price. The breakdown of a price is demonstrated in this analysis of 'the Rentokil pound', the cost of goods and services being high because raw materials are expensive chemicals and the services are mobile. Petrol alone cost £2 million. World-wide sales were £82.1 million, broken down as shown in Table 7.1. From this it will be seen that 84.6 per cent of the Rentokil price went on supplying the products and services; 6.5 per cent was taken in taxation; a mere 3 per cent went in dividends to shareholders; but the company made sensible provision for the future by retaining 6 per cent for the maintenance and expansion of the business. The profit figure is a small percentage of price, £2.4 million out of £82.1 million; whereas wages, salaries, pension and social security contributions amounted to £33.7 million. This is very different from the situation 100 years ago when British fortunes were built on low wages and cheap raw materials, and the living standards of the workers were poor. The parallel to this can be seen in the Third World.

TABLE 7.1

Where it came from £1 sales				How it was used	
2p	Asia	Products	19p	To suppliers	43.5p
5p	Africa	Building services	29p	To employees	41.1p
6.5p	America			To governments (taxes)	6.5p
8.5p	Australia	Contract services	52p		
18p	Europe			To shareholders	3p
60p	UK			To investment	6p

8 The Sales Force

The products or services of a company may be sold by all or some of the following individuals:

1. *Field salesmen* selling to wholesalers and retailers, taking orders which are supplied by head office, the factory or regional depots.
2. *Van salesmen* who carry stocks and supply retailers.
3. *Commission agents* who act as travelling salesmen for a range of similar goods made by different firms, e.g. stationery.
4. *Wholesaler's salesmen* who represent all the brands handled by the wholesaler, e.g. food products.
5. *Brokers* who, as in the insurance business, advise clients and earn commission on the policies they write.
6. *Direct salesmen* who, without use of wholesalers or retailers, sell directly to the customer, house-to-house. This is how the oil business began in the USA, 100 years ago, with the oil companies selling oil door-to-door for lighting purposes. In some countries milk and bread are sold by roundsmen, but the cost of transport is making this more and more uneconomic.
7. *Shop assistants,* the sales force being on the retail premises, which may or may not be owned by the manufacturer.
8. *Telephone salesmen* and especially *saleswomen* who telephone prospects and either make appointments for interviewers (as with insurance firms) or sell direct (as with advertisement space). Telephone selling can be used for industrial products when prospects may be limited in numbers and located far apart. It could appeal in a country like Nigeria which is having a telecommunications revolution.

The above list is a broad one, and some of these salesmen will be reconsidered in Chapter 10 as distributors. The intention here is to show the numerous ways in which people may be employed in selling the product or service. They may not be actual employees of the company, they may earn commission according to their efforts or success. There may or may not be control over their selling efforts, and their loyalties may be divided. The extent of control will therefore influence the marketing strategy. The utmost control will occur when the sales force is employed by the manufacturer or supplier. This will be even more effective when the manufacturer also owns or has a strong interest in the distributor, as in the case of motor-car agents.

CHARACTERISTICS OF SALESMEN

A salesman is not necessarily a persuasive flatterer with a gift of the gab. He has to be sufficiently energetic and optimistic to make many calls on prospective or regular customers who may buy nothing. He has to be presentable so that people will tolerate or even welcome his visit. He has to create a good impression of his company. And in most cases he needs to be knowledgeable about what he is selling, and able to give advice. In American terms he has been called a *drummer* (drumming up sales) or, less complimentary, a *huckster* (one who bargains or haggles).

Selling can be an exhausting experience, and unless the salesman gains promotion and becomes involved in management he may find, like luckless Willie Loman in Arthur Miller's play *Death of a Salesman,* that one's flair can vanish. Selling is therefore mainly a young, or younger, person's calling, and it exploits the enthusiasm and energy of people who can be urged to work very hard. Salesmanship is not unlike other active careers such as most uniformed services.

Consequently five facts of salesmanship need to be considered namely, training; support; reward; incentives and control; which will now be discussed in turn:

Training

A sales force cannot sell effectively unless it is well-trained both in sales techniques and concerning the product or service. If the salesman does not exude confidence, no-one else will. Training may consist of:

1. Induction courses which familiarise the salesman with the company.

2. Technical training courses about the product or service.
3. Courses in selling techniques, perhaps supported by one of the many excellent films which can be bought or hired, or by role-playing exercises and business games. Everyone on the course may learn from the mistakes or successes of others. Tape recordings and video-taping may be used to recall what took place during the exercise.
4. Field training, when new salesmen are accompanied by a senior salesman or sales trainer.

A problem with training is the time it takes and the need for a continuous training programme. It can be costly to take salesmen off the road or out of the shop or showroom, and assemble them at a central or national training centre. The modern trend is to take the training to the salesman. This can be done in the following ways:

1. By distributing informative sales bulletins.
2. By organising training sessions at local or regional level.
3. By distributing audio-tape cassettes, which salesmen can play back at home or in their cars.
4. By distributing video-tape cassettes which salesmen can watch on TV sets fitted with video-cassette receivers, the equipment being supplied to local centres.

The latter may seem costly and sophisticated but it can be less expensive than bringing salesmen to a training centre, accommodating them and losing their sales business during the training period.

Training not only makes a salesman more efficient; it also gives him greater confidence in what he is doing. It is therefore an essential investment, and an important part of the marketing strategy and the marketing budget.

Implicit in this is the behaviour and appearance of the salesman. Three true stories can be told – all, incidentally, about American companies operating in Britain. The first sold plumbing equipment ranging from valves to boilers. The salesmen boasted of the way they socialised with customers, regarding hospitality (mistakenly) as good PR. It was a very weak sales force. The second sold computers, its salesmen gave a 24-hour service, and liquor was banned. The sales record was superb. The third company sold chemicals. Its salesmen were highly qualified scientists. Customers found them boring, and sales were lost to rival companies whose representatives were primarily salesmen.

The lesson to be learned from those three examples is that sales success depends on the salesman's credibility in the eyes of the buyer. Sometimes the customer does not have to be sold so much as made to feel sure. It was the integrity and reliability of the computer salesman which got the business. That company's salesmen also enjoyed great job satisfaction.

Good sales training therefore has to be psychologically right. It is not just a matter of getting your foot in the door, like the proverbial Hoover salesman, or of being cynical and believing there is a sucker born every minute, or relying on good looks, smart clothes, and a smooth tongue. Sales success depends on regular repeat sales that maintain factory output and achieve the sales target which is the culmination of the marketing strategy.

Sales organisation. Obviously, there is no standard sales organisation since everything depends on what is being sold to whom and where the market is. Figure 8.1 is therefore a generalised scheme for a large com-

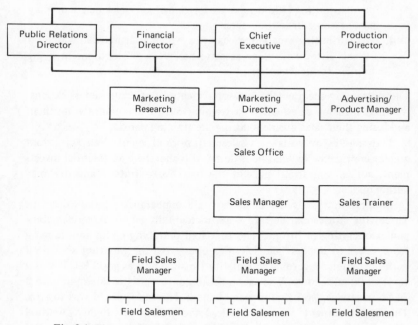

Fig. 8.1. The sales organisation within the integral framework of a manufacturing company.

pany selling over a large area. In the figure the sales manager is supported by a sales office which processes orders, correspondence and other
clerical and administrative back-up. The country is divided into regions
where field sales managers direct teams of field salesmen. The sales
manager reports to the marketing director who is also responsible for
advertising and marketing research. He in turn reports to the chief
executive or managing director. He is also linked to the financial and
production director who also report to the chief executive.

The public relations director reports to the chief executive, and services the financial, production and marketing directors. This, of course,
takes PR out of the marketing director's sphere, and makes it fully related to the total communications of the entire organisation. This
practical positioning of PR makes nonsense of such contradictory job
titles as advertising and public relations manager, that is when there is a
marketing department of which advertising is a part but public relations
is not.

Support

The salesman needs ammunition in the form of sales aids of which the
following are examples:

1. *Sales presenter, portfolio or promoter.* This is a binder which the
   salesman can place on the counter so that he can show the customer sales arguments, prices, samples and specimens of advertisements.
2. *Sample case.* This is an attaché or brief-case container for a range
   of sample products.
3. *Desk-top projector.* Slides, films or video-cassettes can be shown,
   demonstrating the product. Such equipment is portable and light
   for easy carrying, setting-up and display.
4. *Buffer stock.* Salesmen may carry in their vehicles a small stock
   of products to save the customer from being out-of-stock.
5. *Point-of-sale material.* It may help the salesman if he has some
   display material which he can put in position before he leaves the
   customer's premises. There is the example of the salesman who
   places a transfer on the glass of the door of every shop as he
   leaves!
6. *Advertising.* Media advertising may produce enquiries which the
   salesman can convert into sales, *or* the dealer may buy because
   the product is supported by advertising which will create demand.

Reward

The form of remuneration may define the calibre of salesman who is employed.

The commission-only salesman has to be a gambler and he may over-sell or use dubious methods to achieve sales. This type of reward some-times applies to speciality goods, that is, things like encyclopaedias, air-conditioning, security systems or other expensive lines which are sold direct to the user or consumer, usually on a high commission to compensate for a small number of hard-won sales.

The salesman who works on a salary and commission basis has a greater sense of security and regular employment, encouraging him to be a loyal employee. The reward has to be a challenge and provide a satisfactory and deserved income. The basic salary provides a minimum of security while the commission suggests a maximum of effort. The donkey has a warm stable, but he has to work for the carrot.

Incentives

However, the reward may be sugared by additional awards or prizes for special effort. There is a case for and against incentive schemes. They can be unfair to the salesman who has spent longer achieving a sale than does his seemingly more energetic rival, yet he may have no control over the purchasing decision. It could also be said that if the contribu-tory factors of product, proposition, remuneration and support are right all salesmen (if carefully recruited and properly trained) should be capable of achieving target sales. The targets could be adjusted according to the selling conditions of each sales territory.

Even so, it may be company policy to spur salesmen on to be com-petitive among themselves. This may be seen as a lively policy to bring out the best in salesmen for their own self-satisfaction as well as for the gaining of greater sales. It could be a means of weeding out the weaker salesmen on a survival-of-the-fittest criterion.

Incentives may take various forms such as:

1. Holidays and trips, usually for the winner and his wife.
2. Cash awards.
3. Substantial prizes.
4. Bonuses, sometimes in the form of incentive vouchers which can be cashed against a catalogue of gifts.

Incentive schemes can be a guide to promotion to more senior positions such as area or field sales manager. Such schemes can be run on a regular basis such as 'salesman of the month'.

Control

The sales force has two characteristics which affect its control or management. Salesmen, by the very nature of the job, are individualistic. They need to be directed by example, encouragement and reward within the discipline of company policy and sales targets. They are also isolated, lone rangers who are apt to feel lonely, frustrated and perhaps forgotten or ignored by headquarters. The previous four facets of salesmanship (training, support, reward and incentives) all contribute to some measure of control, but here are some more specific methods.

Sales manual. This combines instructions on how to sell and specifically how to explain or demonstrate the particular product or service. While video-cassettes are tending to replace or at least supplement printed sales manuals, the printed manual has the merit of portability. It can be carried in brief-case or car.

Sales meetings. Regular meetings at various levels – branch, area, regional, national – are essential to maintaining unity, good staff relations, direction, instruction and control. Visual aid presentations – charts, slides, videotapes, films, models and exhibits – are effective aids at sales meetings.

Sales bulletins. The sales manager needs to communicate regularly with his men in the field, encouraging, advising and informing them. It could take the form of a letter, newsletter, house journal or video-cassette.

Sales reports and salesman's records. The documents produced by the salesman may, to him, seem to be time-consuming paperwork but they are vital to an effective sales force. Different companies will have their own special requirements but generally the documents are likely to consist of:

1. *Customer record cards* on which the salesman records his calls and results, and so maintains a picture of the kind of orders ob-

tained from each customer. He may also keep, separately, records of prospects who have yet to be converted into customers. This information will help him in planning his calls.

2. *Daily report.* When there is a large salesforce, salesmen working in area or regional groups will send daily reports to their local manager.

3. *Weekly summary of action.* Basically, a diary of his calls and activities (which sometimes includes other things such as account collection, training new staff, attending company meetings or staffing exhibition stands).

4. *Monthly report.* Here we have a more detailed report which provides the sales manager with market intelligence (which will be discussed later) as well as information on the salesman's efforts.

5. *Expenses claim.* Salesmen may have many expenses such as fares, meals, postage, telephone calls, petrol and car expenses and hospitality. On the one hand the salesman must be discouraged from extravagant expenditures while on the other he must be recompensed for genuine expenses essential to his job. The accurate completion of claim forms should provide both sales office control and salesman satisfaction.

MARKET INTELLIGENCE

Salesman's reports call for concise information clearly expressed and written. They should be well detailed but not verbose. Good report-writing can be as big a test of a salesman as his success in achieving sales. The sales manager (or his deputies) relies on these reports for the following information:

1. Numbers and details of calls, interviews, receptions, sales, new business, lost business.
2. Trade reactions to trade terms, product, pack, price, advertising and promotions.
3. Competitor activity — new products, trade terms, promotions.
4. Information which may influence sales forecasting.
5. Information that may call for revision in the sales plan.
6. Regional matters that may affect the sales plan and marketing strategy, e.g. a popular local competitor.

This feedback will assist the whole marketing team, but care must be taken not to use salesmen for primary research. Salesmen have their own job to do, and they are also liable to be biased. Genuine marketing research — that is, interviewing a sample of people — calls for independent research carried out by trained researchers. The independent researcher is disinterested in the answers or views given, whereas the salesman could express bias which could influence and so falsify answers.

The sales force has its own special jargon and some of the terms used are:

Sales pitch. This is the argument or proposition which salesmen are trained to present to their customers.

Sales lead. When enquiries or prospect lists are given to salesmen they are known as sales leads.

Journey cycle. It is usual for a salesman to take a certain period of time to call on his regular customers. This may be every four, six or eight weeks. The complete round of calls is called the journey cycle.

There are two kinds of journey cycle: the *continuous,* which proceeds from point to point and may take a considerable time, and the *quadrant* which embraces a more compact area and allows for more flexible action.

For instance, working on the basis of a national tour, it would take a Nigerian salesman many months to make a journey cycle of continuous calls in Lagos, Ibadan, Ilorin, Kano, Jos, Maguri, Enugu, Calabar, Port Harcourt, Onitsha, Benin City and back to Lagos. How many times a year could that tour be undertaken? That would be the journey cycle. If the sales potential permitted, however, more salesmen could be engaged to cover so many states according to the size of population, number of outlets, or estimated purchasing power. Lagos State would probably merit its own salesman, perhaps more than one, compared with, say, less urbanised regions.

The number of salesmen may be determined by the required frequency of journey cycles. In some trades, goods may be ordered only once or twice a year, while in others turnover may be more rapid. Or the salesman may carry a range of different seasonal goods requiring frequent contact with distributors, e.g. sports goods.

The *quadrant* journey cycle operates over a smaller area, such as a large city, where the journey cycle does not have to conform to a sequential route but can move in any direction within the confines of the area. Thus, some customers can be called on more often than others, while special calls can be made on demand. Generally the frequency of call can be according to value rather than physical opportunity to make the call as occurs with the continuous and consecutive A–B–C–D journey cycle.

Cold calling. When a salesman calls on new prospects without invitation, this initiative is known as cold-calling.

Commando selling. To launch a new product to the trade, teams of special salesmen may be employed to cover sales territories more quickly than normal journey cycles would permit. These *commando salesmen* may also arrange shop displays.

SALES FORCES IN DEVELOPING COUNTRIES

In the West it is easy to operate a well-organised, effective sales force. There are hundreds of cities, towns and villages which require stocks. In most towns there are supermarkets about the size of Kingsway Stores in Lagos, and each supermarket company has a chain of between 250 and 1000 such stores. Selling to them is mostly on bulk terms to centralised buyers. Nevertheless, there are still thousands of independent shops, and in some European countries such as France the smaller shops predominate. The towns or shopping centres are linked to suppliers by excellent road and rail services. Communications are quick and reliable by post, express parcel services, telephone and Telex. All this is strengthened by the fact that everyone has some spending power – even the poor, sick, disabled or unemployed. The mass public is really the population at large. Moreover, in most countries there is a single national language.

This is the background enjoyed by the authors of most books on advertising, marketing and public relations, and by the examiners for those British examinations which attract overseas candidates. The situation in a developing country is very different. Modern marketing techniques, including a well-organised sales force, may seem unrealistic, even irrelevant. Comparisons are therefore necessary, and the following points are offered for consideration against the special backgrounds and conditions of different countries.

Nature of outlets

Shops similar to those in the West will exist in towns, and there will be street markets, but there will also be large numbers of outlets unlike any to be found in the West. There will be numerous small village stalls and lock-up huts, together with itinerant and pavement traders. The street pedlar is a rarity in the West, whereas in some developing countries the pavements will be occupied by them day and night. Shops will vary, too, from the hundreds in Hong Kong which are open from 10 a.m. to 10 p.m., 7 days a week, and the bazaars of the East, to the shanty shack or roadside stall with a small range of goods. In some of the small village stores the stock will consist of one or two cans, bottles or packets of various brands compared with the stacks of goods in a town supermarket. Consequently, it may not be economic to use a travelling sales force calling on retailers, and may be more practical to sell to wholesalers who operate rather like cash-and-carry wholesalers who maintain warehouses from which traders buy their small supplies.

Brooke Bond in Kenya some years ago solved the problem of supplying the small village shopkeeper by sending out small sales vans on weekly tours of these distributors.

Distances and communications

The operator of a sales force may be hampered by distance. In Nigeria, for instance, cities are often hundreds of miles apart with vast rural areas in between. Zambia is a huge country with little physical communication beyond 'the line of rail' and the copper belt. Indonesia, while most heavily populated in Jakarta and Java island, nevertheless has its millions scattered over an area of islands that matches the United States. Few developing countries are as compact as a Caribbean island.

Problems of distance are compounded by poor road and rail systems which are often wrecked by storms and floods. Domestic air services, like those of Nigeria, cannot meet demand. Postal communications tend to be casual, while telecommunications are haphazard. Nigeria's new network of telephone services, and the transformation of its railway services, is a big step forward, but as marketing aids they are primitive compared with those enjoyed by manufacturers in the West 100 years ago. Nigeria's new telephone facility has to be compared with the British situation where there are 80 million subscribers. From a marketing standpoint, Nigeria is entering the nineteenth century which must make almost twenty-first-century marketing techniques difficult to apply. *And Nigeria is far more advanced than many other developing countries.*

While the marketing student needs to understand the sales force concept he also needs to understand its feasibility in developing countries, and the alternatives which work better or are workable in the circumstances.

9 Sales Promotion and Merchandising

Sales promotion is a term which is very loosely and wrongly used, and so it is necessary to understand that it refers only and specifically to those sales aids used *between* the *advertising* to the consumer by the manufacturer or supplier and the actual retail *selling* by the retailer to the consumer or final user. It is a form of advertising which brings the customer closer to the advertiser because it takes place at the point of sale. The point of sale (or point of purchase) means the shop, bazaar or market.

Merchandising also has its special meaning. It does not mean selling merchandise. Merchandising consists of special short-term sales promotion schemes.

Thus, *sales promotion* will consist of continuous sales aids such as give-away sales literature; window, counter and shelf display material; dummy bottles and cans for displays; posters (like those used in the travel industry); permanent displays such as clocks attached to premises and bearing the advertiser's name; and various plastic carrier bags and other means of carrying goods home.

Merchandising, however, will consist of competitions, free gifts, in-store demonstrations, premium offers and other short-term efforts to boost sales.

Some of the terms used may be unfamiliar or confusing so in this chapter we will describe the range of sales aids which come under the headings of *sales promotion* and *merchandising.*

LEGAL AND ETHICAL CONSIDERATIONS

In some countries there are regulations concerning both sales promotion and merchandising. Care is necessary to see that gifts inserted in food packages do not contaminate the contents. Competitions may be subject to lottery and gaming laws. Lottery legislation usually stipulates that a competition must have an element of skill. A lucky draw is not a legal competition because it contains no element of skill. Advertising must not suggest that gifts are bigger or better than they really are, or that premium offers are cheaper than shop prices if this is not the case, or the offered item is not in fact available in the shops.

It is also essential to make sure that a merchandising offer does not provoke complaint because people are disappointed by what they receive or because there is a delay in supplying it. Again, competitors should not be annoyed because they see no publication of the results of a competition. Bad feeling can be created if customers have cause for complaint. It does happen that marketing and product managers will put most of their effort and expenditure into stimulating immediate sales, and forget to consider the interests of the customer who has been encouraged to apply for the gift or premium offer, or enter for the competition. Not surprisingly, the dissatisfied customer feels cheated, does not buy the product again, and may tell his friends about his bad experience. This is poor PR and disastrous marketing.

SALES PROMOTION

Here are some typical forms of sales promotion:

Posters or bills

The standard sizes are crown (381 x 508 mm) and double crown (508 x 762 mm). While shops and offices will have limited space for the display of posters, and it is easy to waste money on posters which get thrown away, really attractive posters are welcomed and well used. In fact, some of the very beautiful travel posters (like those for KLM) will be found in places which do not sell travel services. These are small posters for window and internal use, not the big posters used on roadside hoardings.

Window-dressing services

Large manufacturers such as brewers, cosmetics and cigarette firms may offer a window-dressing service, decorating their clients' shop windows with dummy products, background effects, paper sculpture and other devices. This is a service which applies to urban areas where there are shops and stores, the display being changed at regular intervals by a travelling window-dresser. A similar service might apply where a chain of shops employed its own window-dresser.

Mobile demonstrations

Very popular in developing countries are touring demonstrations which may consist of product demonstrations, film shows, and song and dance teams, the show being driven from village to village. (Note: there are two kinds of 'mobiles'. Already described is the road show type of *mobile*, but a point-of-sale display suspended from the ceiling of a shop so that it swings with the movement of the air is also known as a *mobile*. This type of mobile is very useful in supermarkets where there is little or no space for display material.)

Dealer contests

These can stimulate stockists to sell more goods in order to win prizes. Prizes may be awarded for special efforts like window or in-store displays or for volume of sales with monthly awards and a national annual award for the dealer-of-the-year, as in the motor-car industry.

Co-operative advertising schemes

These are schemes whereby stockists are encouraged to advertise, perhaps on a 50/50 basis, by the manufacturer who may also provide blocks or camera-ready artwork with a space for the dealer's name. This is a method to use when there are *local* media such as newspapers, cinemas and regional TV.

Plastic shopping bags

These are a popular and inexpensive form of sales promotion which provide all-round satisfaction to the dealer who has something to pack goods in, and which the customer can carry away very conveniently; the bag often surviving for a long time as a constant advertisement. It may well pay to fit the bag with strong handles so that its useful life and publicity value is prolonged.

Sales literature

Sales literature of all kinds, but especially that which helps the customer to benefit from the product, can be important sales promotional
material. A paint manufacturer may distribute leaflets, folders or booklets on how to decorate, a food manufacturer may offer recipe leaflets
or booklets, and a sewing-machine manufacturer may supply information on what to make. Or the literature could be straightforward sales
information about the product, giving specifications, performance figures, colours, prices and so on.

Display outers

These are cartons containing small items such as confectionery which
can be opened up so that the lid becomes a display, and the products
can be sold from the open carton which can be placed on the shop
counter.

Display stands

Wooden, plastic, metal, wire and other types of stand or rack may be
supplied from which displayed products can be dispensed. A typical
example is the revolving stand for postcards, paperback books, cassettes
or records. Although identified by the manufacturer's name, the problem does occur that the stand will be so useful that the shopkeeper will
use the stand for rival products!

Sales promotion of a regular or permanent form can take numerous
forms and can be designed to suit the circumstances. If the product has
a container (like a drinks can) which can become objectionable litter,
the supply of suitably decorated litter bins could be a public service and
an asset to the dealer.

MERCHANDISING

Now we come to short-term sales promotional schemes which are more
urgent, competitive and imaginative. They may be used for the following purposes:

1. To launch a new product.

2. As an alternative to traditional 'above-the-line' media advertising in the press or on posters, radio, TV or cinema.
3. As a 'shot-in-the-arm' effort to boost sagging sales.
4. As a means of combating competition.
5. To encourage dealers to stock because the merchandising will encourage people to buy.

Merchandising schemes may consist of:

Competitions. A competition can increase sales of a product if the entry requirement is purchase of the product. The entry form may be supplied with the product or, to prove purchase of the product, some part of the package may have to be submitted with the entry. Great care is necessary when planning a competition and the following points should be remembered.

1. The contest should require purchase of the product.
2. The prize should be sufficiently generous to attract entries and consequently purchases. There should be smaller prizes including consolation prizes to encourage people to feel they have a chance of winning something.
3. It may help if a cash equivalent to the prize can be offered. This is usually possible with a physical product such as a motor-car, but seldom possible with a holiday. A holiday in Hawaii may sound exciting, but if the winner prefers cash this may not be possible because while an airline may be willing to provide an air ticket it is unlikely to provide the cash equivalent. However, if the prize can be, say, a completely furnished house *or* the money value, the beautiful furniture can be illustrated very effectively.
4. Prizes should not be embarrassing. A holiday in Hawaii for two may sound attractive, but it could be an unwelcome prize to an unmarried prizewinner, or one with a family who has to pay a lot extra to take his children on the holiday.
5. The competition should be interesting, require some skill but not be too difficult. If likely answers can be permutated, and a large number of different answers can be given, this will minimise the chance of correct answers being duplicated so that the prize has to be divided. If this is inevitable, a tie-breaking device (such as the writing of a slogan) can be added to the main con-

test. It is better that the big prize is won rather than that its cash equivalent is divided among a lot of people with all-correct answers.

6. It should be a competition, and not merely a lucky draw, or the award of prizes to easily answered questions.
7. There should be a reputable judge, or panel of judges.
8. The rules of the contest should be carefully written to avoid any risk of dispute.
9. The entry form or coupon should be carefully written and designed so that answers can be written simply and clearly, and there should be adequate space for the entrant's name and address.
10. There should not be too long an interval between the closing date of the contest and the announcement of the prizewinners.
11. The results should be announced publicly; say, in the press. Entrants are entitled to know what has happened. It helps if the date and place of this announcement can be stated on the entry form.

Premium offers. These are usually *self-liquidating offers,* meaning that the total *cost* of the scheme including the goods offered is covered by the money sent in by customers, but no *profit* is made. Customers are asked to send in part of the package – a lid-top, a label or a token printed on the package plus cash for whatever is offered, the price being a bargain.

This can be extended into a more permanent sales promotion if people are encouraged to buy the product (e.g. a tea, coffee, soup, breakfast cereal) regularly in order to collect premium offers such as cutlery which eventually make up sets.

If the offer is being advertised, care must be taken to see that shops can be supplied with the product which has to be bought to obtain tops, labels or tokens so that customers will find it in the shops during the run of the advertising campaign.

Premium or cash vouchers. Money-off vouchers may be printed in the press, printed on packages, delivered as mail-drops to houses, or given away in the street so that the customer can obtain a price reduction in exchange for the cash voucher. This is a merchandising offer with many possible applications ranging from money off the next purchase of a food product to a reduced price for a hotel room.

Free gifts. Customers can be offered free gifts when they purchase goods, or a gift can be attached to a product (e.g. a free toothbrush banded to a toothpaste), or an offer can be made in advertising. If it is a 'mail-in' for a gift — the free offer being made in a press advertisement — a closing date or a limit on the number of items being given away should be stated, otherwise the demand may exceed the intended number of gifts. Free gifts may also be distributed as give-away novelties such as balloons, ball-point pens, toys and other items bearing the advertiser's name.

Flash packs. Money-off offers can be made by adding a 'flash' to the package saying that there is a price reduction. This works very well in supermarkets and can induce 'impulse buying', customers buying the product because of the cut price specially printed (or 'flashed') on the wrapper or carton.

Multiple, banded or jumbo packs. More than one unit of a product may be banded together and sold at a special price, or one item may be offered free as, for instance, three bars of soap for the price of two. Or a selection of products may be boxed or packeted, as at Christmas time.

In-store demonstrations and samplings. Goods such as domestic appliances may be demonstrated inside shops by a demonstrator employed by the manufacturer, or samples of foodstuffs, drinks and confectionery may be offered to shop customers.

Trade characters. Some products may be associated with a trade character (like Johnnie Walker of whisky fame), and someone dressed up in the appropriate costume may visit stores, market-places or residential areas to promote the product.

Special displays. Those stockists who give a substantial order may be supplied for a limited period with a special display such as a working model.

Special trade terms. Especially to encourage stocking of a new line, but also to overcome competition or retrieve sagging sales, dealers may be offered attractive special trade terms. A typical example is to offer one free case of products with orders for a certain number of cases. Longer credit could be offered, or a higher discount.

Shopkeepers themselves may indulge in their own merchandising efforts. The *loss leader* is a product offered at a cut price in order to induce people to come into the shop, and perhaps buy goods additional to the special offer. However, this is a practice which some manufacturers dislike because it harms the image of the product; others may welcome the resultant extra sales.

When there is a premium offer, dealers may be expected to display the item which the manufacturer is offering in return for packet-tops, labels or tokens plus cash, and if dealers are allowed to keep the display piece this is called a *dealer loader*. To make sure that dealers have adequate stocks during advertising or merchandising campaigns the manufacturer's travelling salesman will carry stocks in their cars which they can supply immediately to dealers who are out of stock. These are known as *buffer stocks*.

10 Distribution

Without an effective distribution system a manufacturer or supplier cannot supply users or consumers, especially if they are scattered throughout an area, country or the world. *Adequate distribution* means that when a product is advertised it is available in sufficient quantities in the right outlets to satisfy demand. An *outlet* is any source of retail supply, whether it be a shop, market stall, supermarket, department store or even a mail-order trader. The *distribution cycle* is the time it takes for a product to reach the consumer, and this can include time in a wholesale warehouse and on a retailer's shelf. The cycle could amount to days, weeks or months. Obviously, it will be longer for a motor-car, much shorter for meat or vegetables.

Distributors are all kinds of people involved in the chain of distribution, although in the motor-car trade a major dealer (who may act as a wholesaler to small motor-car dealers) is known as a 'main distributor'. Those who sell 'over the counter' to customers may be called stockists, dealers, shopkeepers, traders or retailers.

Middlemen are those distributors who buy goods from the manufacturer, importer or supplier and then sell either to other middlemen or to retailers. The role of the middleman or *wholesaler* is to break down large quantities into the smaller quantities required by shopkeepers. Some goods such as fish, meat, fruit and vegetables may be taken or sent to market by the producer, and national wholesale markets may sell to local wholesale markets before the eventual fishmonger, butcher, greengrocer or fruiterer buys the produce for retail sale. *Agents* and *jobbers* (including manufacturers' agents) sell on commission, and usually represent several suppliers. These agents sell at wholesale prices to retailers in a stated area. *Rack jobbers* are wholesalers who specialise in, say, toiletries and maintain stocks in supermarkets. *Sales brokers* take over the advertising and distribution of non-competing products, and save the manufacturer having to use a sales force.

Brokers tend to give professional advice to clients as well as represent firms; typical examples being stockbrokers and insurance brokers.

Franchisers are those who invest money in a business which sells only the products or services provided by the company awarding the franchise. A number of popular restaurants (with the same name), and several household services such as carpet-cleaning, operate on franchises, thus providing outlets for products through independently managed local businesses.

Factors are not only wholesalers; they also take over the producer's credit operation and collect payment, as with some book distributors, virtually buying the producer's invoices and earning a commission on the collection of accounts.

Cash-and-carry warehouses sell bulk quantities of goods (e.g. a complete case) at wholesale prices provided they are bought for cash and the buyer provides his own transport. Small traders use these services, which are also useful when a shop runs out of stock and cannot wait for delivery by the regular supplier. Private buyers are also accepted, sometimes as card-holders, as when supplies are required for parties or weddings.

Bulk or central buyers are employed by multiples and chain stores who purchase large stocks on practically wholesale terms direct from manufacturers, usually accepting delivery at one point.

These activities incur distribution costs which have to be included in the price paid by the final customer. The manufacturer or supplier, even if he has no absolute control over the final price, needs to work out costings for a list price or recommended retail price which will be both an acceptable or attractive final price, and one which will cover his distribution costs.

Distribution costs will include everything in addition to production costs and profit margin. Items may include:

> packaging;
> advertising;
> warehousing;
> transport to distributors;
> discounts or trade terms for wholesalers, bulk buyers and
>   retailers;
> sales force salaries, commissions and expenses.

Thus, the *selling price* has to cover all these costs, and there may be a series of commissions which continually add to the original price. An example is coal where the 'pit-head price' paid by miners or people in the vicinity of the mine will be very low compared with that paid by a householder hundreds of miles away. The 'mark-up' or difference charged by the retailer will depend on the speed of turnover (e.g. a foodstuff carries a very low mark-up compared with that for a slow-moving item such as a watch, TV receiver or motor-car), and it will also depend on the amount of servicing which the retailer has to provide (e.g. a motor-car). It may also be necessary to include other costs in the price, such as training of retail sales staff, after-sales service and guarantees.

Distribution is thus a major cost, and a major portion of price. A mail-order firm, for example, will have to recover the cost of carriage or postage and packing. Before any profit can be made, all costs have to be recovered, and these will be paid by the customer in the price. The distributor has to regain all his costs in providing a warehouse, transport, staff or shop.

There are many kinds of stockist, dealer, shopkeeper, trader and retailer:

1. *Multiples* are chains of stores or supermarkets and are defined in the British Census of Distribution as firms other than a co-operative society having ten or more retail establishments.
2. *Hypermarkets* are out-of-town or one-stop superstores or mass merchandisers. Their selling area is usually not less than 25,000 square feet, and they have large car parks.
3. *Variety chain stores* (sometimes called bazaars) sell a large range of goods, usually laid out on open counters. Woolworth is a typical example.
4. *Bazaars* can be of three kinds: (*a*) variety stores as described above; (*b*) open or covered markets such as the oriental bazaar; and (*c*) a grouping of similar traders such as antique dealers.
5. *Co-operative stores* are retail societies owned by members or customers who share the profits by means of dividends or trading stamps based on purchases.
6. *Congerie* — a colony of shops selling similar goods.
7. *Discount stores*. These are shops, single or in chains and sometimes quite large, which buy in bulk and sell at cut prices. Merchandise may consist of hi-fi and electronic equipment, domestic appliances, carpets, or knockdown furniture.

8. *Department stores* are large shops with departments for different classes of goods, e.g. Harrods and Selfridges in London, Kingsway Stores in Lagos.
9. *Shopping plazas.* These are high-rise shopping complexes with perhaps offices or flats on floors above, as in Singapore.
10. *Appointed dealer.* Some manufacturers prefer to have a limited number of appointed stockists, perhaps one to a town. Usually for expensive products.
11. *Neighbourhood shop* — a local shop as distinct from one in a city shopping centre.
12. *Shopping precinct.* This is a town shopping centre which has no roads and is therefore free of traffic and safe for shoppers. Malls are similar but at ground level.
13. *Direct selling* means selling direct to the customer on the doorstep. It could mean either home delivery by a milk or bread roundsman, or doorstep selling by salesmen of insurance, household goods, cosmetics and so on. Avon cosmetics are sold direct.
14. *Mail order* or *direct response* is selling by post, using media such as the press, direct mail, catalogues and sales literature. In recent years this has become a major form of distribution and business, and newspapers and magazines carry advertisements for numerous postal offers. Traditionally, some products have been sold regularly in this way e.g. horticulturalists selling plants and seeds; book, record and cassette clubs; mail-order clubs such as Littlewoods; stamp and coin dealers; and many charities sell Christmas cards and gifts in this way. This form of trading is given fuller consideration below.
15. *Party selling.* A housewife invites friends to sample products in her home, where a visiting representative of the company demonstrates products on which she earns commission, the hostess receiving a discount on any purchases made. The hostess receives further discounts if she is able to introduce other hostesses for additional selling parties.

The traditional chart of distribution channels is shown in Figure 10.1.

A totally new concept is introduced by the combination of Prestel (viewdata) and credit cards so that goods may be purchased from the home by means of television and telephones, and payment may be made by credit card (e.g. American Express, Diners Club, Access or Barclaycard with Mastercard facility).

Fig. 10.1. Channels of distribution. N.B. The retailer may be an independent shop, a shop owned by the manufacturer or a mail-order house. The wholesaler may include agents, factors, cash-and-carry warehouses. Direct sales from manufacturer to consumer may be made by a visiting salesman or roundsman or by mail order.)

In developing countries not all these methods may be appropriate. Mail order may have its problems if postal services are poor, or people may be unwilling to trust the distant firm advertising goods by post. Some distributors may be mainly importers and agents for foreign goods, such as Leventis in Nigeria. The market-place and the village stall may be more common than the sophisticated shop in a town.

MAIL ORDER — SPECIAL CONSIDERATIONS

However, provided carriage or postal services are efficient, mail order trading has possibilities and advantages in countries where people are remotely situated and it is difficult for them to visit towns to do shopping. Some of the reasons for the popularity of mail-order trading are therefore worth examining.

Mail order is not a new idea, and it was developed in an interesting and very successful way by such American pioneers of the system as Montgomery Ward and Sears Roebuck. Operating from Chicago in the mid-nineteenth century, they supplied the scattered and distant farmers of the Mid-West with almost anything they needed. They printed huge catalogues of maybe 1000 pages containing thousands of items, and made use of railway and eventually parcel-post services. Later they also opened local depots and shops where the goods were displayed, and Montgomery Ward and Sears Roebuck are today world-famous. As an example of their remarkable services, a hospital in a developing country ordered its entire equipment from one of these firms, by mail order! Perhaps there is a parallel for mail order in large countries like Nigeria?

The reasons for the popularity of mail-order trading are:

1. It provides privacy for buyers who can choose goods at home from a catalogue instead of having to buy in a public shopping place. Some people dislike buying in front of other people, or resent being made to look foolish or ignorant by shop assistants. This is an interesting psychological aspect of *direct-response shopping.*

2. Often, the goods offered are exclusive to the supplier who has made special bulk purchases, or had goods made for them exclusively. They may be the actual producers, as with horticultural growers and seedsmen. There are certain speciality mail-order traders who make and supply curtains, chair-covers, kits for making rugs, or other goods not available from general retailers. Some insurance policies and cash loans, membership of book, record and cassette clubs, coins and other collectors' items, and membership of credit-card promotors are sold in this way. It is a versatile business.

3. Some firms run mail-order clubs with agents, mostly housewives, who recruit customers on a club basis and earn commission on sales. Littlewoods, Freemans, Brian Mills and Grattan are famous names in Britain.

4. Armchair buying — buying from home — is fun for some people who enjoy treating themselves to the goods displayed in press advertisements or catalogues.

5. It is a very convenient way of shopping. The buyer does not have to travel to a shop, and can pay by cheque or credit card.

6. The goods may be cheaper, due to bulk buying by the mail-order firm, and because of special offers.

7. Credit terms may be offered so that it is easy to buy expensive items.

The disadvantages of not being able to see or try goods at first hand, and the high cost of postage or delivery charges, are generally offset by the advantages listed above.

The success of mail order depends not only on a good distribution system but on three other factors:

1. A well-printed catalogue which brings the shop into the home.

2. Suitable media — especially full-colour magazines — in which the offered goods can be advertised realistically. In Britain, the weekend colour magazines issued with Sunday newspapers, the

women's press, and the TV programme magazines carry a lot of mail-order advertising.

3. Trust in the mail-order trader. This can be developed by the newspaper and magazine advertisement departments who vet advertisers and guarantee readers against loss. There have been unscrupulous mail-order advertisers who have not ordered the goods until orders have been received. Then they have found prices have gone up, they have gone bankrupt, and customers have lost money. Nowadays, publishers require an undertaking that the trader is efficiently organised and can deliver in a reasonable time at the offer price. This is necessary because inexperienced advertisers may not appreciate the volume of orders which their advertisements may produce, and they may not have sufficient stock, storage room or packing facilities to supply the goods before customers start complaining to the newspaper or magazine publisher.

Already, in developing countries, people will be familiar with things like correspondence courses and books which are sold by mail-order, while football pools are a form of mail-order trading when coupons, entries and payment are posted.

11 Marketing Research

Although it is not always easy to conduct marketing research in developing countries it is not impossible. In this chapter a broad introduction will be given to the range of research techniques which are in use. We shall also look at the problems which confront the researcher in developing countries, and consider how techniques can be modified to suit special conditions.

Marketing research is based on the same principles as sampling tea, wine or a sack of grain. If a little is tasted or examined this small quantity will give a good impression of the whole. However, too much should not be read into the results of a marketing research survey. A margin of error may have to be accepted. The results may indicate trends rather than facts. People may express interest, but they may not finally buy. A research report needs to be read intelligently. The results will depend on what questions were asked of whom and perhaps when.

A problem with research is that respondents — those who answer questions — may resent being questioned, or be reluctant to give information, or be untruthful. They may not always be aware of the truth, and motivation research is a method by which unknown motives may be revealed. When research (mostly Government) was conducted in Britain after the Second World War unwelcome investigators were dubbed 'snoopers', but nowadays research enquiries are so common that few people object to being questioned. Even so, courtesy and tact is required of researchers.

In developing countries, where people are less familiar with marketing research, people may fear answering questions because they may suspect some ulterior motive such as the gathering of information for taxation purposes. There may also be taboos and customs which make the collection of information — as in census-taking — very difficult so that false results occur. Muslim women may be forbidden to talk to the researcher; in some societies men will wish to prove their virility by claiming to have more children than they really have, while in another society it may be believed that children will die if information is given about them.

DEFINITIONS

Government research is called *social research;* that into market conditions is known as *market research;* while all the forms of research used in advertising, marketing and public relations are more broadly described as *marketing research.* The British Market Research Society defines market research as the 'branch of social science which uses scientific methods to collect information about markets for goods or services'. Being the largest organisation of its kind in the world, with members engaged in all sorts of research, it would be more correct if it were called the *Marketing* Research Society. The two words are often used loosely to mean marketing rather than merely market research. This is clarified very well by Professor Michael J.Baker in his excellent book *Marketing: An Introductory Text* when he says on page 167:

> By definition, market research is concerned with measurement and analysis of markets, whereas marketing research is concerned with all those factors which impinge upon the marketing of goods and services, and so includes the study of advertising effectiveness, distributive channels, competitive products and marketing policies and the whole field of consumer behaviour.

Later, Michael Baker points out that 'marketing research is equally concerned with industrial goods'.

KINDS OF RESEARCH

There are basically three kinds of research: desk research, *ad hoc* research and continuous research.

Desk research

This means the study of *secondary* or existing information which may be contained in Government reports and statistics (e.g. a Census Report); internal sales information as received, for instance, from salesmen's reports; and other published information in directories or survey reports which may be obtained free of charge or purchased. It is quite possible that *primary* or original research has been undertaken already which provides the required information. A Government report may record the number of houses which exist or are built in a year, which would indicate the size of the potential market for, say, corrugated iron sheeting, air-conditioning or even door mats.

Ad hoc research

This means the conducting of a single survey, which may be sufficient to discover, for example, how often property-owners replace their roofs or motorists replace their motor-cars.

Continuous research

This means a series of surveys — maybe monthly, quarterly, or every 6 months, to record trends over time. This could be shown on a graph to show how some kind of situation was changing. It could show the progress or otherwise of sales, a comparison between the sales of one brand and its rivals, or how opinions changed in the light of better knowledge and understanding.

WHO SHOULD CONDUCT RESEARCH?

If it is to be reliable, and as free from bias — one-sidedness — as possible, primary research should be conducted by independent experts such as a professional research organisation. Salesmen should *never* be asked to carry out surveys, neither should other company staff who might bias the enquiry. Very large companies do employ research units (whose services may be commissioned by other firms) but the research staff are skilled specialists. Some of the largest advertising agencies own subsidiary research firms, but they work independently and often for clients other than those of the parent company.

The specialists are psychologists, sociologists and statisticians who understand how to word and design questionnaires, select samples of people, process answers, and interpret results. These are not tasks for amateurs. This also extends to the recruitment, training and supervision of interviewers.

Finding suitable people to conduct interviews can be a problem in developing countries. In the West — and because interviewing is usually an occasional part-time job — interviewers are usually women and mostly either young women of suitable education (e.g. social science degree) or middle-aged women whose families have grown up. The need is for people with a sympathetic, pleasant, mature but unobtrusive personality. The tendency in developing countries is to employ university students, mainly because they are well-educated and available during vacations. They could be too young and inexperienced for such work which requires patience and can be frustrating.

THE RESPONDENTS

It is essential to question the right people. Who are they? Where are they? We may wish to interview various kinds of people of both sexes, different ages, and different jobs or income. We may decide to interview them at work, in the street, or at their homes. There are many possibilities. But accuracy in designing the sample will depend on the availability of reliable statistics.

The most valuable source is a national census of population, which may or may not exist, and if it does exist it may be inaccurate. As a simpler example, if we planned to interview a sample of men and women their proportions in the sample should be identical to their proportions in the national census. If 49 per cent of the population were men and 51 per cent were women, a sample of 500 men and women should consist of 245 men and 255 women. But the sample may have to be broken down more carefully into different kinds of men and women if we wish to discover the views, preferences or motives of a variety of people. (We will return to the types of research necessary for researching views, preferences and motives. The different kinds of sample will also be explained later.)

In many countries, populations are divided into either *socio-economic groups* based on income, or — as in Britain — into the more realistic *social grades* based on occupation. British social grades used in marketing research are as shown in Table 11.1. The A's are not millionaires but the people in top business, academic, civil service, religious, military and other positions. As will be seen, the mass market — the

Marketing

TABLE 11.1. *Social grades in Britain*

Grade		Comprising	Percentage
A	Upper middle class	Top business, social leader	3%
B	Middle class	Senior executives, managers	13%
C1	Lower middle class	White-collar office workers	22%
C2	Skilled working class	Blue-collar factory workers	32%
D	Semi-skilled, unskilled working class		20%
E	Lowest level of subsistence	Poor pensioners, unemployed	9%

people who watch TV and buy popular newspapers (the Cs and Ds) – represent almost three-quarters of the British population. They form the mass of the people – sometimes called the *admass* – who buy at the supermarket the popular brands known as fast-moving consumer goods (FMCG). But they also form the target audience for small to medium-size motor-cars, package holidays, building society savings, household goods and appliances, mail-order clubs and direct response offers. They are the big spenders in terms of volume sales. While not individually rich, their collective purchases absorb factory output.

The picture will be very different in developing countries where TV is not every working man's pleasure, holidays abroad are not commonplace, and motor-cars are not taken for granted. Lifestyles will be dictated by literacy, type of employment, class of housing and income, and the rural population will predominate over the urban. There will also be ethnic and regional differences.

In Kenya there will be relatively sophisticated tribes like the urban Kikuyu and the Masai herdsmen plus Europeans and Indians, but in the remote north there are tribes which have little contact with modern civilisation. Those who live in Lusaka, Livingstone and the copper belt in Zambia will have a relatively sophisticated life style compared with that of the remote lake islanders. The same might be said of the Nupe in Nigeria whose lifestyle is vastly different from that of the people in Nigeria's major cities.

Consequently, in developing countries we find social grades of a pattern such as that shown in Table 11.2. The percentage will obviously vary from country to country and as education and job opportunities

TABLE 11.2. *Social grades in developing countries*

	Grade	Comprising	Percentage
A	Upper class	Royal and well-to-do families	2%
B	Middle class	Educated people in business, civil service, Armed Forces	23%
C	Lower class	The majority, mostly rural, some factory workers, many illiterate	70%
D	Subsistence level	Beggars, disabled, unemployed	5%

improve there will be upward mobility between the grades. But something like the pattern of social grades shown in Table 11.2 will apply to many African countries such as Nigeria, Ghana, Sierra Leone, Kenya and Zimbabwe. The significant difference between the British and the African social grades is that whereas 75 per cent of the British represent the mass market *with* money 75 per cent of the African represents the mass of people *without* money. This is worsened by the fact that 50 per cent of the African people are under 15 years of age and without purchasing power.

The situation is even worse from a marketing point of view in the underdeveloped or least-developed countries where the social grades may be distinguished by the level of education and employment, the educated speaking the national language while the illiterate speak a dialect (see Table 11.3). In such countries purchasing power lies with the

TABLE 11.3. *Social grades in underdeveloped or least-developed countries*

	Grade	Comprising	Percentage
A	University graduate	Professionals	1%
B	Secondary school educated	Clerks, telephonists	5%
C	Partly literate	Unskilled workers	14%
D	Illiterate	Agricultural workers, miners, fishermen	80%

20 per cent minority, most of the 80 per cent being poor subsistence farmers producing little if any surplus for sale.

These are generalities. No two countries are the same. The Caribbean is a good example where no two island communities are the same yet a simple factor like a standard English language helps to encourage educational and literary standards, however local the patois may be.

The significance of this social grades analysis is, as far as marketing research is concerned, that although statistics may be unavailable the research will tend to be limited to the accessible, urban and semi-elitest population who represent the bulk of the purchasing power. The situation will also call for modification and simplification of research techniques as they are known in the West.

Let us now return to the range of marketing research techniques, and consider how they may be used or adapted in developing countries.

PURPOSES OF RESEARCH

What do we want to find out? There are three types of knowledge which marketing research may seek:

What people think or know

This area is covered by what may be called *opinion, attitude, awareness, shift* or *image* research. Such surveys test what people think or believe, or the extent of their knowledge, ignorance or misconceptions; changes or shifts in ideas, knowledge and understanding over a period of time; or the impression or image they hold of the organisation. Mostly, such surveys ask for *Yes, No, Don't know* answers. The Opinion Poll of Gallup Poll fame is a typical example, but many market research organisations conduct such surveys, as is seen at the time of elections. Political polls are sometimes unfairly criticised: the results depend on the kind of sample, the questions asked and the closeness to the event when people finally make up their minds and vote. The poll on the Common Market Referendum in Britian was almost exactly the same as the electoral result.

What people prefer

Research into *preferences* — what people would like to buy or do buy

− is the purpose of most marketing research including consumer, dealer, packaging, newspaper and magazine, TV and radio audience research.

This leads into the question *who buys what*? In an American survey into watch-buying, 46 per cent said they bought a watch because it was an expensive luxury − self-indulgence; 28 per cent because of its quality − rational; while 38 per cent regarded a watch as a necessity − utility. A British survey into clock-buying found that the majority of buyers are C1, C2 middle-aged women who bought clocks as presents. Both products tell the time, but such research indicates very different market segments and distributors, advertisement copy appeals and choice of media. The sexes and ages of buyers, and the time of year for advertising, could be different too.

What motivates people

The underlying reasons why people behave as they do − they may buy to reward themselves for a hard day's work rather than because they prefer one to another − is sought by various forms of motivation research which can be very useful in discovering themes for advertising or reasons for unsuccessful marketing.

RESEARCH TECHNIQUES AND JARGON

Already we have shown three very different kinds of enquiry. There are also different or rival methods of conducting these enquiries. There are as many 'schools' of research as there are makes of motor-car, and the marketer has to be aware of the choices open to him. They are not necessarily better or worse than one another. They may be different ways of getting similar information. One may suit a certain product or service more cheaply or more accurately than another: it depends on the problem. Some of these methods may not suit developing countries, but it is wise to have an insight into this complex subject.

There is a lot of special jargon in marketing research, and words with everyday meanings have special meanings. For instance, a *sample* should not be confused with a free sample. Here, it means the smallest number of people who need to be questioned in order to get an accurate (or accurate within an accepted degree of error) set of answers representative of all the people relevant to the enquiry. The number of people and the degree of error may be determined by the budget. *Population* normally means all the people, as in a census of population, but in research *population* means only those people relevant to the enquiry such as all motorists, teachers or housewives. Different research organisations, researchers, authors or lecturers may use different words for the same thing. *Universe* may be used instead of population; and *retail, shop* and *dealer* audit are the same thing. And as we shall see, when referring to a *random sample* it is not random at all!

Sampling frame

This is the design of the sample, what sort of people are to be questioned, and how and where they are to be found. Thus, we may decide to question all insurance companies and they could all be located in the telephone directory, while mothers with young children might be found at schools or clinics, and motorists might be found at car parks, garages and service stations. These are just simple examples. The actual sampling frame might define certain kinds of motorists, or drivers of particular makes of vehicle.

The sample

There are several kinds of sample, and an interesting exercise will be to decide which samples are possible or practical in the circumstances of a developing country. They can be different from or even the opposite to the experience in industrial countries. Let us take each in turn:

1. *Convenience sampling.* This is the simplest form of sampling, and tends to be unscientific because it is not absolutely representative. It means questioning people who are easily found, such as passers-by in the street. Thus 100 people might be stopped and asked their views or preferences, but without any attempt to find special kinds of people. It will provide information which is better than none, but another 100 people might give different answers. It would be useful if it produced unexpected answers which might never have been anticipated, such as that respondents found the instructions on a package difficult to understand. If only five people said that, it would be a warning to make the instructions clearer.

2. *Judgement sampling.* This occurs when the interviewer selects res-

pondents based on his or her opinion that they form a representative cross-section of the universe being investigated. It could apply to, say, a survey of motorists who might be selected according to the make (and perhaps age) of car they were driving, or the purpose for which they were driving — business, pleasure, car-hire, sports and so forth.

Neither (1) nor (2) is a scientifically designed sample, but for some enquiries it may be adequate, and where population statistics do not exist one of these samples will be a necessary compromise.

3. *Quota sample.* Here, the respondent is instructed to find certain numbers (or quotas) of people of defined types, and the quotas should be in proportion to the total numbers of such people in the population. The quotas may be based on social grades or socio-economic grades. But there could be specified quotas such as non-smokers, cigarette-, cigar- and pipe-smokers and, by asking, the interviewer would find the various quotas. Quota sampling is generally used for one of two reasons: when certain types of people, and not a general cross-section, are to be interviewed or if, for cost reasons, a random sample is too expensive. It cannot be scientifically accurate because it is subject to the bias or error of the interviewer in finding the right people, however skilled and experienced the interviewer may be.

However, in developing countries it may be more difficult and costly to find quotas than in an industrial society. A form of random sample, which is more expensive in an industrial urban society, could in fact be cheaper in a developing country. This is an important contradiction which has to be recognised. We shall return to this situation as we proceed.

4. *Random sample.* A random sample does not mean selecting people 'at random'. A random sample can be of two kinds. Names can be selected on the basis of a set of *random numbers* which can be obtained in ready-printed form. A page may consist of figures which read 4 92 17 33 141 and so on, and these could then be related to names and addresses, in say, a membership list, the 4th, the 92nd , the 17th and so on, name being listed for interview.

However, this is a method more often used in university or social surveys. In marketing, the *interval* or *probability sample* is generally used, the method requiring names and addresses to be selected from an existing list such as an electoral roll, membership list, trade directory or telephone directory, at regular intervals. If the sample was to consist of

1000 people from a list of 10,000 every 10th name would be chosen. Researchers talk of every *n*th name being picked, *n* referring to the length of the interval or gap between names.

The *random* sample becomes more accurate than a quota sample for four reasons:

(a) A mathematical formula can be applied to calculate the minimum number of people necessary for a sample with an agreed degree of error, this degree of error being determined by budget. The smaller the degree of error the larger the sample and the higher the cost of interviewing.

(b) Based on the law of averages the *probability* is that a random sample will be an accurate cross-section of the total population, finding correct proportions of types of people (called 'characteristics') in the total population.

(c) Usually, the interviewer is expected to make three (sometimes more) attempts to interview the named respondent, but following failure to conduct the interview a replacement name may be used.

(d) There is no interviewer bias in selecting respondents since the interviewer is given names and does not have to find people to fit quotas.

Because of the time spent in building the list of respondents, making up to three attempts to interview people at perhaps scattered locations, and also because the total sample is perhaps three times larger, the cost of conducting a random sample survey is about three times the cost of using a quota sample.

The random sample is best when a high degree of accuracy is required, but it is also most appropriate when most or all people in the universe are relevant to the investigation. If only certain people were relevant it could be wasteful and a quota sample would be adequate. Election-time polls are more accurate if a random sample is used, since most adults are voters, but if the survey was limited to, say, housewives of certain ages and certain social grades, a quota sample could be used. Random samples are ideal for readership surveys in a literate country where most people read newspapers and magazines, and for audience surveys where most people watch television.

5. *Stratified random sample.* This version of the random sample is one

based on the make-up of the total population such as the proportions of the sexes or social grades, and is useful if only sections of the total population in census terms are necessary for the survey. This kind of sample could also be applied to trades or businesses if only a certain one or certain ones were to be investigated.

6. *Area sampling and multi-stage sampling.* These are methods of reducing the number of *sampling points* (places where surveys are conducted), and in random sampling a too-widely scattered (and costly) sample is avoided. Area (or cluster) sampling means that the interviews are carried out in groups of towns; multi-stage sampling means that the country is broken down into counties, states or provinces, and then districts, and interviews allocated in proportion to the population in each area.

Another method often used is to take a random selection of the general election polling districts in the country, and to survey only in these areas. One such national survey in Britain is based on 1000 polling districts, thus giving a good cross-section of the whole country.

7. *Random walk or location.* From the above descriptions of random sampling it will be seen that there are sophistications which are splendid where there are census statistics, printed lists of names and addresses, large urban populations, good transportation, and competent interviewers available everywhere. Hardly any of these requirements of random sampling exist in developing countries.

The compromise solution which has been applied in developing countries is the *random walk or location* method. Since most research in such countries may tend to be confined to towns where people with purchasing power live, the technique is a practical way of overcoming lack of statistics. A residential area or township is visited and interval sampling is applied to every nth house in each street. Thus, the interviewer may call at, say, every sixth house according to the number of people to be questioned. But if motorists were being questioned, every nth motorist stopping for fuel at a garage could be questioned. Thus, random sampling can be adapted to local conditions.

The Questionnaire

In most surveys a list of questions is used. The respondent will either fill in the answers, as in a postal survey, or in a field survey an interviewer will read the questions to the respondent and fill in the answers, usually by placing a tick in a box against the given answer. This will depend on the type of question. Preparing questions is a skilled business if correct information is to be obtained. Questions must not be difficult to understand, nor ambiguous.

If people are asked whether they have a car they may say no if the car is owned by their employer, and a different answer would result from asking whether they drove a car or if they bought petrol. Questions must therefore be precise, and this is one reason why it pays to employ research specialists.

There are several different kinds of questions, although in an opinion survey it is usual only to seek *Yes, No, Don't Know* answers.

1. *Dichotomous* questions which call for *Yes* or *No*.
2. *Multi-choice* questions which list items such as makes of motor-car, and the respondent is asked which car he drives, last bought or would choose if he intended buying a car. Such lists can never be complete so it is usual to add a final 'other' category.
3. *Semantic differential.* This is a way of expressing degrees of quality such as bad — poor — fairly good — good — very good — excellent with evaluations such as -3, -2, -1, and 1, 2, 3.
4. *Open-ended* questions are those where the interviewer or respondent is invited to answer freely without being restricted to set or structured questions. The interviewer has to write down the given answer, or at least record the essence of the answer if it is too lengthy to record verbatim. This sort of question gives the respondent the chance to say what he or she wants to say.

A *loaded* or *leading* question, such as 'Don't you think the police are corrupt' should not be asked because this is trying to suggest an answer. Research should be impartial. It should not matter to the interviewer what answer is given.

Structured questions were mentioned above. A survey is structured when there is a questionnaire made up of carefully worded questions. One needs psychological training to write questions, and that is why it is wise to use an independent research unit or a company unit made up of trained researchers. Sales staff should never be used to conduct surveys because they could easily, if innocently, influence the kind of answers given. An *unstructured* survey is one where respondents are free to answer as they wish, and the questions may be put conversationally as in *depth interviews* and *discussion groups.*

Bias

If the interviewer allows personal views, attitudes or feelings to influence answers, bias or distortion occurs. Bias can occur unintentionally through the personality of the interviewer, and so it is necessary to select interviewers whose personality does not obtrude. A student may be considered too inexperienced, a lady may be too pretty or too well-dressed, and a regional accent or membership of a different tribe, or the sex of the interviewer, could provoke bias. When recruiting interviewers, or employing them for particular surveys, these aspects have to be considered. Answers could be distorted or falsified if the respondent liked or disliked the interviewer too strongly.

Product pre-testing

A manufacturer may design a new product which he is confident will sell, but that may be only his opinion. Not everyone is a Henry Ford who intuitively knew that there was a market for an inexpensive motor-car if it could be mass-produced. He was even bold enough to say customers could have any colour they liked provided it was black. Nowadays it is necessary to research what kind of motor-car and what colours people will buy, even what name it shall be called. There are several forms of product pre-testing quite apart from straightforward field surveys using questionnaires.

1. *Blind product test.* The new product and existing products are put in plain packets and respondents are asked to say which one they prefer, and why they like or dislike the different products. They may be asked to rank them in order of merit.
2. *Paired comparison test.* The respondent will be asked to choose between two items, and then between the chosen one and a third. This could be applied to the blind product test, identified products, or subjects such as colours, flavours, containers, wrappings or packages.
3. *Trials.* Respondents may be asked to use a product, perhaps for some days, and then to answer questions at the end of the trial.
4. *Hall-testing.* This is a name given to inviting members of the public, such as passers-by, to enter a building where products are

displayed and respondents are asked to make choices and answer questions, including personal questions to classify the social grade of the respondent. An example might be a typewriter or a sewing machine, and the colour of the case would be under survey.

Packaging research

As already mentioned, techniques similar to product pre-testing can be used to find out preferences for alternative container designs, materials, closures, labels and other aspects of packaging. A special kind of packaging research is the *stand-out* test where people are shown an array of packages, which include the one under test, and they are asked to pick out the one they first notice. The test will be to see how well the new package stands out from the rest.

Postal surveys

When a list of names and addresses of potential respondents exists, when they may be scattered so that it would be prohibitively expensive to call on them, and when the costs are a major consideration, the postal survey may be used. Time may be saved since the questionnaires are despatched on the same day, and a closing date can be given for their return.

However, the economics of this system have to be studied carefully. It may be cheaper to post a questionnaire than to employ interviewers, but interviewers can control the situation and get answers. People receiving questionnaires by post could ignore or mislay them or forget to post them back. Therefore, mail surveys will be effective only if there is some measure of control or inducement. A small gift such as a pen may accompany the questionnaire, or return of the form may entitle the respondent to be entered for a prize. The best control is when the survey is of interest to the respondent so that he or she is willing to co-operate. But a 100 per cent return is unlikely, thus unbalancing the sample and upsetting the accuracy of the enquiry. It depends on the value of what can be learned from the answers which are submitted.

Telephone surveys

Ringing up people unexpectedly and perhaps inconveniently is not the best way of conducting market research. Nevertheless, when used sensibly, this method can be rewarding when important respondents are scattered over large distances. It is ideal for industrial marketing research when the sample is usually fairly small. The respondents are possibly professional men or businessmen who can be written to in advance to make appointments to answer questions over the telephone.

Field survey

This is a general term to cover all outside surveys conducted by interviewers who may question people out-of-doors or at their homes, offices or elsewhere.

Recall research

The expression 'recall' is used in a number of ways in market research. Recall research is a means of measuring recall of advertisements shortly after they have been published in the press, or broadcast on radio or TV. It can also be applied to posters. Respondents are tested to see what they remember of advertisements.

Aided recall

This means using some device to assist people to remember, as when cards bearing the titles or 'mastheads' of publications are shown during readership surveys, and respondents are asked when they last read a copy. In *copy-testing* respondents may be shown a number of press advertisements or TV commercials and are afterwards asked what they remember of each advertisement.

Opinion, attitude or shift research

Well known in political research, this technique is used to determine opinions about persons or subjects (as distinct from preferences or motives). It can be used in public relations to assess what people think about an organisation. If these surveys are conducted periodically as a form of *continuous research* a graph can be drawn showing changes of opinion over time. Percentages can be calculated to show falls or rises in support, awareness or understanding. Random or quota samples may be used.

Image studies

These are also useful in PR to establish the current image — how people see the organisation. The method is to ask respondents what they think about the products, services, behaviour, reputation and so on of a number of rival organisations, one of which is the sponsor although his identity is not disclosed. Then a graph can be drawn showing how each organisation was recorded, topic by topic, and the sponsor is given a comparative breakdown of the way in which he and his rivals are perceived. The *current image* so revealed may be very different from the *mirror image* held within the organisation.

Consumer panel

There are two kinds; the comparatively small one whose numbers collect, test and report on products and the large national consumer panel. The latter will be recruited to receive and complete questionnaires or diaries in which purchases are recorded by date, brand, size and place of purchase. Respondents are thus usually housewives, but panels can consist of other people for more specialised enquiries.

Omnibus survey

Using a consumer panel, the omnibus survey will require respondents to complete questionnaires, usually posted once a month, which are made up of sets of questions paid for by a number of sponsors. This is said to be *piggybacking* on an omnibus survey. This is an inexpensive way of using a ready-made continuous survey to ask a few questions only once or as often as may be required.

Brand barometer

This is another form of consumer panel, except that a researcher calls at the house of the panelist, and notes the branded products stored in the larder, refrigerator or bathroom. This is done regularly, usually monthly.

Dustbin check

The panelist is given a plastic sack in which to keep empty cartons, bottles, wrappers, tubes, sachets and other branded-product containers, and a researcher records these purchases at regular intervals.

Shop, dealer or retail audit

Made famous by A. C. Nielsen 50 years ago, but adopted by other research companies, audit research checks the movement of retail stocks and publishes indexes showing the brand shares held by products in different categories of foods, drinks, toiletries and pharmaceuticals. Panels of representative shopkeepers are visited monthly by an auditor who checks the invoices and stocks and so assesses sales. In the UK, panels are on a TV region basis so that dealer audit surveys can be related to TV advertising campaigns.

Using continuous dealer audit research a manufacturer can compare the performance of his brand with that of other brands (and check the effect of his or rival promotions), while with continuous consumer panel research he can check what kind of people are buying brands in what sizes, how frequently, and where. This is a big advance on merely knowing that salesmen have brought in orders and goods have left the warehouse.

Motivation research

The traditional motivation research introduced by Dr Ernst Dichter in the USA some 30 years ago, uses a fairly small sample of maybe 20 or 30 people and applies clinical and intelligence tests to discover the underlying motives for customer behaviour. The reasons why people buy or do not buy goods may not be revealed by ordinary field research. People may not be aware of the reasons. One of his studies shows that people buy, say, confectionery or drinks, to reward themselves for hard work, not because they like the taste. A famous book, *The Hidden Persuaders,* by Vance Packard, tells of many of Dichter's investigations. Hidden persuaders are market researchers, *not* PROs as supposed by the press.

Discussion groups

A more simplified form of motivation research, and inexpensive, is the discussion group. The leader of the group poses questions which are discussed freely until the leader records a consensus answer. Great care has to be taken to see (*a*) that the group – being small – is representative, and (*b*) that the leader does not bias the answers.

The motivation research and discussion group methods are sometimes criticised because, unlike quota and random samples, the samples are too small and often unrepresentative. Nevertheless, Dichter has achieved spectacular results superior to those using structured questionnaires and large samples. Some very useful studies of agency—client relations have been produced from discussion groups.

The student may be dazzled by all these techniques which resemble the various schools of thought in economics or psychology. The important thing is to understand the various kinds of research, and to know which one is the most likely to produce the best results at the lowest cost. However, cost or budget is usually bound up with the complexity of the enquiry and the degree of accuracy which is acceptable. You tend to get what you pay for.

Even so, strange things can happen in market research. In Britain (and before the creation of BARB in place of JICTARS) the BBC carried out audience surveys with interviewers questioning passers-by in the street. A famous radio programme is the Jimmy Young Show, and Prime Minister Mrs Thatcher was due to be interviewed by Jimmy Young. The questionnaire was issued to interviewers and the questions were asked. The overall result was that Mrs Thatcher's radio performance was rated 'very interesting'. In fact the survey produced an impossible statistic because at the last moment Mrs Thatcher attended a Parliamentary debate on unemployment instead of visiting the radio station studio!

But the impression must not be given that market research is a fraud. In his career the author has employed nearly every technique described in this chapter. On one occasion a client asked him to prepare a campaign for a new product. The author doubted whether there was a market for this product, and asked if a postal questionnaire could be sent to a sample of potential users. Returns were so unfavourable to the product that it was never made, and the client was saved great financial loss. The survey cost only stationery, postage and the time taken up in analysing returns and preparing a report.

On the other hand when large firms like Unilever plan to introduce a new product they invest considerable sums of money on research to arrive at, say, the right name, price, colour, flavour, container, label and so on. Then they test-market the product in an area where it is possible to carry out a miniature of a national advertising campaign -- regional TV helps here — addressed to a typical section of the market to test whether an agreed percentage of sales can be obtained over a period long enough to include repeat sales. They did this successfully with a soft drink in spite of there being 400 brands throughout the country.

In Kenya, East African Industries succeeded in promoting Omo only after they had discovered by means of research why Kenyan women preferred to continue using bars of washing soap, and could not understand an entirely different and labour-saving way of washing clothes.

A lot of interesting research is conducted in Nigeria with its developing domestic markets which companies need to understand more effectively. Both quantitative (head counts and percentages) research and qualitative (psychological) research is carried out. This has to take into account the tribal and regional differences in such a vast and heavily populated country with large cities spread hundreds of miles apart.

For example, while it is possible to recruit multi-ethnic samples for discussion groups and depth interviews in a cosmopolitan city like Lagos, more representative samples of Yorubas, Ibos and Hausas will be recruited in Lagos, Aba and Kaduna respectively. These surveys will be conducted in the particular languages and then translated into English for interpretation and report.

With some 19 Nigerian breweries calculated to meet demand and to encounter great competition, an image study has been conducted to help companies to position themselves in the new market. Similarly, pharmaceutical studies have been made with samples representing doctors, paramedicals, nurses and chemists, and another study has been made concerning domestic insecticides. Most of these psychological studies have used either the discussion group technique or intensive unstructured depth interviews of up to 1½ hours.

12 The After-Market

What happens after the product or service has been sold? Is the customer given the satisfaction of knowing that if any problems arise, or if the product is faulty or breaks down, he can be assured of a solution? Is the manufacturer so jealous of his reputation, so anxious to achieve further sales by recommendation, and future purchases by satisfied customers, that he attends very carefully to the after-market?

Corning, the glass manufacturers, go so far as to make an unconditional promise to give customers every satisfaction. They had to carry out this promise when plastic handles fell off their coffee pots.

But in developing countries it is an unhappy story that many, many importers give no thought to the after-market, especially for mechanical, electrical and electronic goods. The Third World is littered with broken-down products for which there are no spares or after-sales service. It is a lesson to be learned by indigenous firms producing goods for their home market.

The after-market consists of all those things which help to create satisfaction after the product or service has been bought and consumed, used or enjoyed. They are:

1. Guarantees, warranties and promises.
2. Instruction leaflets and manuals.
3. After-sales services such as advice centres, repairs and spare parts supplies.
4. Owner clubs, as with some makes of motor-car.
5. Training of distributors' service staff.
6. External house journals issued to customers.
7. Follow-up offers of service to maintain equipment in good order (e.g. lawnmower manufacturers do this, while opticians remind customers about having their eyes re-tested).

8. Customer service and a facility for dealing with complaints.
9. Maintaining customer interest.

The PR aspect of marketing is very evident here. Failure to nourish the after-market can lead to bad dealer–customer relations, loss of reputation, and refusal by customers to buy the product or service again. PR and marketing are thus interwoven, and the annual report and balance sheet, profits, dividends and share price will reflect the success of that vital relationship. It is therefore a serious matter when marketing people are careless about their PR. Let us look more closely at the nine items listed above.

1. *Guarantees, warranties and promises*

As already stated, some firms no longer issue detailed guarantees but make flat promises to refund money, replace goods or repair them. Some technical products such as cameras have world-wide guarantees. A guarantee should be worth having and not be hedged about by restrictive clauses. In Britain, the law ignores unrealistic guarantees, believing for example that a motor-car should survive much longer than the usual guarantee period. In the USA a company can be fined for a faulty product even if they make remarkable efforts to trace the owners of faulty products, as Corning did over their coffee-pots.

2. *Instruction leaflets and manuals*

Some of these are poorly produced and difficult to understand. It is not sufficient to print instructions in three or four European languages and then export world-wide. Importers need to impress on suppliers the need to simplify instructions and to make generous use of photographs, drawings and diagrams. A simple and excellent example is the instruction card attached to an electric plug, something which became important when the colours of the plastic coatings were changed. A lot of the problems over the misuse of powdered milk could be overcome if pictorial instead of worded instructions were printed on containers and labels.

3. *After-sales service*

When buying a product such as a bicycle, motor-cycle, motor-car, tractor, computer, TV set or sewing-machine, the customer should be assured that he can be given advice, a repair service or spare parts. Computers require considerable technological advice. The customer is entitled to insist on this. Unfortunately customers are often bad buyers, but no-one in the West would buy such a product without proper assurances. Importers of foreign products have had to be careful about this. Of course, unsophisticated people in developing countries are often exploited because of their ignorance about technical products.

4. *Owner clubs*

Some of these may be organised independently, others may be sponsored or supported by manufacturers. They maintain interest in the product and create loyalty towards it.

5. *Training of distributor staff*

This is a major way of maintaining high standards in after-sales service. It gives the customer confidence when he sees certificates displayed showing that service staff have been trained and certificated by the manufacturer. It is a positive way of underwriting dealerships.

6. *External house journals*

Customer interest is maintained and a regular link with the customer is achieved by the issue of external house journals.

7. *Follow-up offers of service*

Even if there is a charge, this is a positive way of avoiding complaints because the customer is encouraged to benefit from well-maintained equipment.

8. *Customer service and complaints facility*

It does a company no harm to invite complaints, or provide an address to which complaints should be made. This is a form of guarantee. It may help the company to correct something and prevent further complaints. Confidence is created if people feel they have the ability and not merely the right to complain. Famous stores like Marks and Spencer have built reputations on such fair-trading methods.

9. *Maintaining customer interest*

This can be achieved mainly by PR techniques such as press articles about product use, documentary films, external house magazines, presence at exhibitions, and sponsorship of sports, culture and other things that make news.

BAD AFTER-SALES SERVICE

After-sales service has become an essential feature of marketing in the West. Neglect of it is a major complaint in the Third World. Careless marketing by international companies is a primary fault but as will be seen at the end of this chapter there are other factors which are peculiar to marketing in developing countries. But first here are some examples.

In the early 1960s Burma bought Japanese Hino buses out of Japanese war compensation funds, but spare parts and after-sales services were not provided. The Burmese Government found that the buses were assembled from bodies, engines and other parts made by separate companies who were difficult to deal with. This resulted in a bad PR situation. As a result, a new deal had to be negotiated through the setting-up of the Heavy Industries Corporation. Burma had the same experience with locomotives and aircraft.

One of the most successful computer firms, selling in Africa and rivalling American and European firms, had been established there for more than 20 years. But in 1976 the fortunes of the company waned when they failed to provide service, spare parts and software because obsolete machines had been sold to the Third World and parts were no longer available. This was almost an abuse of the concept of intermediate technology. So, the company introduced a new computer and promised an end to after-sales servicing problems. Finally, in 1979 there were so many complaints, in spite of using spares from traded-in machines, that they earned the reputation that they had good kits but no support.

The company retreated to another African base to set up a new African regional office, leaving in their wake angry redundant workers. Throughout, there was bungled marketing resulting in bad PR or, what is often the case with some multinationals, marketing which is oblivious of PR. It is the Milton Friedman philosophy of ignoring public affairs.

Toyota seem to have taken greater care, and have a good reputation in most countries. In Malaysia they took the trouble to set up after-sales service depots, and their cars have a good reputation in Kenya. It helps if the company has an assembly plant in the country as Fiat have in Zambia and Peugeot and Volkswagen have in Nigeria.

However, in Asia the Japanese had a marketing problem which did not exist in Africa. After the Second World War there was inevitably hostility towards a former enemy country which had occupied so many Asian territories. Hong Kong, Indonesia, Singapore and Malaysia were at first extremely hostile towards Japanese cars. Markets were won by the price and reliability of products and the attention given to spares and servicing. Datsun and Toyota pioneered this marketing strategy. Today, the European car is a rarity.

A few years ago Datsun entered the Nigerian market at a time when the Morris Marina could have taken the market had the British company persevered. Datsun became very popular. It replaced the fleets of old Morris taxis. Drivers liked Datsun reliability. But scarcity of parts and trained service staff began to cost Datsun its good name. Volkswagen, whose Beetle had won respect although the crude and incompetent Igala was an ugly duckling, set up their own plant in Nigeria and became the market leader, thanks to good after-sales service.

REASONS FOR AFTER-MARKET PROBLEMS IN DEVELOPING COUNTRIES

1. Exchange control restrictions can prevent the purchase of spares from abroad and be an embarrassment to exporter, importer and customer.
2. Foreign manufacturers do not appreciate that harsh conditions of poor roads and extreme climate, including ruts, mud, dust, heat and rain, cause wear and tear not experienced on city roads and motorways in the West and Japan. Nor do they appreciate the traffic conditions in cities like Lagos where an undented car is a rare sight.
3. The scarcity of service stations.
4. The scarcity of trained mechanics.
5. The black market in spare parts, which has become the bane of the Japanese whose marketing strategy is usually to supply adequate quantities of spares.

6. The absence of motoring organisations (like the AA and RAC) with patrols and on-the-road breakdown services, and also the lack of roadside telephones so that help may be called.
7. The mechanical ignorance of drivers and their inability to service their own cars. Many of them cannot understand an instruction manual, which may not be printed in their language. This applies to numerous imported products.
8. The time delay in shipping parts from abroad.
9. The inventory cost of stocking expensive parts. A dealer may not be able to afford to tie up money in spares, and so does not order until they are needed.
10. The fact that some products are not suited to some overseas markets. A little elementary research would show how adjustments or modifications could make their products more acceptable.

It is significant that whereas the German Audi is possibly the most reliable car one can buy in Europe it has been a disappointment in Nigeria. On the other hand, the Peugeot has been consistently the most reliable car throughout Africa for decades.

Before introducing new accounting and computer equipment into Malaysian banks assurances were demanded that the suppliers would have an adequate network of servicing branches stocked with spare parts. Spares had to be immediately available otherwise the banking system would have been at a standstill. Such after-sales service is possible if the market is carefully researched before seeking sales. There follows the need to set up a reliable subsidiary company or local agent, or invest in local production.

Washing machines are notorious for breaking down, and in South East Asia Matsoshita are careful to guarantee spares and after-sales service, otherwise no-one would buy their machines. It is also necessary to have the spares ready otherwise imitation parts of inferior quality might appear on the market and tarnish the good name of the original manufacturer.

It does seem that *buying* attitudes can have some effect on after-sales service. Asiatics tend to be more critical buyers than Africans; Asiatics tend to make their demands before purchase, but Africans seem to complain when it is too late. The Japanese, who are always quick to criticise the inefficiencies of British and American goods, will react very quickly to criticism of their own deficiencies.

Sample Examination Paper - Marketing

INSTRUCTIONS TO CANDIDATES
- (a) **First**, *read through all the questions and do not attempt to answer any until you understand the scope and limitations of the questions you have selected.*
- (b) *Question one is COMPULSORY.*
- (c) *Candidates may attempt* **four** *other questions.*
- (d) *All questions carry equal marks.*
- (e) *Questions need not be answered in numerical order, but all answers must be clearly and correctly numbered.*

1. COMPULSORY QUESTION
Define marketing in such a way that you show that it is more than just the distribution of goods from the manufacturer to the consumer, and that it should be a philosophy of top business management.

2.   (i) Draw a chart of the standard product life cycle, and explain its different stages.
    (ii) Draw additional charts to show variations in the standard life cycle to represent the re-cycled product life cycle, the replacement of an old product by a new

one, and the continued development of a product which does not suffer declining sales.

3.   Give examples of the importance of spare parts and after-sales service — the after-market — when selling to overseas markets, and describe the marketing problems and bad PR which occur when proper after-sales service is neglected.

4.   Draw a chart of the departments of an advertising agency, and name the personnel involved. Describe the special skills and duties of the principal agency personnel.

5.   Write short notes on *four* of the following forms of marketing research:
   (a)   Shop, retail or dealer audit
   (b)   Consumer panels
   (c)   Recall research
   (d)   Readership and audience surveys
   (e)   Discussion group
   (f)   Opinion poll.

6.   In some developing countries a marketing problem is that 50 per cent of the population is outside the cash economy. Explain this situation in terms of the population triangle, forms of employment and earning power.

7.   How does discretionary income and elasticity of demand affect the marketing of expensive products or services?

8.   Discuss the importance of harmonisation in connection with international marketing, giving examples of international conventions and regulations or the harmonisation of legislation within the EEC.

9.   How have new ideas in packaging helped to protect products, or made them easier to use, so that it has been possible to market them more effectively?

10.   What are social grades? Give the breakdown of social grades in your country, and show their relevance to the choice of media for advertising two different products or services of your choice.

11. What do you consider to be the advantages and disadvantages of using the following merchandising methods to promote sales?:

(a) Prize competitions

(b) Money-off offers

(c) Self-liquidating premium offers

(d) Free gifts such as novelties or gifts packed with goods

(e) In-store free sampling demonstrations.

12. (i) What is puffery, and why is it necessary for all PR information such as news releases to avoid puffery?

(ii) Why is it wrong to regard PR as 'free advertising'?

13. (i) Is there any significance in the criticism that a price is high because one is paying only for the name?

(ii) Is it true that you get only what you pay for?

14. American mail-order traders such as Montgomery Ward and Sears Roebuck created a new form of marketing because so many Americans were living in remote places and were often obliged to pay high prices at a local general store. How do you account for the popularity of mail-order trading in a country like Britain which is highly urbanised, with excellent shopping facilities close to most people's homes?

Part Two

Advertising

13 Advertising Defined

Advertising is part of the marketing mix, but it can be used by an individual such as an entertainer or by a non-commercial organisation not engaged in marketing such as a hospital advertising for staff. It is also an activity used by man for centuries, long before modern marketing came about. The earliest recorded advertisement is said to be one offering a reward for the return of an escaped Egyptian slave some 4000 years ago.

The simplest definition is that advertising makes known in order to sell goods or services. A street name or a house name makes known, but does not try to sell anything. *Advertising aims to persuade people to buy.*

Advertising is therefore biased in favour of what it is promoting. But while it will be like the village gong-man beating his gong to attract attention in order to tell the news, and attract attention is the first thing it has to do, advertising will fail if its message is not accepted. Advertising must not be so exaggerated that people are suspicious, or so false that it is disbelieved.

A careful balance has to be achieved. The advertisement is not unlike the dancer who wears a costume different from the clothes of everyday life, so that he or she stands out attractively. African dancers have their feathers, the Chinese dress up as lions and dragons.

Unless a newspaper is bought especially to read certain advertisements such as those announcing jobs, it is normally bought to read the *news*. Similarly people switch on the radio or TV to listen to or watch the programmes, not the advertisements. The advertiser is an intruder: yet newspapers would look dull without advertisements. In many cases we would have no mass media if the proprietors had no revenue from the sale of advertisement space or airtime. In Britain the news magazine *NOW!* was excellent, but after a short life it 'folded' because of the lack of advertisement revenue. In developing countries, where advertisers are comparatively few, media finances can be critical and this will be one reason why media are scarce. The mass media will grow as the economy grows.

ECONOMIC VALUE OF ADVERTISING

The great advantage and role of advertising is that it carries the sales message to a very large number of people, usually to people the advertiser does not know or cannot meet, and who may be scattered throughout a town, region, country or maybe the world. It is this *broadcast* effect which is so valuable. Even though advertising costs a lot of money, a skilfully used advertising campaign can be the cheapest means of reaching the market. Advertising is expensive only if it fails to produce sales, but for successful advertisers it can be very cheap. It is therefore important to realise that the cost of advertising is relative to results.

To put this more forcefully, if thousands of pounds, dollars or naira are spent on advertising, and the results can be counted in millions, the advertising will be inexpensive, a profitable *investment*, in fact. If advertising does not produce that sort of result it certainly is expensive and, more than that, it is a waste of money. It is therefore wrong to say a medium is expensive just because the rates are high.

Let us take an imaginary example. If a newspaper sells 100,000 copies daily, £100 is spent on an advertisement and 1000 sales are received, the cost per sale is £100/1000, which is £0.1 or 10 pence (the example is easily translated into other currencies). But the cost per thousand buyers of the newspaper is £100/100,000 which is £.001. Either way, the cost of reaching people, and the cost of each sale, is very small and so the *apparently* high cost of advertising becomes economical. There is no point in advertising unless it is an investment which produces results.

Thus advertising becomes a distributive cost, and part of the overall marketing budget. It is just as important as the cost of packaging or that of despatching the product to shops or customers. The cost of advertising does not come out of profits but is an investment in making profits. It is not a question of what the advertiser can afford to spare on advertising but what it will cost (as one part of the marketing strategy) to achieve the sales target.

WHO PAYS FOR ADVERTISING?

This is a question often asked in examinations. There are many possible wrong answers but only one right answer.

The advertising agency is legally responsible for paying the media for space or air-time under the 'agent acts as principal' rule, so the agency might be said to pay for advertising. In allowing the agency a commission (which to a large extent covers a lot of planning and administrative costs for which the advertiser would otherwise be responsible) the media-owner may, in a curious way, be said to contribute to the cost of advertising. (We will return to these topics again.) And what about the advertiser who wanted the advertising in the first place, and who is ultimately responsible for paying the advertising agency? Doesn't the advertiser pay for advertising? After all, he is always complaining about what he can or cannot afford! No, the advertiser does not pay for advertising. He does not pay for it out of his profits so that it is a loss.

Advertising is a *cost* like raw materials, labour, production, packaging, warehousing, despatch and delivery; trade terms to wholesalers, retailers, agents, factors and other distributors; commission to company salesmen; after-sales service and the cost of meeting guarantees. All these costs, and sometimes many others, have to be built in to price plus gross profit. Thus, profit consists of sales minus costs, of which advertising is a part.

How the costs are made up will vary from place to place and product to product. In Britain as much as 70 per cent of price may be taken up by wages, and we saw the Rentokil example in Chapter 7 on prices. But if one shops in Hong Kong cheap and excellent clothing may be purchased which has been made in mainland China where the cost of labour is minimal. In petro-economies like Nigeria and Trinidad, where standards of living are rising and so are costs, labour is becoming more expensive, and prices will include a correspondingly higher proportion of labour costs. Wages and prices tend to rise together.

The cost of advertising is largely related to value, that is, the size of circulations (and readerships if researched) or audiences, and also to demand by potential advertisers. There is a value for money supply and demand situation. When one says TV advertising is expensive in Britain one has to consider that for a very popular programme there could be an audience of 20 million viewers. TV advertising could therefore be a very cheap and effective way of promoting a repeat-selling mass consumer product and maintaining economic factory output.

Thus the cost of advertising will be related to employing labour and machinery at maximum capacity. If the factory output can be maintained at a certain level the selling price can be low because the advantages of scale (mass production) can be enjoyed. To do this may cost millions of pounds, dollars or naira in advertising, but the unit cost per, say, packet of detergent, will be fractional.

Press advertising in the *Daily Mirror* or *The Sun* (each having daily circulations around 4 million copies) justifies rates much higher than those for small circulation newspapers like *The Times* or *The Guardian* which sell only about 400,000 copies, or *The Financial Times* which sells only 200,000 copies daily.

But a bank could find it profitable to advertise in *The Financial Times* and a waste of money to take space in *The Sun* which in turn could be excellent for a chain of supermarkets. This situation has to be contrasted with that in developing countries where there are fewer publications. Newspapers like the *Straits Times* in Singapore, the *New Straits Times* in Malaysia and the *Hong Kong Standard* and *South China Morning Post* do have their business sections, and there is the Nigerian *Business Times,* but generally speaking banks and supermarkets have to advertise side by side in most newspapers like the Nigerian *Daily Times* and *New Nigerian* or the papers already mentioned. The *Straits Times,* although faced with some rivalry nowadays, is an English-language journal with a large number of pages, and it is an omnibus newspaper covering every interest.

It may therefore be a problem in developing countries that media are less economical, and will represent a higher cost, than in countries with a greater number and variety of media and competition between rival media. This could be a problem peculiar to countries where press media are limited to the literate. The situation differs from country to country.

When the total population of India is more than 600 million it follows that the literate elite may be counted in millions and greatly exceed the total populations of many developing countries. Yet it is true that many unemployed Indian graduates cannot afford to buy a newspaper. In contrast, Hong Kong's five million Chinese support nearly 100 daily newspapers, and pavement newsvendors flourish on every corner of the busy streets.

The economic value of advertising media depends on their ability to reach enough potential customers in order to influence profitable sales. Consequently, in some parts of the world, press, radio, TV, static cinema, mobile cinema, posters and signs, direct mail, exhibitions and so forth will be more or less effective. The media that work in the West may, for ethnic, language or literary reasons, be less effective in the Third World. For that reason, European or American textbooks on advertising may be largely irrelevant outside their countries of origin.

It is noticeable that in a country like Nigeria, where educational and literary programmes are active and the economy is strengthening, new newspapers and magazines are continuingly appearing. Political interest since the advent of civil government has led to the appearance of new newspapers such as *National Concord* and *Sunday Concord* and associated Hausa and Yoruba newspapers. In recent years more Nigerian evening and Sunday newspapers, and more business, trade and special-interest magazines have appeared. The growth of the press is a sign of a thriving and more literate society.

EFFECT OF ADVERTISING ON SOCIETY AND THE ECONOMY

As a society develops, towns grow and they are linked together by transport systems, it becomes economic to produce goods in one place and sell them to people in other places. In order to do this, people have to be told that the goods are on sale. This is the job done by advertising. Without advertising people would not know that the goods existed nor where they could be bought. They would not know the virtues, nor the cost, of these goods. This happens even in Russia and China too where one might think advertising would be frowned on as a capitalist device. There are plenty of posters and signs in the streets of Moscow and Peking.

The student may argue that there is no point in advertising something with which he is familiar, and that this is a waste of money. Moreover, since we are agreed that the customer pays for advertising why should he pay to be told about something he knows is in the shops waiting to be bought?

There are four answers to this challenge.

First, in a competitive society there is not only competition between rival advertisers but choice between their rival products or services. Which bank or airline shall we use; which cigarette or soap shall we buy? Advertising presents the choice, and we pay for the privilege of being told the advantages of this and that bank, airline, cigarette or soap.

Second, people forget very easily, and the biggest advertiser in the world would go bankrupt very quickly if he stopped advertising. It's like the singer or the pop group – a new record, another hit, is necessary otherwise they are finished. If all the Coca-Cola signs were taken down all over the world people would forget to ask for Coca-Cola in less than a year. As a test of memorability, the following is a list of countries which have changed their names. How many of their new names do you know?

Formosa	Siam	British Guiana
Ceylon	Straits Settlements	British Honduras
Dahomey	Madagascar	Gold Coast
Basutoland	Nyasaland	Bechuanaland

These were all once well-known countries. How many did you get right? This test may have helped to show how easily once well-known names can vanish and be forgotten. The modern names for these countries are:

Taiwan	Thailand	Guyana
Sri Lanka	Malaysia	Belize
Benin	Malagasey	Ghana
Lesotho	Malawi	Botswana

A practical effort to establish the geographical location of Malawi is the map which appears on the back of Malawi airletters, showing the country in relation to neighbouring Mozambique, Tanzania and Zambia; a very commendable piece of communication.

A name has to be repeated many times for it to be remembered. A famous cigarette company thought it could save money by cutting out advertising. The effect was so disastrous that it took three years for this manufacturer to regain its former position in the market.

So a supreme task of advertising is to make sure that when people need something, or go to the market or store to buy something, they remember the name, or when confronted by the product they recognise the name and have faith in it.

Third, as just mentioned, familiarity with a name helps to create confidence in it. There is a psychological factor which is at the root of all good human relations, and that includes race, foreign and all kinds of relations between people. *We like the things we know best. We dislike the things we know least.*

From this stems the fact that people tend to be conventional and conservative. There is a saying, that familiarity breeds content. People feel safe with things that are the same, suspicious of things which are strange or different. We are unsure of people whose skin is a different colour, who speak a different language, who come from another village, town, region, state, country or part of the world. The advertiser has to deal with the same sort of hostility. World-famous names like Guinness, Cadbury, Ford, Dunlop, Berger and Honda have been established for years. But it was not just plugging the name which did the trick: products had to live up to the name.

Fourth, if a product or service is to be introduced, or simply made available, it is necessary to tell people of its existence, and this role of advertising can be observed even in Communist countries.

Advertising makes people *know, remember* and *trust* the familiar name, but in promoting a company or brand name the advertiser does stake his reputation on it. That places a high social value on advertising. On the whole, advertised goods are to be trusted. This is because, by declaring his responsibility, the advertiser lays himself open to criticism. It is therefore foolish to risk one's reputation by making misleading claims. Ethics become economics for it is more profitable to be honest.

This concept of advertising may seem strange to readers in some developing countries where advertising may appear to be exaggerated and even misleading, where the creators of advertising make the mistake of being over-dramatic and where the reader tends to be sceptical. There are often great social contrasts between those involved in marketing and those likely to buy. These contrasts would scarcely exist in the West where generations of consumers have been brought up on advertising over the past 100 years.

Consequently, it is noticeable that advertising in developing countries contains simple, direct and powerful appeals. Explanatory pictures are very important. The subtleties of Western advertising will not work. Indeed, the copywriter in a country with different ethnic, tribal and religious groups — however literate they may be — has to be a very clever writer if he is to communicate selling messages which are easily understood. In fact, the advertisement may have to depend more on pictures than words, an advantage which can be exploited on posters and on TV.

14 The Three Sides of Advertising

Most commercial advertising (as distinct from private advertising) is divided into three separate sections which, if the advertising is to be successful, must work together very carefully. The roles of these three sections are quite different, and each calls for special knowledge and skills. Figure 14.1 shows the interplay between the *advertiser,* the *advertising agency* and the *media owner.*

Note that the *advertising* manager is employed by the advertiser and buys advertising, but the *advertisement* manager is employed by the media and sells space or air-time to the agency or advertiser. Note, also, that *media* is plural and *medium* is singular so that one should never refer to the press, radio or TV as 'a media'. Collectively, all three comprise 'media', but each is a 'medium'.

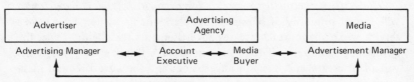

Fig. 14.1. The Three Sides of Advertising

Figure 14.1 shows that there may be direct contact between the advertiser and the media. This can happen in three ways:

1. The advertiser may not be large enough to use an advertising agency.
2. The advertiser may be so large that he maintains a complete advertising service department, and does not need an agency. Such as advertiser would need to advertise constantly to justify the employment of full-time staff similar to those found in an advertising agency.

3. The media sales organisation may contact the advertiser direct even though an agency is used, and bookings (if any) will eventually come through the agency.

The type of personnel employed by the three sides of advertising are different in the following ways:

The advertising manager should have all-round knowledge of the advertising business, know the organisation or industry which employs him, and be a good administrator able to budget, control budgets and supervise staff and agency work.

In most consumer product organisations which have either a large range of products or a number of product divisions, e.g. many brands of confectionery or special product groups such as foods, drinks, proprietary medicines and household products, the advertising manager is usually replaced by a number of *brand* or *product managers*. Each product manager will be responsible for the total promotion of his product or group of products. He will work closely with the sales manager for his product or product group, and he will be responsible to the marketing manager or director. He will also deal with the advertising agency.

The advertising agency personnel, as will be explained more fully in Chapter 16, will consist of a team of specialists and the extent of the division of labour will depend on the size of the agency and the range of services it offers.

The staff of the media owner's advertisement (or sales) department will consist primarily of salesmen, but some media owners may have a service department which creates advertisements for clients. Thus, the advertising manager will tend to control advertising; agency personnel will plan, create and execute advertising; and the advertisement manager will sell space or time like any other product or service.

It is essential that good relations exist between these three sections of advertising if the advertiser is to enjoy successful advertising, if the agency is to retain and gain clients and earn revenue, and if the media owner is to operate profitably. All three depend on each other if they are to stay in business.

TRIPARTITE NATURE

The tripartite nature of advertising is shown in Britain in the following ways:

1. Independent media research is conducted by Joint Industry Committees representing all three sides, e.g. JICNARS, BARB (replacing JICTAR), JICPAS and JICRAR dealing respectively with press, television, poster and radio readership or audience surveys.
2. The Advertising Standards Authority operates the British Code of Advertising Practice on behalf of all sides of advertising.
3. The Advertising Association is a federation of all kinds of advertising bodies.
4. The Communication, Advertising and Marketing Education Foundation (CAM) organises professional examinations for all sides of advertising.

Similar collaborations for common purposes exist in other countries.

It is important, therefore, that the advertising manager understands media and is familiar with the characteristics, costs and statistics concerning all media which may be useful to him. This will enable him to appreciate or criticise agency proposals.

Similarly, he should understand how an agency works, and be able to work with agency personnel, especially with the account executive. He should know how to select an agency, judge presentations when agencies are 'pitching' for his business or 'account', and buy agency services. Ideally, he should accept the agency as an extension of his department, but appreciate that he is only one client and is sharing agency facilities according to the size of his account.

The agency needs to understand the various businesses that clients are in, and be able to advise and provide the most cost-effective campaigns. The agency and client must share confidences and work together in harmony. Good agency-client relations is an art which can lead to long association. It is very frustrating for both sides if a working partnership does not exist. It can be poor policy if clients change agencies frequently.

But the agency is in the middle like the fulcrum in a balance, and also has to enjoy good relations with media owners and suppliers such as printers, photographers and point-of-sale producers. The agency is a buying agent on behalf of his principles even though *in law* he acts as the *principal* and is liable for payment: Historically, he is a commission agent paid by the media. This will be explained in the next chapter.

A delicate financial situation exists. The agency has to be an expert buyer of what the client needs and authorises. Yet, on the one hand, he has to pay the media owners promptly in order to maintain 'recognition' or 'accreditation' and be entitled to commission, while on the other hand he must exact prompt payment from clients. Because of the inevitable time-scale involved (clients seldom paying the agency as promptly as the agency has to pay the media), the agency must have adequate cash reserves to maintain cash flow.

The personalities of those involved becomes important to the satisfactory interrelationships between the three sides of advertising. Sincerity, trust and efficiency are human values which make for good relationships all round and successful business for all concerned. The advertising manager who bullies his agency, the agency which behaves inefficiently, and the media owner who sells short can only contribute to disastrous advertising.

This situation of interdependence is very different from that in PR where the PRO – who is often much more of a jack-of-all-trades person – may well be entirely responsible for planning, creating and executing a programme such as a house journal, slide presentation or private exhibition, engaging and directing his own technicians such as printers or photographers. Even in a press relations programme, the PRO handles everything short of the actual publication since he has no control over the editor's decisions and no space is bought.

The greater division of labour between advertising and PR is largely because more money is involved, but even so, the greatest advertising cost is for press space, air-times or poster sites which are to be occupied by advertising. Less may be spent on PR, but the greatest PR cost is man-hours.

15 The Advertising Department

Some advertising departments may consist of little more than an advertising manager and his secretary and perhaps an assistant. They will administer and control or supervise advertising which is mainly planned, created and executed by an advertising agency. Such a department will be concerned with interpreting management policy to the agency, scrutinising and approving agency work, recording results, and checking agency expenditure so that payment may be made. It is a responsible role even if it is not creative. The agency has to satisfy the advertising manager if it is to keep and renew the account.

In contrast to this there is the advertising department which does the whole job, and no agency is used. Or perhaps an agency may be used merely to place advertising in the media. Such self-sufficient advertising departments are fairly rare, but in some businesses they may be necessary. The department store or supermarket chain is a good example. Prices may change so suddenly, and rivalry between stores may be so fierce, that advertisements have to be created and placed so quickly in the daily press that there is no time to deal with a third party. Another example is the big package tour agency such as Thomas Cook where the main task is the creation and production of holiday and travel brochures, and the job is best done 'in-house'.

Between these two — the non-creative and the highly creative — there is the advertising department which supervises the agency but undertakes other forms of advertising on which the agency earns no commission. This follows the division between *above-the-line* and *below-the-line* advertising. These expressions do not imply that one form of advertising is superior to the other. A mail-order advertiser might never use above-the-line advertising, concentrating on, say, sales literature and direct mail. Neither are they *primary* and *secondary* media, that is spearhead and supporting media. To take the mail-order advertiser, his catalogue could be his chief or primary medium, and occasional press advertising his minor or secondary medium.

Above-the-line media consist of the five media on which advertising agencies traditionally earn commission, namely press, radio, TV, cinema and outdoor (including transportation).

Below-the-line media are all other media, on which no commission is earned (and on which an agency would add a percentage or a service charge if the agency handled it). These comprise direct mail, exhibitions, sales literature, sales promotion, point-of-sale display material, calendars, diaries, give-aways and novelties. Note that PR is not involved, simply because it is not a form of advertising.

From this division it will be seen that an advertising manager may control a large and busy department, and he or his assistants will have to buy directly from many suppliers such as artists, designers, photographers, printers and other specialists.

All this may be represented as shown in Figure 15.1. As the figure shows, the advertising manager is responsible to the marketing director and works in liaison with the PR manager, the sales manager and the

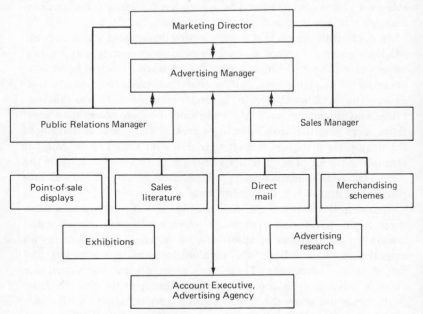

Fig. 15.1. Advertising department handling below-the-line
advertising.

agency account executive. Under his command he will have artists, designers and copywriters, either on the staff or working outside as freelances. He will conduct research to evaluate the effectiveness of media and advertisements, either by recording enquiries and business resulting (cost-per-reply and cost-per-conversion), or by using outside research units as when measuring the extent to which people recall advertisements or the extent of impact of advertisements. Merchandising schemes could include the running of competitions, self-liquidating premium offers as when customers submit parts of packages together with cash for a bargain price offer, and in-store demonstrations.

THE APPROPRIATION

In conjunction with management and, ideally, in consultation with the advertising agency, the advertising manager is responsible for budgeting and budgetary control. The total advertising budget is called the *appropriation*. Divisions of the appropriation for specific expenditures such as press advertising, research or exhibitions are known as *allocations*.

There are many ways of arriving at the appropriation, and the choice may depend on the type of organisation or the purpose of the campaign. The cost of advertising is a distributive cost which has to be included in the price. Ultimately, like every other cost from product research and development to the retailer's margin of profit, plus the manufacturer's profit, it has to be recovered by sales. Advertising is not paid for out of profits! But advertising is an investment in success, and it is important to budget sufficient money for the advertising to be effective. Some of the methods are:

1. *Arbitrary*. This is a rule-of-thumb method which is little more than a calculated guess or what the advertiser thinks he can 'afford'. The arbitrary method is not to be recommended unless the advertiser can base his hunch on experience.
2. *Historic or percentage of past sales*. At least this method is based on some financial knowledge, but it tends to assume that sales will be static.
3. *Percentage of future sales*. This is a better method since it is based on an estimate of advertising costs required to achieve a sales cost.
4. *Unit cost*. Suitable for fast-moving small-unit consumer goods, an

advertising cost is built in to the price of each unit — litre of petrol, packet of cigarettes, or carton of detergent. The appropriation is thus geared to actual sales and can be adjusted from time to time since sales produce an automatic advertising fund.

5. *Target method.* The simplest form of target method is to estimate the cost of the weight of advertising necessary to reach a given percentage of the market. Thus it may be calculated (if audience ratings are available) that in order to reach 60 per cent of all housewives a TV commercial has to appear so many times. This may have to be repeated so many times a year in order to maintain repeat sales.

6. *Composite method.* Probably the most practical method, the composite method considers everything which will influence sales and looks at past and future targeted sales. The success of the campaign may be influenced by the political and economic situation, the extent of competition, the co-operation of distributors and the general state of the market.

Control of the budget will require scrutiny, criticism or acceptance of agency and supplier estimates, and similar attention to accounts when they are rendered. This is not always as simple as it seems. Prices may change and bills may exceed estimates. The appropriation and its allocations may need revising. A supplementary budget (see Table 15.1) may be necessary if the reserve or contingency fund is inadequate to cover higher prices.

For a complete and realistic internal budget, the advertising manager would also have to include the salaries of the advertising department staff, travel and hospitality costs, rent and rates of office, stationery, postage and telephone, and overheads such as light, heat (or air-conditioning) and office-cleaning, plus hire charges or depreciation for office equipment such as Telex, typewriters, copiers, furniture and fittings.

A serious problem can be in approving agency accounts, and money squabbles can sour agency—client relations. There are two problems. Under the commission system agencies have to pay their accounts within 30 days, sometimes in advance, whereas clients may pay the agency less promptly. For cash-flow reasons, the agency will render accounts as quickly as possible.

Now, the client has approved a total budget, but he gets invoiced as

TABLE 15.1. *Typical advertising budget or appropriation*

	£/₦/$
Press advertising (as media schedule)	XXX,XXX
TV advertising (as airtime schedule)	XXX,XXX
Radio advertising (as airtime schedule)	XX,XXX
Outdoor advertising (as site schedule)	XX,XXX
Cinema advertising (as cinema schedule)	XX,XXX
Artwork and photography, model fees	XX,XXX
Production costs, press	X,XXX
Production costs, TV	XX,XXX
Production costs, radio	X,XXX
Production costs, outdoor	X,XXX
Print costs, posters	XX,XXX
Catalogues, artwork, design, print	XX,XXX
Display materials, artwork, design, print	X,XXX
Exhibition	
charge for stand space	X,XXX
designing and building	X,XXX
servicing and manning	X,XXX
Advertising gifts and novelties	X,XXX
	X,XXX,XXX

parts of the campaign are executed such as photography and artwork. In approving accounts he does not know whether the accumulated bill is going to equal the original estimate. It is difficult, for instance, to know how '15 per cent production costs' is working out when it consists of many items done at different times in the course of a year's campaign. Thus the budgetary control skill of the advertising manager is one calling for practical experience of what things cost.

Ability to buy a great many services requires knowledge of everything bought, whether it be print, photography, films and other audiovisuals, display material, exhibition stands, market research, and last but not least advertising agency services. The latter will begin with choosing an agency, briefing it and judging presentations by rival agencies.

CLIENT–AGENCY RELATIONS

After appointment comes the testing time of achieving good agency–
client relations. The client who continually criticises the agency will be
a bad client. Their points of view are different and have to be harmon-
ised. The good advertising manager regards his agency as an extension
of the advertising department, not as an outsider. It is said that an
agency is as good as the advertising manager permits it to be. That, of
course, implies understanding how an agency works, and it may pay the
advertising manager to 'sit in' at the agency for a few days to see how
it operates. Good client-agency relations are therefore the key to successful advertising, and the following are ways in which a sound
relationship can be established.

1. The advertising manager (and other members of his organisation,
   such as top management) should be frank and honest with the
   agency, and keep it well informed about company affairs and
   policy. Sharing confidences is important.
2. To support the above, the advertising manager should supply the
   agency with all useful background and essential information such
   as the house journal, annual reports and accounts, sales literature,
   lists of stockists, figures on response to advertising, samples of
   products and packs, and early information about developments
   or changes such as new prices.
3. The advertising manager should work with agency personnel
   other than just the account executive, especially with creative
   people like copywriters and visualisers. They should be supplied
   with samples and invited to visit the plant or showroom and so
   become familiarised with the product. This does not always
   happen, and too often bad campaigns result from too restricted a
   relationship between advertising manager and account executive.
   This applies the other way round, too, and the account executive
   should know company personnel. There is the true story of the
   agency which won a contract for a furniture account. The copywriter visited the works, and he went up to a man who was
   upholstering a chair. 'What's so wonderful about that chair'? he
   asked the man. 'It's sprung on springs', replied the craftsman.
   Those words became the slogan of a long and successful advertising campaign.
   Similarly, 'Guinness is good for you', a slogan long disused in

the UK but still remembered and still used abroad, resulted from asking people, many years ago, why they drank Guinness. Creative people do not necessarily dream up brilliant ideas: they are often waiting outside the agency to be picked up.

4. The agency principals should be invited to attend client functions such as dinners, sales conferences, sports events, annual general meetings, Christmas parties and so on. It is a good idea for an agency representative to address salesmen at their annual conference and explain what the advertising campaign aims to do for them. The same thing can take place at dealer conferences when a new product, or a new advertising campaign, is being launched to the trade.

A good advertising manager is thus not only an asset to his company but a great help to the advertising agency. The agency business tends to be a young one and it is not surprising that experienced advertising managers are often agency account executives who have developed their careers by moving over to the client side. Sometimes this is welcomed by agencies because it is much easier to work with an agency-trained advertising manager. But it can work the other way round, especially with technical agencies, and a skilled advertising manager may branch out and set up an advertising agency.

16 The Advertising Agency

During the past 200 years advertising agencies have developed from space-brokers who simply earned commission on space they sold for newspaper publishers to the modern service agency which can provide every form of advertising. The change from space-broking to providing service came in the mid-nineteenth century when newspapers began to use display type faces in different sizes, and it also became possible to reproduce pictures. Then, the space-broker began to compete for business by offering to write and design advertisements.

Today, a big agency will handle radio and TV advertising as well as press, it will offer marketing and market research services, and it may engage in special work such as recruitment advertising, merchandising and sales promotion exercises, overseas campaigns and public relations.

Basically, a client will seek two main services from an agency: (1) creativity – the writing and designing of advertisements including radio and TV commercials; and (2) the planning and purchase of space and air-time – the recommendation of media and the placing of advertisements. These are the areas where the advertiser usually lacks expertise, whereas they are the specialities of the agency. To achieve these two services the agency has the back-up skills to plan and execute campaigns.

The agency, however small or large, represents a team of experts which the advertiser does not require continuously and so it would be uneconomic for him to employ such people full-time. By using an agency the advertiser is able to share the services of the agency team. Moreover, he can change agencies, which is easier than changing staff.

Whether it be a great international agency like J.Walter Thompson or a one-man office in a Third World city, all advertising agencies have four things in common.

1. Getting and keeping accounts (clients).
2. Planning advertising campaigns.
3. Creating advertisements.
4. Placing advertisements according to the available media.

This is exemplified by the definition of advertising used by the Institute of Practitioners in Advertising, the British trade association of advertising agencies which states:

Advertising presents the most persuasive possible selling message to the right prospects for the product or service at the lowest possible cost.

THE COMMISSION SYSTEM

The agency relationship is a paradox based on the historical space-broking origins of the system. Strictly speaking, the agency is the agent of the media, not the advertiser. Except where a fee system is used, the agency is paid by the media under the 'commission' and 'recognition' or 'accreditation' systems. If the rate card price of space or air-time is, say 1000 pounds, naira or dollars the media charge the agency 850 and the agency charges the client 1000, thus earning 15 per cent commission. There are variations on this. Some agencies surcharge the client 2½ per cent in order to earn 17½ per cent.

There are always arguments about whether the commission is enough, and adjustments are made. A technical advertiser may use trade and technical journals with small circulations and correspondingly low advertisement rates, and to compensate for small commissions the agency will charge a service fee. It costs the same to produce an advertisement for a journal with a circulation of only a few thousand copies as it does for a newspaper with a mass circulation; more if the ad is in colour.

Commission usually covers the advice of the account executive or client representative, planning campaigns, copywriting, visualising, media buying and production. The client is then charged for all artwork, photography, typesetting, blockmaking, printing and other physical work such as making TV commercials, plus any special services such as market research, public relations and so on. Agency income is also gained from further commissions on purchases or by adding percentages to, say, print bills. If the agency employs any outside services it adds an 'on-cost' or handling charge.

This is very different from the PR consultant who is mainly selling his time and expertise and therefore, since he earns no commission, is obliged to charge professional fees based on man-hours and an hourly rate. Some advertising agencies do this by 'returning' commissions (charging clients the discounted rate) and then charging for the work they do. This is a much fairer and more professional method of remuneration.

An agency is 'recognised' for the purpose of receiving commission from the media owners, that is, from publishers, radio and TV companies, cinema and poster advertising contractors. The agency is recognised by the organisations representing each kind of media, e.g. the Newspaper Publishers Association which represents British national newspapers. Recognition is not given by the advertising bodies such as the Institute of Practitioners in Advertising or the Advertising Association, a mistake often made by examination students.

Recognition does not mean that the agency is of approved professional status, a mistake often made by clients. All it means is that the agency is able to show that it has sufficient cash flow to pay its bills promptly, accepts the British Code of Advertising Practice, and is capable of producing professional advertisements. In the case of TV advertising the agency does have to prove to the Independent Television Contractors' Association that it is capable of producing commercials.

The Nigerian recognition system is known as accreditation, and it operates differently from the British system. There are three grades. A new agency is ranked C grade and is allowed a 5 per cent commission. If, a year later, the agency's turnover has reached a certain figure, 10 per cent commission is granted to a B grade agency. And if the agency has a studio, and about four times the turnover of a B grade agency, it is classed as A grade and is given the full 15 per cent. Other variations and different commission rates apply in other countries.

However, agency fee systems are resisted by both advertisers and media owners. The agency is caught in the middle. Under a fee system the advertiser has to pay more because under the commission system he is subsidised by the media owners. That is to say, the advertiser does not have to pay for many services that he would otherwise have to provide himself, to mention only the account executive's time, planning campaigns, copywriting and all the clerical account and administration work of booking space and delivering advertisements on time. The media owners like the commission system because it enables them to demand quick payment from a much smaller number of customers.

The media owners 'recognise' or 'accredit' agencies mainly on their cash flow ability to pay them quickly while extending up to 3 months credit to their clients. To survive, the agency has to be financially strong, something which deters newcomers from setting up agencies and encourages amalgamations.

If the advertiser is very big and is a constant advertiser it may pay him to set up a fully-staffed advertising department and buy space and air-time direct.

While the commission system lingers on, to the unfair advantage of advertiser and media owner, it is nevertheless true that some of the most successful agencies in the UK and in the USA have for some years adopted the more professional and satisfying fee system.

AGENCIES AND THE LAW

Three legal aspects apply:

1. It is a 'custom of the trade' *that the agency acts as principal* in making purchases on behalf of clients. Consequently, the agent is responsible for all accounts he incurs and if the advertiser defaults the agent has to pay up. This could bankrupt an agency, and it has actually happened in the UK where an agent has booked space for an advertiser who has himself gone bankrupt. Some agents are cautious enough to demand payment in advance!
2. Under the law of contract any creative work produced by an agency remains the copyright of the agency, even though it was produced for an advertiser, *unless* the agency has assigned all such copyrights to the client. Some agencies take the wise precaution of refusing to assign copyrights until the client has paid his final bill; something which is very necessary to cover occasions when contracts end and clients transfer to a new agency.
3. When an agency is appointed there should be a contract of service written by the agency and signed by both sides, and it is in this contract that immediate or later assignments of copyright can be agreed.

AGENCY DIVISION OF LABOUR

A feature of the advertising agency is its division of labour on the basis of departments containing specialists. Even a small agency is made up of people with special skills, for example, dealing with clients, creating advertisements and media purchase. Different agencies have particular forms of organisation. Some agencies have *creative groups* including account executive and TV producer which are assigned to certain clients. Others have departments which service all clients. Some have production departments which direct the flow of agency work, handle mechanical production such as typesetting, and despatch finished advertisements to the media. The alternative to this is to have a traffic department which is responsible for the progress of work through the departments of the agency.

Figure 16.1 depicts a general chart of a complete service agency. In practice, there will be variations of this. In a small agency a smaller number of staff will amalgamate tasks, or certain work like copywriting and visualling may be done by freelance workers not on the agency full-time staff. In fact, it is now possible for a visualiser to work from home and design layouts on a computer with a display unit! Agencies like Ogilvy Benson and Mather have for many years performed their media planning and buying on a computer which produces a daily print-out of insertions, costs, TV commercial appearances and audience ratings.

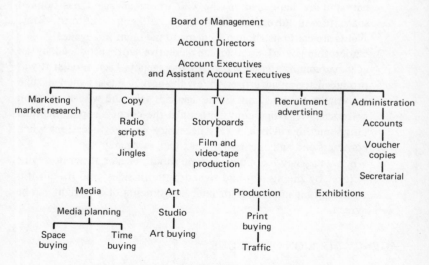

Fig. 16.1. Chart of a service advertising agency

Copywriting has not yet been reduced to word-processing, but the advertising agency of the near future is likely to be reduced to little more than a computer centre.

Some advertising agencies also offer PR services and others have subsidiary PR consultancies. These services are described in Chapter 27.

AGENCY PERSONNEL

In a large advertising agency the division of labour will be represented by the following specialists, although in a smaller agency more than one job will be undertaken by a smaller number of associates, partners and staff.

Account executive

The account executive is the liaison between the agency and the client. He may be a graduate, hold a professional qualification such as the CAM Diploma, and be a good all-round advertising man with a knowledge of how the business world operates. He has to advise the client and convey the client's needs and wishes to the agency. He may seek new business but he tends to be a client service executive rather than a sales representative. It is more likely that new business will be negotiated by the head of the agency.

No two agencies are quite the same and they develop round the talents and special interests of the principal or principals. In large agencies there will be *account directors* who supervise the work of *account executives* who are responsible for groups of accounts or clients and may be aided by *assistant account executives*. The old term was 'contact man', and he was mainly a business-getter. Today other titles are used such as *account superviser, client service executive* and simply *representative*.

Media planners and buyers

In a small agency one person will be responsible for both jobs, but in a large agency one person, the *media planner,* will study research reports and other information and plan campaigns which, to quote the Institute of Practitioners' definition of advertising, will reach 'the right prospects ... at the lowest possible cost'. For example, which newspaper or magazine, or how many spots on radio or TV, will reach the required number of prospects of a certain kind, e.g. housewives, motorists or tourists?

Given knowledge of circulation, readership or audience figures it is possible to compare costs and produce a media schedule that will reach the maximum number of prospects at minimum cost. This is a skilled job and even greater skill and knowledge is required when reliable figures are not available.

The buyers of space in the press and air-time on radio and TV are skilled in bargaining for the best rates or for getting the best positions and times.

Creative services

The creative side may be organised differently according to the way different agencies operate. There are, however, three main creative areas: copy and script writing, artistic presentation, and TV commercial production. They may all come under a creative director, or operate separately, or there may be creative groups which concentrate on particular accounts. Nevertheless certain people specialise in particular jobs. The *copywriter* (who may work under a *copy chief*) usually creates the *copy platform* or theme of the advertising and will write the wording of advertisements, sales letters, sales literature, radio and TV scripts, and create jingles and slogans.

The *visualiser* (who may work under an art director or be the art director) translates the copy ideas into visual presentation. He produces rough sketches known as visuals, roughs or scamps.

The *layout* man will eventually produce carefully measured layouts or plans of the advertisement which will show exactly how the advertisement is to appear.

The *typographer* is an expert in type faces, and he will mark up the copy with instructions regarding the names of the type faces and their sizes and weights (bold, medium, light) which will be followed by the typesetter.

However, in a small agency one artist will combine the tasks of visualising, producing layouts (and *adaptations,* that is, variations on the basic layout to fit different size or shape spaces), and marking up the typographical instructions for typesetting.

With letterpress printing, complete stereos (metal copies of entire advertisements) will be supplied ready for printing, but with offset-litho printing camera-ready copy will be provided for photography by the printer. Note that another meaning has now been given to *copy*. In the agency copy means words, but to the printer or publisher copy means everything which is to be printed, including artwork and photographs.

Production

The *production manager* or *traffic-controller* is responsible for progressing the flow of work through the agency. In an agency, production means producing the finished advertisement and despatching it to the media. This will include aspects of printing such as ordering typesetting, blocks and stereos, and preparing camera-ready copy, such as advertisements, complete as a piece of typographic and pictorial artwork ready for the offset-litho printer's camera. He will also buy print, knowing the best printers for particular jobs, dealing with print representatives, obtaining quotations, supplying the printer with copy ready for printing, handling proofs and corrections, and chasing delivery.

Large agencies separate mechanical production from progress-chasing, and the *traffic department* is responsible for controlling the flow of work through the agency. The traffic department ensures that copy and artwork is produced on time, the client's approval is obtained by the required deadline, any necessary corrections are made, and the advertisements are issued to meet copy dates laid down by publishers and broadcasting stations.

Marketing and market research

Some clients may not have a marketing manager and the agency *marketing manager* can advise on marketing strategy including branding, packaging, pricing, distribution and target markets. This may call for the use of market research, and the agency may have a market research expert who knows which outside market research unit should be used to obtain certain information.

Is an opinion survey required? Can motivation research reveal hidden objectives or buying motives? Should there be a field survey? Should new packaging ideas be tested? Can the client benefit from consumer panel or dealer audit reports? Perhaps forms of advertising research are required such as copy testing to determine the best appeal, or some form of impact or recall research may be desirable to test whether people remember seeing an advertisement and what in particular they remembered.

SOME AGENCY TERMS

The agency world has its own jargon and the following terms are worth explaining:

Plans board

The plans board consists of the account executive and the departmental heads concerned with the planning of an advertising campaign. These are the creative director (or it could be the copy chief and the art director), the media planner and the marketing manager.

The plans board will first meet after studying the account executive's report on his briefing by the client. The executives will discuss various ways of planning the campaign, and then go away to their departments to produce creative ideas and prospective uses of media. At the next meeting the campaign will be taking shape, and the client's advertising manager will be invited to see the proposals and make his comments. Eventually, the complete campaign will be produced in 'mock-up' form for showing to the advertising manager and top client management. In some large agencies an independent *review board* – another group of executives not working on the campaign – will be invited to examine the proposals before they go to the client.

Presentation

This word has more than one meaning in agency circles. It can mean either the general appearance of an advertisement – the way it is presented – or it can mean showing and explaining a proposed campaign to the client.

TV producer and director

Within the agency, the person who creates the idea for a TV commercial – this being presented to the client in the form of cartoon drawings of action sequences known as the *storyboard* – is called the *producer*. The outside head of the unit which films or makes a video-tape of the commercial is called the *director*, and he and his unit will be appointed by the producer.

Contact report

After the account executive has attended a meeting with the client he writes a form of minutes called the *contact* report, but sometimes called a *call* or *progress* report. This is probably the most important item of paperwork produced in the agency for it not only reports the essential business of the meeting but records decisions and individual responsibilities. The contact report has a ruled-off column on the right-hand side in which all future actions are recorded with the initials of those responsible for taking the action. Thus an item in the contact report may read like this (AB being the advertising manager and CD the account executive):

The estimate for printing the new catalogue was approved.	AB to supply CD with new prices.

The contact report should be written and despatched immediately after a meeting so that any inaccuracies or disagreements can be resolved quickly. The contact reports are collected in the agency *facts book,* and the complete file is extremely valuable when writing a report to a client on the year's work.

Voucher copies

These are copies of publications containing advertisements which publishers send to agencies, and agencies send to their clients as proof of insertion.

CLIENT ATTITUDES TO ADVERTISING

Clients in developing countries are sometimes sceptical about the need for advertising, and four points may be made by the agency to the client.

1. It is sometimes thought that *competition* does not exist in a developing country because new things will be in short supply and will be snatched up in a seller's market. But competition is a sign of a developing country as distinct from an underdeveloped country. Paint is a good example in countries like Kenya and Nigeria where perhaps a dozen companies compete for the growing business. Beer selling is now very competitive in Nigeria.
2. It is not always realised that one has to *invest* money in advertis-

ing, that one has to buy one's way into the market, and buy one's continued place in the market. It is like using fertiliser to make crops grow. To people who are used to selling face-to-face with customers in the bazaar, market or local shop, it may seem a strange idea that money needs to be spent if sales are to be made to unknown buyers in other parts of the country. But the product or service has to be made known. Demand has to be created. Buyers have to be directed to the place of sale.

3. Advertising can be *a waste of money* if the budget is insufficient. It is like sowing seed. The crop will be disappointing if too little seed is sown. But with advertising there could be no crop at all if the impact was feeble, and this would be like crops dying for lack of water. Advertising has been described as the life-blood of business.

4. It is folly to stop advertising because the product is so successful that advertising may seem to be unnecessary. Long-established products like Guinness and Coca-Cola would be forgotten if they were no longer advertised. A product has to be kept known and remembered — constantly! To stop advertising would be to surrender to one's competitors, and virtually to commit business suicide.

In selling agency services in developing countries the client may have to be convinced on these points.

17 The Media Advertisement Department

The media owners do not sit waiting for advertisers and advertising agents to send them bookings for space, air-time or sites. They have to *sell* empty space in the press, future time on the air, blank poster sites, and exhibition stands or booths which are just areas on a plan.

Media owners therefore have sales departments (sometimes termed marketing departments) and their purpose is to sell space, time or sites like any other product or service. The department is headed by an *advertisement manager* (*not* advertising manager), sales manager or marketing manager. He employs salesmen or representatives who sell to advertisers or advertising agencies. These salesmen have various titles such as space salesmen or, as the fashion is nowadays, marketing executives. The staff in the office maintain dummies of publications, programmes of air-time, lists of poster sites, or plans of exhibition-stand space on which are marked the spaces, times, sites or stands which have been booked.

The rates depend on *quality* and *demand.* For example, prime time costing the highest rate on TV will be the time when most people are watching and advertisers want to be seen by most people. This is usually in the middle evening between return from work and going to bed. Similarly, a space on the most popular page of a newspaper — perhaps the front page — will command a higher rate than elsewhere in the paper. A poster site in a main shopping centre costs more than one in a side street. And an exhibition stand with aisles on all four sides rates more highly than one with an aisle on only one side. The media owner will therefore try to get the best price for the best advertising proposition, and his *rate card* is a price list based on this principle.

AIDS TO PROMOTING SALES

Press

1. *The rate card* is the principle selling aid, and this gives the fullest possible information about the medium which the advertiser or advertising agency requires. This information is also published in the UK in the monthly *British Rate and Data.* Similar media guides are published in other countries (e.g. Germany, France and Italy). Rate card information consists of:

   Title of the publication.

   Address and telephone number of the head office and of any branch offices or overseas agents. The name of the advertisement manager is usually stated. There may be separate managers for display and classified advertisements.

   When it is published – morning, evening, weekly, quarterly, annually, together with publication day or date.

   Rates for whole pages and divisions of a page; single column inch or centimetre; classifieds; run-of-paper (inserted at the publisher's discretion) and special positions; black-and-white, spot colour or full-colour; special classes of advertisement such as mail order; and various discounts that may be offered, such as for a series.

   Printing process – whether letterpress, photogravure or lithography – and mechanical details regarding page and column measurements, half-tone screen, and requirements for camera-ready copy, colour transparencies, etc.

   Copy dates for black-and-white and colour.

   Press date for corrected proofs.

   Cancellation date.

   Circulation figure – audited net sales (e.g. ABC figure).

   Agency commission.

2. Brochures describing readership statistics quoted from independent surveys (e.g. Joint Industry Committee for National Readership Surveys – JICNARS – in the UK), or from surveys commissioned by the publisher, and audited net sale or circulation figures (e.g. Audit Bureau of Circulations). Calculations may be given breaking down the advertisement rate to show the cost-per-thousand readers or circulation. This provides a means of comparing costs with other publications with different rates, circulations and readerships.

3. Brochures describing circulation areas, demographic profile of readers, or penetration and coverage of certain groups of readers.
4. Dummies of new publications or forthcoming issues, or specimen dummy page, when there is to be a special feature, section or supplement.
5. Advertising features (e.g. the special reports in *The Times, The Financial Times* and other newspapers which are not produced by the editor but by a special editorial team within the advertisement department). Such features or supplements will be used to attract special advertising associated with the topic.
6. Brochures to promote advertising in special advertising sections such as staff recruitment, mail order, books, property, sales and wants, entertainments, holidays, hotels and travel, education and so on.
7. Advertisements in the trade and business press.
8. Sales letters to accompany the promotional literature already described or accompanying specimen copies of publications and rate cards. These may be contained in a special folder or wallet.

Television

Similar aids to those used for the press may be used but with statistics on audience figures such as those produced by the Broadcasters' Audience Research Board (BARB).

1. Advance information about forthcoming programmes so that advertisers may book time to coincide with programmes which are of sympathetic interest or which promise particular or large audiences.
2. Brochures giving geographical details of the area covered by the TV station, and of the demographic profile of the area.
3. Case studies of the successful use of the medium by advertisers.
4. Package deals will be offered for combinations of prime time and less popular time.

Radio

As with the press and commercial television, promotional information will be issued about rates, audiences and future programmes, and in the

UK independent audience figures are produced by the Joint Committee for Radio Audience Research (JICRAR).

Outdoor

1. Lists of sites and sizes and their rates for various periods of display.
2. Package deals for combinations of sites.
3. Brochures setting out statistics based on surveys such as the Joint Industry Committee for Poster Audience Surveys (JICPAS) based on traffic counts or opportunities-to-see by people surveyed regarding their travelling habits.

Transportation

Promotional material may be similar to that regarding outdoor advertising sizes and periods of display but the variety of positions will be greater and some additional information can be given based on numbers of passengers carried. There will also be special facilities such as monopoly advertising on one vehicle or 'painted buses' and sites will be offered on transport property, e.g. London Underground stations.

Exhibitions

Exhibition promoters use the following forms of promotion:

1. A plan of the venue, showing available stands or booths.
2. Brochure describing the exhibition and, if the event has been held before, listing previous participants and quoting attendance figures.
3. Rate card, based on area and position.
4. Offer of inexpensive shell schemes, that is, a simple stand requiring no elaborate design.

Direct mail

While a direct-mail house is not exactly a media owner, it does offer services which have to be sold, using the following methods:

1. Catalogues of mailing list subjects, with total numbers of ad-

dresses stated, and costs for mailing operations.
2. Brochures setting out services offered, including the writing of sales letters, special forms of personalised mail, and mailings for special purposes such as coverage of various categories of retailer in TV areas to coincide with TV advertising.

From the above analysis it will be seen that the media owner has to sell and compete like any other businessman. Advertising agencies, armed with statistics, experience and computers, are expert buyers and the media owners have to present convincing arguments. One way of presenting a good sales argument may be to combine their media with rival media to show how an economic schedule, to achieve the advertiser's target audience, could be planned, using their publication, station or sites as the case may be.

18 Above-the-line Media

The expressions 'above-the-line' and 'below-the-line' are attributed to the detergent manufacturers, Procter and Gamble, as a means of distinguishing between 'media advertising' and 'sales promotion'.

Above-the-line advertising consists of the five traditional mass media: press, radio, TV, outdoor (including transportation) and cinema.

Below-the-line advertising consists of all other media including direct mail, exhibitions, point-of-sale material, merchandising schemes, calendars, sponsorships, gimmicks and give-aways.

Advertising agencies may offer a complete service, but 'traditionally' they usually prefer to concentrate on the five media from which they earn a commission or discount. If they undertake below-the-line work they have to add a percentage or handling charge, or charge a service fee. Agencies tend to be in the percentage rather than the professional-fee business.

The expressions *primary* and *secondary* media are used but the above-the-line and below-the-line media do not automatically fall into these categories. The reverse may be true. For a mail-order trader the catalogue and direct mail may be his primary media, press advertising his secondary, and he might never use the other four above-the-line media.

You will notice that PR is not included in either group since it is not to be confused with advertising. Some marketing authors use confused terminology, calling PR 'publicity' and including it in the promotion mix. They are usually authors with no practical experience of PR.

Let us now consider the characteristics of each of the five above-the-line media.

THE PRESS

In the industrial world the press remains the leading advertising medium in spite of the challenge from television because:

1. It can accept a greater variety of advertising, either for products which do not suit the mass audience appeal of TV or because it offers a greater choice of advertisement spaces from whole pages to classifieds.
2. With so many different kinds of publications the press can offer specialised readerships.
3. Press advertisements can be retained.
4. Publications have mobility and permanence, and can be read anywhere at any time, and can be referred to at any time.
5. The sales message can be more detailed and informative.
6. Response can be urged by means of coupons and reader services, and it is easier to give addresses and telephone numbers in the press than on other media.
7. TV itself has generated new interests which have resulted in the introduction of journals covering these subjects, or newspaper and magazine features on them.
8. Press advertisements can be inserted quickly, whereas it takes time to produce TV commercials, or even to design and print posters, while desired sites may not be available immediately.

It would be false to claim that the press is cheaper than TV because costs are relative to results. The high cost of TV advertising will be justified if a high volume of profitable sales result, as happens with massmarket goods which could not be promoted so effectively in the press. Cost efficiency must be applied to any medium.

The situation may be different in the Third World, due to ethnic and literacy problems, and other media such as radio may predominate. Even in an industrialised country like South Africa, scarcity of advertising media made commercial TV welcome to advertisers.

SPECIAL CHARACTERISTICS OF THE PRESS

One of the problems overseas students have when taking British examinations is that they may be unfamiliar with UK media concepts, and can judge only by their immediate experience. For instance, the trade, technical and professional press may not exist, whereas in industrial countries every trade, industry and profession will be represented by its own group of journals. In Britain the building industry is served by more than 50 publications, yet most developing countries will have no building industry press at all.

What is loosely called 'the trade press' is actually divided into three sections. There are the *trade* journals read by distributors such as wholesalers and retailers – the people who *sell* things; the *technical* journals read by technicians – the people who make things; and the *professional* journals – read by *professionals* such as accountants, doctors, lawyers, teachers and PR practitioners.

Similarly, the concept of the 'the local press' (sometimes called provincial or regional) is not always understood by people living in countries where most newspapers are national or, as in Nigeria, based on cities such as Lagos, Ibadan, Enugu or Kaduna, mainly regional but often available nationally. The Nigerian *Daily Times, New Nigerian, National Concord* and *The Punch* are virtually national even if the *Daily Star* is fairly restricted to the east.

But when Nigerian students visited the *Croydon Advertiser* in Britain some of them found it difficult to understand why the circulation was confined to Croydon instead of being sold nationally. Croydon, situated 15 miles south of central London and a London borough, has a population of 300,000 and can sustain its own local newspaper with weekly sales of 90,000 copies. Every city and large town in Britain has its own weekly newspaper, and some have more than one.

It is as if Ikeja, Aba or Owerri had its own weekly newspaper. There are about 1000 in England, Scotland, Wales and Northern Ireland. The advertisements in them are almost entirely placed by local firms, and there are usually many pages of small classified advertisements for jobs, sales and wants, second-hand cars, houses for sale and holiday accommodation. The popularity of such advertising is confirmed by the title of the paper mentioned above, the *Croydon Advertiser*.

TYPES OF PUBLICATIONS

The press can be divided into the following categories, and each will have its special value for advertising purposes. The volume of advertising carried is sometimes a good way of judging the pulling power of a publication. A few publications, such as *Exchange and Mart,* may carry no editorial and be bought entirely for the advertisements. But newspapers such as *The Daily Telegraph* and *The Sunday Times* carry more editorial than most newspapers and also the most staff recruitment advertisements. Each journal has its own 'character'. Understanding media is one of the skills of advertising. It is not just a case of 'placing' ads: they have to be placed where they are most likely to produce the most sales at the least cost.

It may cost more or less to buy space in the *Daily Times* or the *Daily Sketch* in Nigeria; the *Hong Kong Standard* or *The Star* in Hong Kong; or the *Trinidad Express* or the *Trinidad Guardian* in Port-of-Spain. What matters is what do you, as an advertiser, get for your money in terms of circulations, readership, types of reader, geographical distribution, reproduction quality and actual response? For instance, some journals produce a bigger return of coupons than their rivals, while others have reader-service systems so that readers send all their requests for offered information to one editorial addresss.

National dailies are morning newspapers circulating throughout the country. *Regional dailies* are morning newspapers with local circulations.

Evening newspapers may have national or regional distribution but are usually fairly limited to the city of publication. The first edition may be in the morning with subsequent editions coming out during the day, including perhaps a racing edition, but the biggest-selling edition will be when people are going home from work.

National Sundays are popular newspapers often having bigger circulations than dailies, perhaps because the news content is often small and the magazine or entertainment content is large, and also because Sunday is a good day for reading.

Weekly colour magazines are usually distributed with certain Sunday newspapers such as the *Observer* and *The Sunday Times* in Britain and *The Sunday Times* in Singapore. They are printed on better-quality paper than the accompanying newspaper, and are excellent for full-colour advertising.

Regional or provincial weeklies are newspapers circulating either within a town or throughout a region. Very large-circulation weeklies operate as series with different title pages for separate areas. For example, the *Croydon Advertiser* is part of a series, other titles with more localised news pages covering neighbouring towns. Advertisers may take space in one, some, or all editions. Other series may be more regional and cover hundreds of miles, appealing to rural readers. People are literate everywhere in Britain.

Free sheets are newspapers which are distributed free of charge house-to-house throughout towns. The editorial is mostly of domestic or popular interest, and the saturation distribution attracts local consumer advertising which makes the publication a profitable proposition.

Consumer magazines are popular ones with big circulations such as the women's, but sometimes the term *special interest magazines* is used because numerous interests, sports and hobbies are covered by separate journals.

Trade, technical and professional magazines have been described already, but in each case there can be two kinds: those which have a *cover price* and are sold by postal subscription or by newsagents' shops and street newsvendors, and those which are posted to readers free of charge and have *controlled circulations*. You may ask which is best, a magazine which people take the trouble to order or buy, or one which arrives, perhaps uninvited, through the letterbox? From the advertiser's point of view the latter may well be the better proposition because its readers being selected by the publisher (with the addition of requests from readers), the controlled circulation (cc) journal will have the bigger circulation, and therefore the greater penetration of the market. It may therefore pay the advertiser to pay more for this bigger circulation than pay less for a lower, paid-for, circulation.

Regional magazines are those of local interest − local industry and commerce, culture, history and events. They range from Chamber of Commerce journals to ones of more general interest to people living in the area.

House journals are private or sponsored PR publications, either internal or external, but some may be good advertising propositions for certain advertisers, either because of big circulations or special readership.

Directories and yearbooks. There have been some infamous directory rackets, advertisement space being sold in directories which were never published! However, there are hundreds of reputable annual publications which, because they are used repeatedly as reference books, can be useful to some advertisers. A printer may find it worthwhile to advertise in *Advertiser's Annual*, while the Nigerian Daily Times Group Publications, the Singapore Times Group of Newspapers and the Trinidad *Guardian* newspapers advertise in *Benn's Press Directory*. Among the annuals are also the yearbooks published by trade associations and societies and timetables published by transportation companies. Telephone directories, and especially the Yellow pages type of trade telephone directory, may be essential advertising media. It can pay to advertise where people are looking for you.

PRESS TERMINOLOGY

When dealing with the press it is important to understand the 'jargon', much of which will appear on rate cards. Some typical expressions are:

Sc.cm – the single column centimetre (but in some countries still the single column inch (sci)) is the unit of measurement on which rates are based, particularly in newspapers. Space may also be sold by the page and divisions of the page. A double-page spread will be two facing pages.

Type area is the area of the page that is printed, or the area of the advertisement space that has been booked.

Bleed means that half-tone pictures are printed right to the edge of the page. The printing plate is actually slightly larger and the page is trimmed to give the bled-off effect. A higher rate is charged for bled-off advertisements.

Display advertisements are laid out with different type faces and illustrations.

Classified advertisements are those which appear under headings such as Situations Vacant, Houses For Sale, Educational Services and Flats To Let. They may be displayed, or semi-displayed in a border, or run on line after line as 'smalls'.

Run-of-paper insertions cost the least and are placed at the advertisement manager's discretion.

Special position is an advertisement placed exactly where the advertiser wants, and various special positions claim higher rates according to demand. There is usually only one advertisement on the front page of a newspaper. The publisher may create special positions in order to obtain higher rates – on, say, the leader page.

Next matter or facing matter is a kind of special position, it being guaranteed that the advertisement will be inserted next to editorial content and not on a page full of advertisements.

Solus position is again a special position, there being no other advertisement on the page.

Spot colour means printing some part of the advertisement, such as the brand name or logo, in a single colour other than black.

Copy date. This is the latest date for delivery of the advertisement.

Press date. The date of publication.

Ears or title corners are the small ads which appear on either side of the title or masthead of a newspaper.

Voucher. This is a copy of the publication showing proof of insertion of an advertisement. Voucher copies are sent to advertising agents, or to advertisers if the space has been booked direct.

Web-offset is a printing term meaning that the newspaper is printed by offset-lithography using a web or reel of paper.

RADIO

While commercial radio is a comparatively new medium in Britian, it has been established for decades in most developing countries. There are three reasons for its popularity in the Third World:

1. Not everyone can read or afford to buy a newspaper, and its distribution may be hampered by lack of roads or bad roads affected by weather conditions. Given a powerful enough transmitter, radio can reach rich or poor, literate or illiterate, anywhere, and often in local languages.
2. The transistorised radio, public broadcasting loudspeakers and rediffusion services bring radio programmes to people far and wide. The car radio is another means of listening in.
3. Unlike the British system where listeners pay an annual licence fee to the BBC, the only income available to radio stations is that derived from selling air-time, unless there is a state subsidy.

Some of the advantages of radio advertising are:

1. Since people listen for pleasure it is effortless for them to absorb the advertising messages when they are broadcast.
2. The cost of air-time is usually fairly low.
3. The cost of producing radio commercials is low compared to other media, but it still pays to have expertly written scripts and presenters with pleasant-sounding voices.

4. Stations are usually on the air for many hours, and it is possible to time advertisements to reach particular audiences when they are most likely to have their sets switched on.
5. Commercials can be repeated, either to achieve impact through repetition or to reach different audiences at different times of day or different days of the week.
6. Radio programmes, such as plays, pop music or sports events can be sponsored by advertisers.

Radio is not, however, without its disadvantages which are:

1. It is the one medium which cannot be seen. The advertiser has to rely on the human voice, perhaps supported by musical and sound effects.
2. It is difficult to assess audiences in developing countries since sets may go unrepaired and batteries may be unreplaced, because of cost or difficulty in getting replacements.
3. The message quickly passes and cannot be retained like a press advertisement.
4. It is not always easy or possible to write down details given in the commercial.
5. Special language broadcasts may be limited to certain times and days.
6. Reception may be poor in some remote areas.

Although the number of advantages and disadvantages are identical, there is no doubt that radio is a powerful and penetrating medium. The audience is usually so vast compared to any other medium in the Third World that it is a very economical and profitable advertising medium. In a huge country like India radio has predominated among all media. Even within one country, media predominance may vary region by region. While press advertising tends to lead in Lagos and the south of Nigeria, radio advertising tends to dominate in Kano and the north.

One of the big advantages of radio advertising is the ability to use local-language scripts. For example, in Nigeria *Omo washes brightest* becomes *Omo fo aso mo* in Yoruba and *Uno de Omo we dembo* in Ibo, and *Guinness is good for you* translates into *Ginies di nma maka ngi* in Ibo and *Ginies otin to da* in Yoruba. Nigerian radio reaches more than half the population; probably about 65 per cent.

Zambian advertisers such as Zambia Bottlers (Coca-Cola, Sprite,

Fanta), and Colgate and Palmolive Zambia (Choice soap, Cold Power detergent, Colgate toothpaste) make good use of local-language facilities on radio. The languages are: Eastern Province (Chinyanja), Northern Province – the Copperbelt (Chibemba), Southern Province (Chitonga), Western Province (Solozi), North Western Province (Lunda), and Lusaka Province – containing the capital (Lenje). There are also broadcasts in English.

TELEVISION

Commercial TV usually means that the TV company or the programme contractors sell advertising air-time. Sponsored TV is different in that advertisers sponsor whole programmes and insert commercials throughout the programme. Public service broadcasting (either radio or television) is conducted by state authorities, unlike American television which is produced by numerous local private stations plus national networks run by private companies. These different forms of TV vary from country to country.

In Britain, the British Broadcasting Corporation runs programmes paid for by annual licence fee, and there are no advertisements. At the time of writing the BBC (and ITV) are objecting to televising football matches played by First Division team Coventry City because the players will be wearing shirts advertising Talbot cars. This would infringe the 'no advertising' rule for screened matches. This is somewhat contradictory because the cameras cannot help but pick up the arena advertisements on boards around the pitch!

The Independent Broadcasting Authority provides transmitters and issues contracts to companies such as Thames and London Weekend to produce programmes. These programme contractors receive their income from selling air-time to advertisers, and from selling programmes to other TV companies at home and abroad. Thus, a popular programme such as 'Coronation Street' is produced by Granada in Manchester and networked to all other British regional companies. It is also sold abroad to places such as Australia. There is no such organisation as ITV, this being an expression to distinguish independent television from the BBC. Advertisements are limited to 6 minutes per hour, and are usually presented in 2 minute slots containing commercials occupying 5, 10 or 15 seconds, but on very important occasions such as a royal wedding or a state funeral no advertisements appear.

There are fifteen British TV programme contractors, London having two, Thames operating during the week and London Weekend at the weekend. An advertiser may book air-time on a single station, a group of stations, or network nationally. Since the national audience could be 20 million viewers, the cost is obviously prohibitive except for a big national advertiser of popular consumer products. But the audience size does justify the production of first-class commercials made by production units which also make feature films. This survey of British TV may help the overseas student to understand why the situation is different in his own country.

Audience figures are likely to be lower for the following reasons:

1. People cannot afford to buy TV sets.
2. TV rental services may not be available and even if they are only a small number of people can afford to pay rent.
3. Outside urban areas (such as 'the line of rail' in Zambia) there may be no electricity.

Nevertheless, TV audiences are growing in the Third World for the following reasons:

1. Community viewing centres have been set up in many developing countries such as Nigeria and Malaysia. However, since the medium is most attractive to advertisers of domestic consumer goods the absence of women from these centres is a disadvantage. Moslem women will not visit a community viewing centre, and in many countries women do not go out at night.
2. In some African countries nomads will pitch their tents on the outskirts of towns and will have TV sets.
3. In South East Asia, especially Indonesia, viewers have Japanese sets run off 12-volt car batteries. TV can be enjoyed anywhere in this vast country, irrespective of electricity, and thanks to a satellite system. But Indonesian viewers are conservative about their choice of programmes because of the cost of re-charging their batteries.
4. Urbanisation is bringing more people into cities where they are likely to swell TV audiences. Improvements in education also bring people to work in cities.

For all these reasons, TV is becoming less of an elitist medium and

much more of the popular mass medium that it is in developed countries. With its advantages of sound, vision, colour and movement it
becomes increasingly attractive to advertisers.

Language problems are overcome by using local languages, as in the
north of Nigeria where whole programmes, including drama, are conducted in Hausa. In multi-lingual countries it is also possible to use
sub-titles. Because, say, Chinese viewers in Hong Kong or Singapore
wish to watch English-language programmes they are sub-titled in
Chinese. However, in Indonesia no English is permitted and all programmes and commercials are in the Indonesian language. Moreover,
commercials are restricted to certain times of the evening so that
programmes are not interrupted, and viewers are attracted by playing
the latest pop records in between commercials. The Malaysians forbid
foreign-made ads, and their TV commercials have to be produced in
Malaysia using Malay characters speaking Malaysian in Malaysian
situations.

OUTDOOR (INCLUDING TRANSPORTATION)

These two media have been put together but there is a difference.
Transportation advertising includes advertisements inside public service
vehicles and on transport property such as railway and bus stations and
at airports and seaports. Because the travelling public may have more
time to absorb messages, the wording can be more detailed than on
posters and signs along the highway. The London Underground, for
instance, provides an advertising medium which is totally different
from poster advertising in the streets above ground.

Outdoor advertising is one of the most significant media in developing countries, although a problem may be scarcity of sites since
there may not be the walls of buildings, high buildings, or building sites
surrounded by hoardings which are common in heavily urbanised
countries. Few countries have streets almost roofed with lighted signs
like Hong Kong, yet even in Russia, where advertising might seem
unexpected, street posters and illuminated signs are to be seen in
Moscow and Leningrad. However, for the benefit of tourists posters
are not permitted on Kenyan roads if they might obscure sight of
Moscow and Leningrad. However, for the benefit of tourists, posters
have disappeared from the road to Cairo airport.

The special characteristics of outdoor advertisements are:

1. They are usually large and dominating so that they can be seen from a distance. This requires that their content be brief and simple, seldom more than a slogan, picture and name display.
2. Because posters lend themselves to big pictures it is possible to convey advertising messages quickly to people who are illiterate or irrespective of the language they speak. Family-planning campaigns have made good use of pictures suggesting that two children are enough if the children of a family are to enjoy good health, attention and educational opportunites. The use of products can be explained pictorially. Malaysian posters make exceptional use of explicit pictures.
3. Special devices can be used to attract attention, such as strips and spangles which flutter in the breeze. These are very striking in South East Asia, and recently they have been introduced into Britain.
4. If printed in fluorescent inks, posters can be made visible at night, a technique well used in Ghana. Large supersite posters or painted panels can also be floodlit for night viewing.
5. They have long life, perhaps from a week to 3 months depending on weather conditions. This leads to them being seen repetitively, especially if the same poster is displayed on many sites.
6. If well placed in busy places the audience will be very large, and the cost of renting sites will be based on assessment of the possible audience.
7. Some forms of transportations advertising offer the opportunity to carry the message among people or from one community to another. Posters on the fronts, sides or backs are seen by many people other than passengers. In some countries whole buses are painted on behalf of a single advertiser and become a complete mobile advertisement. Painted buses were popular in Britain at one time. Among the reasons for discontinuing them was that passengers looking for, say, a red or a green bus for certain routes were confused by the painted buses. But they are to be seen in many parts of the world, Hong Kong for example. In Britain, taxi-cab advertising has become popular, an advertisement panel being fixed to the exterior of the nearside front door.

Some of the special terms used in outdoor advertising are:

1. *Billboard.* This word has two meanings. In the USA 'billboard advertising' means poster advertising in general, but in Britain a billboard is a small poster fixed to a board which may, for instance, be placed on the pavement outside a shop.
2. *Bulletin board or supersite.* This should not be confused with a small notice board. Bulletin boards, or supersites as they are more often called nowadays, are specially constructed and very large sites for posters or painted panels, the sort of thing often seen beside a main road out of town.
3. *Newscasters.* Not to be confused with the announcers who read the news on radio or TV, newscasters are electronic signs with illuminated words moving from left to right to spell out news items interspersed with advertising messages.
4. *Projected advertisements.* Advertisements on slides are projected at night from the window of one tall building to the wall of a facing building.

CINEMA

Although the public cinema has, in the West, lost its audiences to TV, a certain amount of cinema advertising has survived and advertisers take the opportunity of making a longer filmlet when producing a brief TV commercial. The death of the popular cinema has not occurred in developing countries because TV has not yet taken over, drive-in outdoor cinemas are popular, and cinema vans are an excellent way of taking advertising to the bulk of the population who live in the countryside. The mobile cinema is an ideal advertising medium in countries like India, Kenya and Nigeria. It may be accompanied by other attractions such as singers and dancers, and product demonstrations may be given.

Advertising films have similar characteristics to TV commercials. They have the realism and entertainment value of sound, vision, movement and colour, but the screen is larger, there is more audience participation, and there can be better concentration (especially in a cinema) because of the lack of counter-attractions.

For the mobile cinema, visiting country people, the message should be presented as simply as possible and repetitively.

19 Below-the-line Media

Below-the-line media are all advertising media other than press, radio, TV, outdoor and transportation, and cinema. There are numerous below-the-line media, and some of them may be extremely valuable to the advertiser. They may supplement the above-the-line media, as when a catalogue is sent to those who respond to a press advertisement. They may be quite different media used for special purposes such as exhibitions and direct mail. Each has to be considered on its merits. An advertising campaign will combine the media most likely to achieve the sales target at the lowest cost.

It may be necessary to have a chain of media which direct the customer to the final purchase. A missing link in that chain could ruin the whole campaign. For instance, the initial impact could be made by press, radio or TV advertising; on the way to the shops the customer can be reminded by posters; at or in the shop there can be display material; and this can be supported by a give-away leaflet. The design of the container or package can complete the campaign. Many different combinations can be organised according to the nature of the product, or even according to the extent of competition with rival products.

EXHIBITIONS

Exhibitions may range from small ones held in a hotel lobby or room to a giant event such as an international trade fair at permanent quarters, as in Accra. They may be held once, or occasionally, or regularly like the London and Paris Motor Shows, and they may be private, public or trade events. With the exception of, say, agricultural shows they are held indoors in the West but in hot countries they will often be held out-of-doors.

Exhibitions offer the opportunity to actually see things and sample them or watch how they work. There is a face-to-face situation which encourages confidence although sometimes criticism can be welcome, especially if a prototype is displayed for inspection. People like exhibitions. It's a day out. Sometimes it can be a family outing. In such an atmosphere business can be conducted pleasantly. Some exhibitors use exhibitions in a PR sense, simply to meet customers or distributors and perhaps offer them hospitality.

But it can be a costly medium, and the cost has to be justified. Is it worth exhibiting? Will participation in a show be more or less cost-effective than the same expenditure placed differently with other media?

If you have built a new aeroplane there may be no better medium than the Farnborough or the Paris Air Show. But motor-car manufacturers no longer wait for the Motor Show to launch their model; they bring it out with press, TV and poster advertising when the moment seems right. There are traditional shows which fit into a marketing pattern as when toys are exhibited at the Toy Fair in January, are sold throughout the year, delivered in the Autumn, and sold at Christmas.

Exhibition costs are not limited to the rental of the site, stand or booth. It has to be designed, built and furnished. Staff have to be taken away from their regular work to attend the stand. Give-away literature has to be printed. Hospitality may have to be provided, and other costs may include gas, electricity and water supplies, hiring demonstrators, insurance and security, transportation of exhibits, and travel and accommodation for staff.

Nevertheless, an exhibition may be the focal point of a sales and advertising campaign, a major facet of the marketing strategy. 'As shown at the so-and-so exhibition' could be used as a sales plug for months after the event. The message of the exhibit can be extended through advertising and PR to many people who do not or cannot attend and visit the stand. Again, some participants go from show to show, actually selling from the stand. Necchi sewing machines are sold in large numbers at the Ideal Home Exhibition in London.

DIRECT MAIL

This medium depends on three things: good mailing lists, a good mailing shot, and a reliable postal system. While the postal system may be irregular in remote areas, this medium can still be effective in developing countries where there are Post Box services in cities.

The advantage of direct mail advertising is that the sales message can occupy a solus position in the reader's hand, conveying the message in a person-to-person fashion, and doing so more intimately than is possible through any other medium.

The important rule is to post the shot to prospective customers, and not broadcast it on a hit-or-miss basis to people who may or may not be interested. The compiling of selective mailing lists is therefore one of the skills of direct mail. Moreover, lists should not be kept too long since people move, change jobs, get married or die and lists go out-of-date after about 6 months. Names and addresses can be collected, as when department stores ask customers for these details when writing out bills for purchases, or they can be taken from membership lists, directories and other published lists. The telephone directory may provide a list. Mail-order traders who advertise in the press create lists of those who answer their advertisements. Insurance companies watch out for marriage and birth announcements.

It is absolutely essential that the mailing shot is created so that it will produce the desired response. There should be a well-printed letterheading for the *sales letter*. It should not begin 'Dear Sir/Madam' which is insulting. Don't you know the recipient's sex? The letter should be written in a friendly yet persuasive style — not in dull government department language nor in an offensively aggressive tone. It should be interesting, and try to make an offer that cannot be refused. The first paragraph is all-important because it must win the reader's attention. It could ask a question such as 'Do you know how many goals Clemence has saved?' and then go on to show how the reader can save money by accepting your proposition.

A great many sales letters fail because they are dull and boring, full of awful business-letter jargon, and lacking the personal touch. The format of a sales letter is as follows:

1. the introduction;
2. the sales argument;
3. the admonition.

The last sentence should urge action, or make it easy for the reader to do what you want such as filling in an order form and writing a cheque, picking up the telephone or visiting the showroom.

A vital part of the mailing shot may be whatever accompanies the letter. This may be a leaflet, catalogue, order form, reply card or sample. Never bewilder the reader with too many loose bits and pieces.

One-shot mailings can be effective, and a covering letter will not be necessary if the shot is self-explanatory such as a mail-order book list complete with instructions on how to order, and a clearly worded order form so that the right books are ordered, the correct payment is sent, and the full postal address of the customer is given. This sort of mailing shot requires the advertiser to think of every possible doubt or problem the prospect may have, and every mistake he may make such as failing to give a complete address.

Finally, timing is important. The shot should be mailed to arrive when it is most likely to achieve a favourable response. The day, week, month or season may be vital. Someone returning from a holiday will be confronted by accumulated mail. Your shot should not be among it. It is easy to avoid public holidays by posting after they have happened.

POINT-OF-SALE (POS)

Sometimes called point-of-purchase, this medium embraces all the support material that can be displayed to help distributors to sell. It could be elaborate and expensive like the model aircraft supplied to travel agents by airlines, attractive and effective like the wall posters supplied to cafes and restaurants by soft-drink manufacturers, useful like beer mats provided by brewers, or permanent like transfers which can be stuck on shop doors by the salesman on leaving.

Money can be wasted if POS material is issued carelessly for shop-keepers have only a limited amount of display space. Supermarkets have practically none; and scores of other people will want their share of the display space. Meanwhile, to create fresh interest, the shop-keeper will change his displays from time to time.

Sometimes it pays to offer display material to retailers, rather than send it to them uninvited. An order form may be mailed, describing the available material, or the travelling salesman could show samples, take orders for items, or carry supplies in his vehicle which he himself could arrange in the shop. Expensive display pieces such as working models may be offered on loan if a sufficiently large order is given.

Display material may consist of the following:

1. *Dummy packs.*
2. *Price tags, or crowners* such as those which slip over the necks of bottles.
3. *Mobiles* which dangle on a string from the ceiling. These are ideal for supermarkets.
4. *Dispenser packs or display outers* which are containers for small items such as confectionery, the lid being folded back to form a display and the whole being placed on the counter so that the items are sold from it.
5. *Wire stands* for displaying goods such as books or records.
6. *Show cards* for the window, counter or shelf.
7. *Small posters* or bills for display on doors, windows and walls.
8. *Dumpers or dump bins* which can hold a lot of items such as canned goods in a supermarket.
9. *Display stands and cases* in which items such as clocks and watches can be shown.
10. *Trade figures* such as the Michelin Man.
11. *Models,* either static or working, such as scale models of aircraft or ships. One of the most attractive models in any sort of shop window is a toy train-set, for few people can resist watching the train going round and round. In Britain, building societies which have rather dull things displayed – mostly figures of interest rates – borrow all sorts of interesting material such as toy soldiers, paintings, postage stamps, collections of clocks and so on which attract attention.

MERCHANDISING SCHEMES

Merchandising is a term which should not be confused with 'selling'. It consists of short-term sales promotion schemes, and sales promotion may be described as special promotional effects between advertising and selling to the customer. They help to bring the manufacturer closer to the customer. They include:

1. *Free gifts* such as a toothbrush attached to toothpaste.
2. *Flash packs,* a price reduction being printed on the pack.
3. *Competitions* in which customers are invited to compete for

prizes, completing an entry form, and submitting proof of purchase such as part of the package.

4. *Mail-ins,* free gifts being posted to those who submit proof of purchase.

5. *Premium offers, premium vouchers, money-off offers,* whereby customers may claim a price reduction by giving the retailer a voucher worth so much, cut from a pack, from a newspaper advertisement, or as delivered house-to-house as a mail-drop.

6. *Self-liquidating premium offers – not* means of getting rid of old stock but an offer to mail low-price goods if the customer sends the manufacturer cash and proof of purchase (e.g. a packet-top). Self-liquidating means that the payments from customers are equal to the cost of the offer, the aim being to sell more products, not make a profit.

7. *Gift coupons* inserted in packs, these being collected to claim gifts from a catalogue.

8. *Cash dividends* are similar to gift coupons except that stamps or tokens from packs are collected on a card and sent to the manufacturer for a cash refund.

9. *Free samples* of products may be offered in advertisements or given out at the point-of-sale.

10. *Cash awards for use of product,* money being given to customers (in the street or at home) who can show that they are using the product or products.

11. *Multiple or jumbo packs,* these being an economical way of buying products in bulk, several items being contained in one package at a price lower than if the items were bought singly. A variation on this is something like 'Buy six, get one free'.

12. *Banded packs* are similar, say, two or three bars of soap banded together at a special price.

These special promotions may help to recover falling sales, compete with rivals, maintain sales during a dull selling period, encourage retailers to stock up and help them to sell, introduce a new product, or provide an alternative to traditional media advertising. They work well in supermarkets where they encourage impulse buying. Those which involve collecting packet-tops, labels, vouchers and tokens can create habit-buying, and can ensure that the customer does not buy a rival product. For example, breakfast cereal manufacturers have offered cutlery and crockery sets which have involved customers in buying the product for months in order to get sufficient packet-tops.

Scores of these offers take place simultaneously in Britain. Whether they are feasible or not in developing countries will depend on factors such as the reliability of the postal system, the ability of people to follow printed instructions, facilities for handling applications, packing and despatching offers. British manufacturers use specialist firms for receiving applications and despatching offers.

Alternative merchandising schemes which may be more practical and more attractive in developing countries can be those involving the after-use of the container. A large can is very useful for carrying liquids.

This can be an important aspect of marketing strategy in poor countries, especially in the less developed countries with their per capita rating of 100—200 US dollars. In countries such as Bangladesh nothing is wasted. Every waste item is collected, sold and re-used, which is rather different from the situation in some African countries where Coca-Cola cans litter the streets. In Bangladesh broken biscuits are sold to rural areas in cooking oil cans which have further uses. Every scrap of paper is saved to make paper bags. Other materials may be used for fuel. Beer cans are collected and sold and converted into other goods such as crown cork tops, lamps, or for patching-up rick-shaws. Elementary merchandising can therefore be a matter of pack-aging policy.

Care must be taken that a merchandising offer does not recoil and create bad customer relations, that is, bad public relations. This can be a delicate matter in developing countries where people have to spend their money wisely. Powdered baby-milk firms have created ill-will by high-pressure promotional schemes, offering gifts if two or three tins are purchased, so that mothers have been persuaded to spend more than they could afford. The old criticism, that advertising per-suades people to buy things they do not need, can have some truth if multi-nationals do not appreciate that the merchandising schemes that may be acceptable in the West are unsuitable in poorer markets.

SALES LITERATURE

All kinds of promotional print can be included under this heading, and it may be essential to successful selling that the customer can obtain leaflets, folders, brochures, catalogues, reply cards, price lists or order forms. Some businesses may require special print such as technical data sheets for building products; timetables for transportation firms; instruction booklets for cars, cameras or computers; recipe leaflets and books for foods and drinks; proposal forms for insurance; colour charts for paints; and how-to-do it charts or advisory leaflets for tools, sewing machines or other equipment.

They have to be written in clear, explicit language so that the customer is not confused and does not fail to get full enjoyment or value from the product.

CALENDARS

The value of a calendar is that it carries good-will and occupies a permanent position in the home or office for a long time. In fact recipients often look forward to receiving the next one, and request cards can be included. They do not have to run from January to December; some are issued during the year and others are issued quarterly. A company can do its own photography and print its own individual calendar, or there are firms such as Eversheds of St Albans who produce a range of calendars on which the advertiser's name and other details can be printed.

DIARIES

Like calendars, diaries also extend good-will and have permanent value, although this can be more personal, whether they be desk or pocket diaries.

SPONSORSHIPS

The sponsoring of sports events, cultural events, books, maps, educational bursaries and support for charities such as a sponsored film, may have a blend of advertising, marketing and public relations value. It may be that the product is appropriate to the sponsorship, as when Bata Shoes in Nigeria sponsor certain sports.

In Britain, Cornhill Insurance sponsors test cricket, the aim being to familiarise more potential insurers with the name. Previously, Cornhill had been a less familiar name because its business had been mostly conducted though brokers. When the French petrol, Elf, was first introduced into Britain the British motorist knew the name as a result of watching the Elf-sponsored motor-racing team on television. Many famous names such as Whitbread and Schweppes are associated with horse-racing trophies. And in the spheres of horse-racing and show-jumping, horses are sponsored with names such as Son of Schweppes and Sanyo Sanmar.

Sponsorship obviously costs money, and it is very expensive to sponsor a motor-racing team, but whatever the expenditure the objective has to be clear. A wealthy company may wish to show that it is socially responsible and the sponsorship may be mainly a PR effort. But most sponsorships aim to achieve a specific advertising or marketing objective if only to plug the name repeatedly, as with consumer products such as milk, beer or tobacco which are consumed by large numbers of people who will be aware of the sponsorship.

A novel use of sponsorship has been that of the Japanese whisky, Suntory, which has sponsored golf in Britain in order to benefit from publicity when the TV coverage was obtained in Japan.

A mistake made by some overseas candidates is to confuse sponsored advertising on radio and TV with the form of sponsorship mentioned here. When, say, a football match is 'sponsored' on TV that is a form of advertising, and one of the ways in which some television companies outside Britain obtain revenue. It contrasts with commerical TV where the advertiser buys air-time during commercial breaks in programmes wholly provided by the television company.

MISCELLANEOUS MEDIA

There are also many below-the-line media which would be tedious to discuss in detail here. Among them are: give-aways such as ball-point pens, cuff-links, balloons and toys, and specialist media such as bus tickets, carrier bags, book matches, playing cards and almost anything which can carry advertisements. A medium growing in popularity is the hot air balloon, or the tethered balloon or airship, bearing an advertising message.

20 Planning an Advertising Campaign

Advertising is one element of the marketing mix or strategy, and it will usually follow decisions on product policy, branding, pricing, packaging and distribution. The client may approach an advertising agency with a ready-made marketing proposition, seeking a campaign to promote either an existing product or service or a new one on which everything else has been finalised. Alternatively, and this is more practical, the agency may be approached at the ground-floor stage and invited to contribute ideas overall. There may be a prototype product with no name, no pricing policy, no market segment defined and no method of distribution decided. Let us consider how an advertising agency, large or small, goes about planning a new campaign, assuming it has been appointed to undertake the assignment.

We will assume that the agency operates the *plans board* system, which is no more than the heads of departments meeting together, which they may do without giving it a special name. In a small agency the executives will be responsible for more than one function.

First, the account executive or client representative will meet the client at either his or the agency office. The fullest possible information is required about the company and the product or service to be advertised. It is best, therefore, if the account executive prepares a questionnaire covering everything he needs to know.

After this initial briefing meeting with the client the account executive writes a detailed report. He may first of all discuss this with his account director or managing director. This is important for policy reasons. The account executive may receive advice from his chief on how to handle the account. It could even happen that because the campaign will conflict with that for another client, or because it is for some reason an undesirable assignment, the account executive may be told to resign it.

Copies of the report are then sent to the members of the plans board who are likely to be the marketing manager, media planner and creative director. If there is a PR department or subsidiary, the PR manager will also receive a copy. At this stage the production department is not involved. However, in some small agencies 'production' is a general term including the creative side.

A few days later the members of the plans board will meet under the chairmanship of the account executive. A frank discussion will follow. Members may like or dislike the product, different and maybe contradictory ideas will be expressed on how it should be advertised and media should be used. This can be a very lively meeting! Finally a measure of agreement will be reached, and the account executive will direct each member to go away and do his specialist task.

The marketing manager may be asked to do some desk research on available statistics about the market; the media planner will be instructed to produce a media schedule to fit the budget, and perhaps to consider alternative costs for using either press or TV; the creative director will be responsible for working up a copy theme and visual ideas to suit the various media.

During the next few days these agency executives will probably have informal meetings to discuss how the campaign is being worked up. There could be further meetings of the plans board to discuss ideas, problems and costs.

When all the members have their schemes roughed out there will be a meeting of the plans board when it may be sensible to invite the client's advertising manager to attend for a preview of the proposed campaign. At this stage there could be more than one possible copy theme. If artwork will eventually call for the hire of models and expensive photography it will be sufficient at this stage to take, say, Polaroid pictures of office staff, in order to give a general idea of the intended artwork. The media schedule could, at this stage, be a permutation of possible media uses. The advertising manager is given the opportunity of expressing his opinion and giving his advice. The agency could be on the wrong track or one proposal might be distinctly more acceptable than others. There may be a case for copy-testing the different themes to discover which one has the most impact on a sample of the relevant public.

As a result of this meeting, and possible tests and revisions, a complete campaign will be prepared for presentation to the client. This meeting may be attended by a group of client directors and executives.

The account executive will make his presentation, using such visual aids as may be necessary such as a flip-over chart on which he has prepared his proposals, copies of the media schedule, mock-ups of press advertisements, a storyboard of the TV commercial, a tape-recording of the radio commercial and so forth. The bigger the campaign the more elaborate this will be, and the longer it will take. It is normal for the client to pay the cost of such a presentation, even if he rejects it.

There will much discussion. Some of the people present, having had no previous association with the planning, will prefer ideas which have been considered and dismissed in the agency days or weeks earlier. If the client's advertising manager has been brought into the agency's preparations he will be able to support the proposals. Eventually, the client will take a decision. The campaign may be accepted as it stands or some changes will be agreed. The account executive will return to the agency with his instructions.

Now the media buyer can finalise the bookings of space, air-time, poster sites and other requirements. The creative director can proceed with the preparation of copy, layouts, drawings, photography, scripting and filming. And this is where the production manager or traffic controller will come in to produce and control a time schedule of operations, and the final production and delivery of advertisements.

At various times, client approvals will be required for copy, layouts, artwork, radio tapes and previews of TV commercials. The production manager will be keeping people to deadlines, checking each day to see that every job is moving along correctly.

When the campaign breaks, the account executive and the advertising manager will check to see that everything has happened as planned. Things can go wrong. Ads can appear on the wrong page, or print badly. An agitated client may ring up and complain about something. It is rather like the first night of a play. Then the campaign starts rolling. Research may be undertaken to check the recall of a sample of the public. New business may start coming in. Distributors may have comments to make.

The agency has a living to make and it must make sure that every cost incurred on behalf of the client is billed to him. Likewise, the agency has to pay all its suppliers. And because the work may be spread over weeks or months the agency may have to charge the client for some costs as they occur. Control of expenditure will be maintained by a job number system so that everything purchased is identified in respect of the particular client.

This is a brief account, but it can be read in conjuction with other chapters in this part of the book, especially Chapter 16 on the advertising agency. It should be remembered that this will be only one of the many assignments for different clients which the agency is handling at the same time. They will all be at different stages of planning and execution. The production manager has to control the smooth throughput of work. Similarly, the client may have other advertising campaigns in progress for associated companies or products, either with the same agency or with different agencies.

21 Copywriting

The word *copy* has more than one meaning, so it is important to know what we mean when discussing the writing of advertisement copy by the copywriter. We may speak of a copy of a newspaper, meaning a single issue, or a copy of something which may be reproduced on a copying machine or when we copy somebody else's work and perhaps infringe copyright law. All the materials such as words and pictures supplied to a printer will be called 'the copy'. A copycat is a person who copies other people's behaviour. But when we speak of advertisement copy we mean *only the words contained in an advertisement.*

The art of copywriting is to write words which compel people to act as the advertiser wishes.

That does not mean that they will so act. They may not want to buy. They may be unable to buy. So, it is a contest between seller and possible buyer. Advertising is about bringing the two together, and a successful sale is a satisfied buyer as well as a gainful seller.

The copy will not work unless it is combined with the right media, the right time and an attractive presentation. Copy has to be written as one part of this combination. The copywriter does not write to please himself, or his client or employer, but to please the reader. He pleases the reader by telling him something worth knowing about something worth buying.

Bad advertisements are those which are dull, vague, false or boastful. Even so, they must be lively and borrow something from the world of nature where the colours and shapes of flowers and creatures make them attractive.

The first two rules of copywriting are that copy must be *precise* and *concise*. Say what you have to say in the fewest necessary words, even if long, detailed copy is necessary. Words which are strange to the reader stop the flow of reading. This book is full of jargon, words the reader may never have met before, but the attempt is made to explain them, sometimes by giving an alternative word. Remember, readers will know less about the subject than the writer, and the reader's vocabulary may contain fewer words than the writer's. It is not so much a case of writing down to people as making sure that anyone will understand.

Copy needs to be *simple* and *sincere*. The copywriter should believe in what he is writing. He is not trying to hoodwink the public, although bad advertisements give the impression that they are insincere. Words may have special relevance to certain people. *Works like magic* could be meaningful to an African while *Be a lucky owner* could appeal to a Chinese. Sometimes words like *fantastic, exclusive, stupendous, remarkable, unique* and *incredible* are really weak words because they have suffered over-kill by being used too often. People no longer believe them, and advertisements must be credible if they are to work. The AIDCA formula helps in the planning of copy that does work:

AIDCA formula

The five elements are: an advertisement must

1. attract *Attention;*
2. stimulate *Interest;*
3. create *Desire;*
4. inspire *Conviction;*
5. influence *Action.*

The design of the advertisement can also follow this formula, and although design is discussed separately in the next chapter the two go together. The copywriter and the visualiser need to work as a team, and in a small agency one person may create the whole advertisement.

ATTRACTING ATTENTION

While the size and position, the use of colour, the layout and the typography (choice of type faces) may all help to attract attention there are copywriting techniques which also do so, or which contribute to the overall effect.

By one means or another, the reader's attention must be claimed.

It is unlikely that the reader has bought the publication for the sake of the advertisements, although this can happen. Unless it is noticed, unless the reader is *persuaded* to even *look* at it rather than at something else, the advertisement will be ignored and it will be a waste of money. In attracting attention it may have to *select* particular readers who are potential customers. People cannot be expected to read every advertisement. The same people are not necessarily interested in banking, beer, bicycles or brassières although advertisements for all these things may appear in the same journal.

Some of the copywriter's special attention-getting devices are:

1. A compelling headline such as *There's only one service to West Africa!* (UKWAL Lines).
2. A catchy, memorable slogan, which may or may not be the headline. Modern advertisements end with a *signature slogan,* e.g. *We never forget you have a choice* (British Caledonian), *The reliable airline of Holland* (KLM) or *The best international connections* (Nigeria Airways).
3. The bold display of price or prices, e.g. *Rate £1.00 per kilo* (JCTI).
4. The display of selling points such as:
   Regular Express Freight Service between
   　　U.S. GULF PORTS and
   　　WEST AFRICAN PORTS
   (Freetown, Monrovia, Abidjan, Takoradi, Tema, Lagos/Apapa, Doula, Warri)
5. The use of sub-headings to break up the copy with contrasting black type, directing the reader's eye through the text copy.
6. The bold display of special selling words like that favourite of advertising — FREE! Even an information leaflet can be *free.*

From the above it will be seen that copywriting is not just a matter of writing a title, a description, and a name and address. The words may have to be broken up so that they appear in larger or smaller, bolder or lighter type. The copywriter has to *see* how his words will look. Their arrangement can help to attract attention.

STIMULATING INTEREST

The attention may be gained but has it been captured? How can attention be converted quickly into interest so that the reader is curious to know more? The opening words of the text must grip the attention. The UKWAL advertisement whose headline was quoted above had an opening paragraph which read:

> *Only one service offers you twelve sailings a month to more than sixteen West African ports and ten groupage bases.*

To an exporter or freight forwarder that could be good news. This short paragraph gives a lot of facts in simple English.

CREATING DESIRE

It is no use the reader enjoying the advertisement unless he is moved to want to own or enjoy the product or service advertised. Desire, the wish to have, use or do something, must be prompted. The Nigeria Airways ad creates the desire to fly by their airline rather than by a rival with the paragraph:

> *Heathrow has better connections, better facilities, a more central location and, of course, far better duty-free shopping than Gatwick.*

Very competitive! British Caledonian use Gatwick.

INSPIRE CONFIDENCE

But however much the reader may want what the advertiser has to offer, he may still resist making a decision. So, he has to be convinced that the product is value for money, that it is worth buying more than something else, is all that is claimed for it, or that purchase can be made possible. Proof may have to be offered, a testimonial may help, a guarantee may be convincing, or an easy payment service may have to be explained. The KLM ad whose signature slogan aims to inspire confidence also had this paragraph:

> *We've 60 years of airline experience and we're setting new, higher standards. Because we know just how important reliability and customer service really are. And that's why we train our ground and cabin staff to give you nothing but the best.*

INFLUENCING ACTION

Finally, we come to the *admonition,* some means of urging the reader to go to the shop, visit a showroom, accept a free sample, telephone an order, fill and post a coupon or even simply *remember* when next making a purchase. This latter action could occur when buying, say, soap or cigarettes or even, at some future date, when buying a motor-car or booking an air-ticket. Getting the reader to *act,* to respond, is the hardest job which the advertiser has to achieve.

Now let us consider the full wording of the Nigeria Airways full-page advertisement which had at its foot a drawing of a DC10 taking off. It followed the modern trend of headlining displayed sentences in bold type, and they filled two thirds of the space. The three paragraphs of text copy were set in two columns.

Daylight flights.
Fastest onward
connections.

Nigeria Airways
to London Heathrow.

Fly to London with us by day, any day of the week. Land at Heathrow, London's major airport, and the major gateway to all destinations in Britain, Europe and, indeed, the rest of the world. No transfer problems: connections the same day to almost everywhere you want to go.

Heathrow has better connections, better facilities, a more central location and, of course, far better duty-free shopping than Gatwick.

Or fly overnight for an early morning start: with ten flights a week, Nigeria Airways gives you the best choice. And the London Airport – Heathrow.

NIGERIA
AIRWAYS

the best international
    connections

The interesting aspect of this advertisement is the way in which, without mentioning names, it subtly competes with British Caledonian over the advantages of arriving at Heathrow rather than at Gatwick. This will be clearly understood by potential passengers. Knocking copy is negative and should be avoided, but here there is some refined knocking which is justifiable, especially if one is flying on from London.

ACTION WORDS

A device which helps to make a copy flow is the use of short verbs, and the following are words which are very useful to the copywriter:

Buy	See	Try	Give	Put
Ask	Get	Go	Start	Come
Do	Let	Write	Tell	Phone
Call	Send	Taste	Look	Pick
Save	Trust	Take	Use	Smell

Words such as these help in that most difficult task of urging action. Instead of saying 'You are invited to visit our showrooms' it is more positive to say 'Come to our showroom and see . . . '.

The above is typical of how one comes to write copy. Rough ideas are written down first and then they are polished to become sparkling diamonds of salesmanship.

22 Layout and Typography

The first rough designs for an advertisement are known as *visuals,* and the perfected designs, carefully measured and marked up for typesetting, are called *layouts.* Different size layouts for various size spaces are called *adaptations.* Display lines only are written or drawn on the layout. Other copy is represented by lines. The full copy for typesetting is typed on a separate sheet of paper. When advertisements are submitted for offset-litho printing they are usually in the form of camera-ready copy, this consisting of finished artwork and typeset copy.

Even though one may not be an artist it is useful to have sufficient 'sense of layout' to be able to plan a rough layout. The following are the basic rules of design of which balance and contrast are the two most important:

THE LAW OF UNITY

An advertisement may consist of a headline, picture, text, sub-headings, name, address and telephone number, logotype and signature slogan. There may also be a coupon which should be placed where it is easiest to cut out. All these elements need to be arranged so that they form a unified whole like a person's clothes.

THE LAW OF VARIETY

If everything is too black or too grey the advertisement will be monotonous so changes, such as between bold type and light type, big type and small type will create variety.

THE LAW OF BALANCE

In art and printing the 'centre' of balance is not at the exact centre — the middle — but one-third down, rather like the hilt on a dagger or short sword. To achieve this sort of balance an advertisement can be divided into one-third and two-thirds or vice-versa as in the examples shown in Figure 22.1. These simple outlines represent the proportions and balance to be found in a great many well-designed advertisements. The headline or picture may occupy one area, the text may fill the other. Or one area may be filled by the picture and the headline could be set above the text in the other area.

Fig. 22.1. Proportions and balance

THE LAW OF RHYTHM

The eye should move naturally throughout the design, and not be encouraged to dart about. Thus the eye should be guided by the sequence of elements such as the headline, text and sub-headings, down to the advertiser's name or the coupon. Photographs should be taken, chosen or trimmed to help achieve this effect, and the same applies to drawings.

THE LAW OF HARMONY

The parts of the layout should be arranged harmoniously but not monotonously. The human face with its arrangement of forehead, eyebrows, nose, mouth, cheeks and chin is a very harmonious layout. Three eyes or two mouths would be ugly.

THE LAW OF PROPORTION

Most sheets of paper, books, newpapers, magazines, catalogues and leaflets are longer in one direction than the other, and arranged either vertically or horizontally. These proportions are more attractive than a square. The shape of the whole advertisement can be important to its appeal.

THE LAW OF SCALE

Dark areas advance and light areas recede. Dark or bold colours such as red and orange stand out while paler colours such as blue and mauve tend to fade away into the distance. We are now into the business of achieving contrast with black headlines and grey text.

The designer has to resist the temptation to emphasise too much, for all emphasis is no emphasis. The outlines shown in Figure 22.2 demonstrate good and bad contrast. While the left-hand outline has contrast the right-hand outline has none, although both are well proportioned and balanced. One of the greatest aids to contrast, also an effect which pleases the eye is *white space*. Even the indenting of paragraphs (as on the pages of this book) provides white space.

The use of white space, by comparison with the outlines above, is now demonstrated in Figure 22.3.

TYPOGRAPHY

The skilful choice of printing type is essential to the effective presentation of the copy. There are hundreds of type designs to choose from but the typographer should be careful to create a blend of faces, sizes, and weights which enhance the appearance of the advertisement and

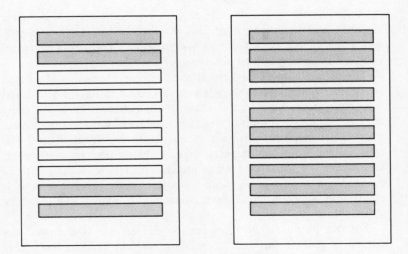

Fig. 22.2. Good (left) and bad contrast

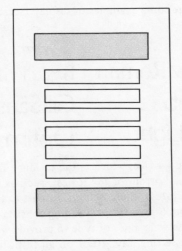

Fig. 22.3. The use of white space

make it easy and pleasant to read. He should not have such a mixture of type styles that the advertisement becomes jazzy and confusing. Harmony is important here again.

A *face* is the distinctive design of a type, a *fount* is a complete alphabet with numbers, signs and punctuation marks in one face, and a *family* consists of all the weights (extra bold, bold, medium, light, italics and any special variations) of one face.

Typesetting may be mechanical and use metal characters. Monotype typesetting machines set single characters, while Linotype and Intertype set type on *slugs* to the width of the columns. There are many different kinds of photo-typesetting machines, some computerised, which photograph standard-size characters to any required size. The copy can be stored on magnetic tape or floppy disc and corrections are more easily made than when metal characters or slugs have to be changed. An advantage of photo-typesetting is that each character is identical in quality whereas metal characters are individual and can be imperfect.

For our purpose type faces can be divided into two classes: the display faces which are more decorative, and the book or text faces which are used for the paragraphs of text. It is of course possible to use larger and bolder versions of the text type for display purposes.

The following are some examples of display faces:

Times Bold   *Palace Script*

Times New Roman   Baskerville Old Face

Univers 55   Gill Sans

Helvetica Light   Optima Medium

Type is specified by size, which is the distance from the top of the highest letter to the bottom of the lowest, such as a 'y'. This is measured by the *point system,* there being 72 points to the inch. Type sizes usually measure from 6 pt to 72 pt. Leading consists of spacing which is sometimes placed between lines of type to provide white space, but this can be achieved by setting, say, 10 pt on an 11 pt body to permit 1 pt of space between the lines.

One has to be careful not to set small type to too wide a measure or width. To be legible, small type should be set to a narrow measure; larger type to a wider measure. Thus, if there is so much copy it has to be set in small type it may pay to cut the copy in order to set in a larger and more readable size type.

23 Advertising Research

Market research techniques can be applied specifically to advertising in the following five ways:

1. To establish the copy theme or platform.
2. To test the effectiveness of different media for media planning purposes.
3. To test copy to discover which of a variety of advertisements is likely to be most effective.
4. To test the impact of advertisements when they have appeared.
5. To test what is recalled when advertisements have appeared.

1. ESTABLISH THE COPY THEME

Forms of motivation research are used to find out what motivates people to buy. The reasons may be quite different from those believed or suspected. If they can be discovered, the advertisement can be written and designed to appeal to the correct motive. These reasons cannot be obtained by the normal use of a questionnaire because people may not know why they really buy. They may *say* they buy confectionery or beer because they like the taste, but the underlying reason may be that they buy these products to reward themselves for hard work.

Motivation research methods range from the clinical and intelligence test kind of research conducted by Dr Ernst Dichter in the USA to simpler and less expensive discussion groups. Although there is sometimes criticism that the sample is too small to be truly representative, this objection is overcome if the participants are very close to the subject being investigated. For instance, there have been some very good discussion groups on advertising agency—client relations, the members being clients of agencies. There have also been good discussion-group studies in Nigeria where it is sometimes less easy to do field surveys.

Care has to be taken that the leader of the discussion group — who presents the topics, concludes the talk on each question by producing a consensus view, and then writes the report — does not bias the answers in any way. It is important that the spontaneous answers encourage frank and sincere information which might not be forthcoming from a structured questionnaire. These revelations will then help in creating a realistic copy platform and show what sort of selling points need to be stressed.

MEDIA RESEARCH

Surveys are conducted by independent bodies and also by the owners of media themselves. These surveys analyse the readership of newspapers and magazines, the audiences for radio, TV and outdoor advertising, and the attendances at exhibitions. These analyses may also go into age and income groups, sex, interests (e.g. having a motor-car or telephone) and geographical breakdown. With this infomation, the media planner can select media which are most likely to reach the right people at the lowest cost and with least duplication.

Two terms need to be understood regarding the press. Circulation means the average number of copies per issue which are *sold*. An audited net sale figure is one from which free copies and returns are excluded from the number printed. Readership, produced by research, is an estimate of the number and kind of people who read a publication. This could be three or more times higher than the audited net sale or circulation figure. A newspaper may be read by the whole family, a business newspaper or technical magazine may have a pass-round office readership, while a magazine may be read by many people in waiting rooms. Readership is not therefore limited to original buyers of the publication. *The Financial Times*, for example, has a small circulation but a large and influential readership.

ABC figures of circulation are those certified by the Audit Bureau of Circulations, which issues audit forms to member publishers who keep a daily record of sales. The actual audit is the responsibility of the publisher's accountants, and the figure finally authorised by the ABC is usually a six-monthly one.

JICNARS (Joint Industry Committee for National Readership Surveys) represents publishers, advertising agencies and advertisers and conducts a regular survey with 30,000 interviews and publishes a comprehensive report on the demographic profiles of national publications.

JICPAS (Joint Industry Committee for Poster Audience Surveys) has undertaken studies into the numbers and kinds of people who have opportunities to see outdoor advertising.

JICTAR (Joint Industry Committee for Television Advertising Research) was replaced in July 1981 by BARB (Broadcasters' Audience Research Board) which now measures both BBC and ITV television audiences. This combines the methods previously used, electronic meters attached to a sample of sets plus diaries kept by viewers (as used by JICTAR) and the street interview daily survey as previously used by the BBC. As a result the National Top Ten is produced for BBC1, BBC2 and ITV.

Table 23.1 lists a typical BARB weekly Top Ten, the BBC programmes being seen nationally, the ITV programmes being networked over all ITV areas. The names Granada, Yorkshire, ATV and Thames are the TV companies in Manchester, Leeds, Birmingham and London responsible for producing the show which was networked to all regions.

Advertisers are given advance notice of programming so that time can be booked in the most suitable segments. In addition to these popularity ratings actual estimated audience figures are given. This enables an advertising agency to plan a series of spots which will achieve a given total audience figure over a period. To avoid saturation advertising, which could bore viewers, the aim will be to show the commercial only until such time as it has been seen by a given number of people a certain number of times for it to be effective.

JICRAR (Joint Industry Committee for Radio Audience Research) conducts periodic surveys, using interviews and diaries, to estimate the audience for each commercial or independent radio station in the UK.

Attendances at exhibitions are recorded at the turnstile or by the collection of admittance tickets.

COPY-TESTING

The object of copy-testing is to discover which of a number of proposed advertisements is likely to be the most successful. Whatever method is used, measurement is made of the extent to which a sample

TABLE 23.1 *The National Top Ten*

BBC1
1. It Ain't Half Hot Mum
2. Nine O'Clock News (Thursday)
3. Gambit
4. Nine O'Clock News (Tuesday)
5. Summertime Special
6. Top of the Pops
7. Citizen Smith
8. The Monday Film: 'Young Billy Young'
9. The Good Old Days
10. News and Sport (Saturday)

BBC2
1. Bringing Up Baby
2. Secret Army
3. The Leopard Man
4. James Dean
5. On the Beach
6. Gardeners' World
7. Rhoda
8. Laughter in Paradise
9. Innocents in Paris
10. Top Crown

ITV

1.	Coronation Street (Wednesday)	Granada	All areas
2.	Coronation Street (Monday)	Granada	All areas
3.	Winner Takes All	Yorkshire	All areas
4.	A Sharp Intake of Breath	ATV	All areas
5.	Seagull Island	ATV	All areas
6.	Crossroads (Wednesday)	ATV	All areas
7.	The Big Top Variety Show	Thames	All areas
8.	The Krypton Factor	Granada	All areas
9.	Crossroads (Tuesday)	ATV	All areas
10.	Quincy	ATV	All areas

of relevant people respond to or remember the message. The advertisement achieving the highest score will be the one used or recommended to the client. A TV commercial will be tested on an audience in a hall or small cinema, or different commercials will be shown on two different TV stations, and next day a recall test will be carried out to see which one was remembered best.

The folder technique may be used for testing press advertisements, a series of different advertisements (among which is the one under test) being inserted in the plastic sleeves of a folder. Respondents will be asked to look at each advertisement in turn. After returning the folder to the interviewer, the respondent is asked to state what he or she remembers of each advertisement.

TESTING IMPACT

Rather more intensive than a recall test is the reading and noting test. A sample of people are asked whether they read the previous day's issue of a newspaper in which the advertisement appeared, and if they did they are questioned on every part of the advertisement. Percentages of men and women readers reading and recalling, say, the headline, the text, the sales points, the advertiser's name and so on are recorded.

This technique can be used for pre-test purposes if the advertisement can be printed in a limited edition — say, the London-only edition — of a national newspaper. As a result of what is learned it may be found necessary to amend the advertisement for national publication.

TESTING RECALL

This method is used after an advertisement has appeared to check how well a press, TV, radio or poster advertisement has been remembered. As an example, people in the USA were interviewed and asked to name the last six Presidents. A certain percentage was gained. Then a poster was displayed listing the names of the last six Presidents. Another survey showed that following display of this poster the percentage of people knowing the Presidential names had increased greatly. This test was used to demonstrate the effectiveness of poster advertising.

Armed with such techniques and the information provided it is possible to plan advertising campaigns in keeping with the IPA definition that *advertising presents the most persuasive possible selling message to the right prospects for the product or service at the lowest possible cost.*

Finally, dealer audit research and consumer panel research, subscribed to or conducted by the marketing department, will also demonstrate movement in sales, and any changes of the share of the market held, following or during an advertising campaign.

24 Advertising Problems in Developing Countries

Advertising in the West (or North) may be more sophisticated than it is in what is now known as the South, but in many ways it is much easier to plan and mount a campaign because of the special problems which confront the advertiser in the developing world. In this chapter we will summarise the problems that have been apparent in this book.

Literacy is enjoyed by 20 per cent or less of the population, and it can be a limited literacy since vocabularies may not be large. There is also the problem of lost literacy among those who left school but found no job requiring literacy. Illiteracy hampers the growth of the press which is one of the most economical media.

Languages are often so many that the creation of advertising is complicated by the need for special-language versions, while the circulations, readerships and audiences of different language media are in uneconomic quantities. Advertising becomes more expensive than in the West.

Different ethnic groups with their tribes or races, languages, taboos and traditions provide more complications. The same products cannot always be sold in the north of Ghana or Nigeria as in the south, due to Muslim preferences in the north. Thus appropriate products may use the *Daily Times* in the south of Nigeria and the *New Nigerian* in the north. In Ghana, the choice may be between the *Daily Graphic* in the south and the Hausa-language programme on radio GBC1.

Lack of media may result from some of the above problems or because of balance-of-payments problems which restrict the import of newsprint, as in Zambia. The growth of TV may be hindered by the lack of electricity in the hinterland. There may be few poster sites. Poor roads may make it difficult to transport newspapers and mail. Direct-mail advertising may be difficult to conduct because of the lack of mailing lists and unreliable postal systems. Radio – always thought to be the great medium of these countries – is often a less efficient medium because of unrepaired sets, non-replacement of batteries and poor reception.

Scepticism of advertising is often natural for people who are conservative in their ways.

Poverty constricts the size of the market for many goods, and this may affect 80 per cent of the population, while the population is such that 50 per cent are usually under 15 years of age and outside the cash economy. At least 300 million are jobless, according to VSO.

Distribution of goods can be uncertain so that it is difficult to advertise goods in the certainty that they can be bought. This is partly due to the lack of transport, warehouses, wholesalers, telephones and retailers able to stock adequate supplies, but again due to the poverty of countries which cannot sustain a normal distribution network due to the lack of demand and cash flow.

Imported products may be difficult to promote because the country of origin is disliked, or the products represent different cultures and the manufacturers fail to research the special needs of different people. The product may be the wrong colour, or its name may have an unfortunate meaning when pronounced in the overseas market. Or measurements may be required in order to use the product, and no means of measuring exist. When the meat substitute Metex was advertised in Nigeria housewives were told it would make a pound of meat. This was meaningless to those who bought meat by the piece and not by weight. It was also infuriating when it was discovered how little a 'pound' was.

Datsun were wise in Ghana when they employed translators throughout the country to educate people about the suitability of the Japanese car under tropical conditions, its low fuel consumption and durability on country roads. Catalogues were printed in local languages and left with people to read at their leisure.

Yet, in spite of all these problems, advertising is necessary in order to make known in order to sell.

Sample Examination Paper - Advertising

HIGHER STAGE

THE LONDON CHAMBER OF COMMERCE AND INDUSTRY

SPRING EXAMINATION 1981

MONDAY 27 APRIL—6 to 9 p.m.

ADVERTISING

INSTRUCTIONS TO CANDIDATES
  (a) **First,** *read through all the questions and do not attempt to answer any until you understand the scope and limitations of the questions you have selected.*
  (b) *Question 1 is COMPULSORY.*
  (c) *Candidates may attempt* **four** *other Questions.*
  (d) *All questions carry equal marks.*
  (e) *Questions need not be answered in numerical order, but all answers must be clearly and correctly numbered.*

1. COMPULSORY QUESTION
Write the copy and draw the layout for a whole page upright black and white advertisement for a tourist holiday in another country. The advertisement should include a coupon so that the reader may request a free brochure. The advertisement is to appear in a suitable magazine. Name the magazine of your choice.
  Elaborate drawing is not necessary. If layout is clearly indicated, full credit will be given.

2.   Briefly explain the following terms:

    (i) Account executive   (vi) Presentation
    (ii) Media buyer   (vii) Media schedule
    (iii) Visualiser   (viii) Layout
    (iv) Typographer   (ix) Contact report
    (v) Traffic controller   (x) Voucher copy

3.   What kinds of research may be termed continuous research, and how does the information gained from continuous research differ from that of an *ad hoc* survey?

4.   'Our product is firmly established as the market leader', says the managing director of a tea company. 'There is no longer any need to spend money on advertising.' What do you think the position would be after a year without advertising? Explain why you think the position you describe has been brought about.

5.   (i) Why are pictures reproduced better in newspapers printed by offset-litho than by letterpress?
    (ii) Why are large circulation colour magazines printed by photogravure instead of by letterpress?
    (iii) Why is the silk screen process used for printing on non-flat surfaces such as bottles or ashtrays?
    (iv) Why does photo-typesetting produce better print than hot metal typesetting?

6.   When television advertising was first introduced it was feared that this advanced medium would bring about a reduction in press advertising, yet press advertising has survived and retained its importance. Explain why this has happened.

7.   The British Government and the EEC have proposed various legal controls of advertising which have been resisted by the Advertising Association and the Advertising Standards Authority. What are the strengths and weaknesses of a self-regulatory voluntary control system compared with legal controls?

8.   It has been said that public relations informs and educates but advertising persuades and sells. It is also said that the task of public relations is to create understanding after which advertising takes on the selling role. Furthermore, it is claimed that advertising may not work unless the market has been educated through preliminary public relations activities. Develop these statements

to show the differences between public relations and advertising as forms of business communication, so that you make it clear that public relations is not a form of advertising.

9. Advertising media are often best suited to certain advertising campaigns. Give an example of a particularly appropriate use of each of the following advertising media:
   (i) Direct mail
  (ii) Commercial radio
 (iii) Bus posters
 (iv) Bulletin boards or supersites
  (v) Television programme magazines, e.g. *Radio Times, TV Times*
 (vi) Professional journals, e.g. *The Lancet, Architect's Journal*
(vii) Financial and business journals, e.g. *Financial Times, The Economist*
(viii) Mail drops
 (ix) Commercial television
  (x) Scale models as point-of-sale displays

10. Explain how the plans board operates from the time the account executive brings in a new account to the day when he presents the proposed advertising campaign to the client.

11. (i) What would be your main considerations when planning a competition to increase sales of a popular consumer product?
   (ii) What would influence your choice between offering a motor-car or a holiday abroad for two as the main prize, assuming they were of equal cash value from the winner's point of view, although cash could not be taken as an alternative prize?

Part Three

Public Relations

25 Public Relations Defined

INTRODUCTION

Inevitably, public relations (PR) has been mentioned already in Parts One and Two on marketing and advertising. This does not mean that PR is either a part of marketing or a form of advertising, but that it is associated with both. Some people like to make a mystery out of PR. Few marketing and advertising people understand it. Management often misuses it. So let us say first of all that PR concerns the total communications of any organisation or person who has to communicate with others. Like the weather, it exists whether we like it or not, but it may be good or bad public relations. Before analysing some well-known definitions let us first discuss some of the popular misconceptions about this subject.

MISCONCEPTIONS ABOUT PR

Free advertising

A false and glib saying is that advertising is paid-for publicity and PR is publicity that is not paid for. Let's first appreciate that publicity is the *result* of making known and, as every public figure knows, publicity can be good or bad. Two other sayings bear on this: *bad news is good news, good news is no news* and *if you cannot stand the heat in the kitchen you should stay out.* In other words, most people prefer disaster stories because they are more exciting than success stories, and people 'in the news' must expect criticism.

Having realised the implications of publicity let us consider whether PR is free advertising. First, it is not advertising because advertising aims to persuade and sell (which PR does not), and it lacks the control over appearance and message content which is possessed by advertising. If he wished, an editor could cut, re-write or destroy a news release, whereas the advertisement manager will print our advertisement as supplied provided it does not offend any code of practice or law. Second, it is not free for two reasons: editorial space or programme airtime is priceless and cannot be bought like advertisement space or commercial/sponsored air-time, and all PR work bears the cost of time, materials and expenses to produce media coverage.

Part of the marketing mix

Public relations is not – like advertising – part of the marketing mix. It is concerned with the total organisation, of which marketing may or may not be a function, and every element of the marketing mix has PR implications. Feedback which may influence product design, naming and branding, labelling and packaging, pricing, instructions, dealer and customer relations, market education, selling, advertising, merchandising and after-sales service all have their PR aspects. When people refer to PR as part of the marketing mix they are probably thinking of press relations support for the marketing strategy, but this is a minor and limited approach to PR. However, it is a typical marketing misunderstanding of the role of PR. Some marketing writers, especially American, even make the mistake of referring to PR as 'publicity'!

Favourable image

A common error (which is popular in Nigeria) is that PR is to do with creating a favourable image for an organisation, or with achieving a 'favourable' climate of opinion or 'favourable' mentions by the media. This attitude has the unfortunate effect of encouraging the media to think that PR practitioners promote good news only and hide the bad news, and that PR information is therefore biased, faked or unreliable. It is not the job of PR merely to put a good face on things and try to pretend that nothing bad ever happens.

PR, if it is to be trusted, must be *credible*. It must deal with the facts of both good and bad events as they occur. If there is an electricity failure, a postal strike, a railway accident, an air crash or a loss at sea, accurate information about these misfortunes has to be issued just as readily as good news. Some organisations – especially public service ones – may have great difficulty (perhaps through no fault of their own but sometimes because of their inadequacies) in achieving favour. During the past decade this has been true of Nigeria Airways, Nigerian Railways, NEPA, Barclays Bank and British Petroleum. Their public relations officers (PROs) have nevertheless had the sometimes thankless task of presenting the facts. Sometimes it is enough to be understood even if that does not mean that one is loved. It is therefore foolish to think PR can pretend things are what they are not. In fact that could be termed *propaganda,* a very different thing from public relations.

Confusion with propaganda

In developing countries, especially where there are one-party, dictatorial or military governments, it may be difficult to distinguish between propaganda and PR. Propaganda is biased information to gain support for a cause, creed or belief, but PR is concerned with achieving mutual understanding. A government or a political party may engage in propaganda to win supporters, but a government department may use PR techniques to create understanding of a policy or service such as road safety, a census or an educational programme.

Conning the press

Perhaps because of the unprofessional behaviour of bad PROs, PR is misunderstood (by management on the one side and the media on the other) as a confidence trick. But if PR is to work there can be no question of 'conning the press', 'twisting editors' arms' or bribing the media to publish stories. It is unfortunate for the image of PR that, in West Africa especially, journalists are sometimes given payments such as banknotes attached to news releases, handed 'envelopes' containing money at press receptions, or paid 'taxi money'. Reporters may accept such payments, perhaps thinking that big companies can and should afford them, but editors continue to publish stories on their merits irrespective of bribes taken by their staff. Such practices bring public relations into disrepute. No doubt these malpractices will diminish as the authority of the Nigerian Institute of Public Relations grows.

THE RANGE OF PR

From these remarks it will be seen that public relations is a larger and more embracing activity than either advertising or marketing. It enters into every corner of an organisation, and is very much to do with how an organisation is seen to *behave*. Moreover, it concerns both commercial and non-commercial organisations, in both the public and the private sectors. It is significant that in developing countries, where there are so many new services and products to explain, and where lifestyles are changing with increased literacy and prosperity, PR has a valuable task to perform.

To take Nigeria as an example, the agricultural, educational, energy, transportation, steel, water, telecommunications, industrial, financial and other programmes all depend for success on factual information and clear understanding. Similarly, the economic and social development of Zambia calls for PR commitments. Zambia, so long penalised by events in neighbouring countries, needs PR to help its recovery programme and to exploit its cotton, tourist and other industries. The world needs to know about what is happening in developing countries, whether this be to attract investment, trade, tourism or simply recognition. Too long the world has heard only of wars, revolts, famine, floods and earthquakes.

THE IMAGE

Reference has been made to the *image,* and to the nonsense of talking about a favourable image. An image can only be what it is, favourable or unfavourable. An image cannot be invented or polished, although it can be changed. If, through bad behaviour, products or services a poor opinion results, this can be changed to a good one if it is deserved by good behaviour, products or services. You cannot pretend something is what it is not, for the deceit will be discovered sooner or later. An image can also be changed if there is a change of policy or activity. And the image (impression or character) can be developed as people learn more about its subject.

For example, if a country has a poor tourist image this could change if new roads were built, modern hotels were opened, and facilities and attractions were developed. This has happened in the Seychelles. Hong Kong became a great tourist attraction for the British once the British Airways monopoly was broken and British Caledonian and Cathay Pacific were allowed the route. Six new hotels were opened in a year! Zambia is regaining its tourist industry — and it has the attraction of wonderful game parks — and earned valuable foreign exchange from its modest 57,000 tourists in 1980.

There are some special images which will be discussed again when dealing with the planning of PR campaigns. The *mirror image* is that held by management, which may well be different from that held by outsiders who have a *current image* based on their knowledge and experience of the organisation. The *multiple image* occurs when different representatives of a company, such as salesmen, present personal images rather than a uniform image of their organisation. The *corporate image* is that of the organisation itself, based on its reputation, activities and behaviour. A *product image* is that based on the quality, performance, selling points or distinctiveness of a product.

THE PR TRANSFER PROCESS

The role of PR can therefore be demonstrated by the model of the PR transfer process shown in Figure 25.1. The model demonstrates the task of public relations.

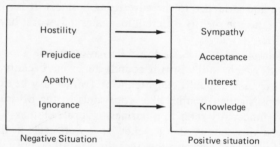

Fig. 25.1. The PR transfer process

People are hostile to change, or to things with which they are unfamiliar. In a developing country the PRO will be confronted by many instances of these. Tribal hostility is a typical example, and it is often based on fear of other people because they have different languages, customs, religions, dress and so on. Again, people are often prejudiced by the ideas, beliefs and attitudes common to their environment and upbringing. But people may be disinterested in things outside their job, family or village, while everyone in the modern complex is ignorant about many things.

A PR programme may well have to overcome all or some of these negative situations. A perfect state of knowledge is unlikely, but the ultimate objective of the PR transfer process, of PR, is to achieve *understanding*. Understanding is very difficult to achieve, yet that is what PR is all about. Beyond that may lie advertising, and advertising campaigns are unlikely to work unless people understand what is being advertised. Equally, people are unlikely to co-operate with census-takers unless they understand why a census is necessary.

PR DEFINED

PR has been defined by many people. British and American definitions tend to be rather different, mainly because the British are rather preju-diced about selling, and the media dislike PR which resembles adver-tising, whereas the Americans are less inhibited about selling and advertising. American definitions may refer to 'persuasion' and 'influ-encing attitudes', whereas British definitions are broader and leave persuasion and influence to the advertising business. It is a question of credibility and the slightly different meanings that words have in differ-ent countries.

For example, in the USA Edward Bernays may talk about 'engineer-ing consent' which, to the British, sounds somewhat deceitful, while the Nigerian expression 'public enlightenment' (which may be exactly what it says to a Nigerian) sounds like propaganda to the British. Nigerians may quite innocently refer to a business or profession as 'a game', but to a Briton this sounds like a racket. It is noticeable in the Nigerian press, and in general conversation, that the slang of colonial days, which is no longer used by British people, remains as normal English. To British reader an expression like 'Bad eggs arrested' is almost meaning-less, or at least bad English, yet it is a headline often seen in the Nigerian *Daily Times.* Imagine the effect of such language on an English examiner who is unfamiliar with overseas expressions

Moreover, an overseas student may read both British and American textbooks with very contradictory uses of apparently English words. An example is 'piggybacking' which in the USA means putting a con-tainer or vehicle on the flat wagon of a train, whereas in Britain it means inserting questions in the questionnaire of an omnibus market research survey sent to a consumer panel.

In this book we shall stick to a British definition and one accepted internationally.

The definition used by the (British) Institute of Public Relations (IPR) reads: *Public relations practice is the deliberate, planned and sustained effort to establish and maintain mutual understanding between an organisation and its public.*

The two most important aspects of this definition are its emphasis on *planned* public relations, and on two-way understanding. Mutual understanding means being understood by other people and understanding other people, that is not just informing other people but being informed about *their* wishes and attitudes. For example, what is the current image, what is the extent of external understanding or misunderstanding?

A very interesting modern definition is the Mexican Statement which was the product of an international conference of PR institutions held in Mexico City in 1978. It reads: *Public relations practice is the art and social science of analysing trends, predicting their consequences, counselling organisation leaders, and implementing planned programmes of action which will serve both the organisation and the public interest.*

This is probably the most helpful and practical definition that has ever been produced. First of all it introduces the need for research to audit or assess the situation (the current image) and to consider the implications of what is discovered. Second, it stresses the advisory role of PR, its service to management. Third, it shows that PR programmes must be planned. We do not work haphazardly on a day-to-day basis. Finally, PR action must not only benefit its sponsors, but must be socially responsible.

PUBLICS

The IPR definition refers to 'public' but it is normal in PR to use the plural 'publics' since we communicate with many different groups of people. It is necessary, as we shall see in Chapter 35, to define publics and then choose the media with which to reach them. There are certain basic publics:

1. *The community* — people who live near the organisation or its premises (e.g. factory, office, college, airport, seaport or whatever kind of premises it may have).

2. *Potential employees* – who may live locally, work for rival organisations, be students in colleges or universities, or live overseas.
3. *Employees* – who will include people such as management, office, factory, warehouse, sales, service or transport staff.
4. *Suppliers* of services and materials.
5. *The money market* – bankers, insurers, shareholders, brokers, analysts and investment advisers.
6. *Distributors* – wholesalers, retailers, brokers, agents and so on.
7. *Consumers and users*, past, present and future of both sexes and all ages.
8. *Opinion-leaders* – all kinds of people – parents, preachers, politicians, TV and radio presenters and others who express opinions and influence attitudes towards the organisation.

The above is a basic list, but for any one organisation there will be a special list of all the groups of people with whom the organisation does, should or could communicate.

THE COMMUNICATIONS PROCESS

Communications follow a process of disseminating information (known as *encoding*) and receiving information (known as *decoding*). The information may be issued by any form or medium of communication which may be simple ones like the voice, drum, music, smoke signal, flashing light, flags or semaphor, or more sophisticated ones such as print, photographs, drawings, charts, Morse code, signals, deaf-and-dumb signs, Braille, radio or TV. However, the message will be understood only if there is a *common field of experience or understanding,* and as was demonstrated in the PR transfer process, the chief objective of PR is to achieve understanding.

The PRO has to communicate effectively. The overlap of the field of common experience is called the *extensional bargain.* Both sides must share at least some of the same experience if there is to be mutual understanding. All this can be very simply shown in Figure 25.2.

As an example of a breakdown in communication and understanding, the case can be re-quoted of the Ugandan farmers who lost their cattle because they failed to protect them from tsetse fly in spite of the fact that they were supplied by the Government with free insecticides. Unfortunately, the foreign manufacturers of the insecticide printed pic-

Fig. 25.2. The extensional bargain

tures of huge tsetse flies on the containers. The farmers thought they had been sent the wrong material because their tsetse flies were not as big as those illustrated. In the West it is common to picture things larger than life. This is the sort of dramatic effect often used in advertising and marketing and on posters and packaging. The Ugandan farmers accepted only what fitted in with their everyday experience, and giant insects did not. This is perfectly understandable, unless you happen to be a designer in Europe or America.

In a similar way, a major communication problem occured when the Mass Transit Railway in Hong Kong, an underground railway system under the harbour, was being constructed. The majority of Hong Kong people are Chinese. To them a tunnel is a place for burying the dead. The extensive PR programme had to overcome fears and create experience and understanding of the tunnel as a cheap, safe, comfortable and quick way of travelling from one side of the harbour to the other.

The same thing applies to banking and insurance in many developing countries. These are concepts outside the experience of simple country folk, and even some town people think banks and insurance companies are not to be trusted. The mobile bank is an interesting marketing device which adds credibility to the service and shows a good sense of PR in communicating the idea of a bank to people who are unfamiliar with it.

In the West it is not difficult to communicate, and the field of common experience is extensive and can be increased easily. This is not so in developing countries, so that there is great need for PR methods which in turn have to be employed with skills and under difficulties unknown in the West.

There may, of course, be different experience or understanding of the same thing. There are PR implications in advertising which will fail if the message collides with a wall of conflicting or non-existent experience and understanding. For example, a British confectionery manufacturer called a chocolate bar Lion and put up posters with the headline *Man Eats Lion* and a roaring lion was shown on the illustrated wrapper. One wonders whether the subtlety of this advertising message would have gained the same response in Africa?

EDUCATION, TRAINING, EXAMINATIONS

At the time of writing no British University offers a degree in public relations, although there are degrees and diplomas in mass communications and communication studies, which are not quite the same thing.

The British professional qualification is the CAM Diploma in Public Relations. The third year Diploma examination is preceded by the CAM Certificate in Communication Studies.

The London Chamber of Commerce and Industry offers a Higher Certificate in Public Relations. There is also the LCCI Marketing Diploma for passes in Marketing, Advertising and Public Relations, sat and passed together. Distinctions gained in these subjects rank for exemption from the same subjects in the CAM certificate examinations.

Addresses are:

Communication, Advertising and Marketing Education Foundation, Abford House, 15 Wilton Road, London, SW1V 1NJ.

London Chamber of Commerce and Industry, Commercial Education Scheme, Marlowe House, Station Road, Sidcup, Kent, DA15 7BJ.

26 Role of Public Relations in Commercial and Non-commercial Organisations

Not all organisations are engaged in marketing; some may never use advertising or they will use it only on special occasions to recruit staff or to sell property. A hospital does not advertise for patients, a fire brigade does not advertise for fires, nor does an army advertise for wars. Yet all three are active in PR. It is easy to see from this that PR extends far beyond industry and business. Just as it embraces the total communications of an organisation so does it do so in any kind of organisation.

More than that: *PR exists whether we like it or not.* Any two people are involved in PR. It concerns individuals as well as organisations, and only a person with no human relations and no communication – a hermit – is without PR. It is not necessary to have someone labelled PRO to have PR, for it is inherent in human relationships. It has been going on ever since man created signs and speech.

The profession of PR applies techniques to communications to spread knowledge and create understanding, but people have been doing this badly or well for thousands of years. The modern world demands that it be done efficiently. In developing countries where life-styles are changing and new things are happening, the techniques of PR have a vital part to play.

Commercial products, business services, Government policies and programmes, social services, education, roads and transportation and many other subjects have to be explained in developing countries both to the 20 per cent who may be urban and literate and to the 80 per cent who are rural and illiterate.

It is a massive PR task quite outside advertising, marketing and propaganda. The media are scarce, the audience is vast, and the messages are often strange. The field of common experience may be slight or non-existent. It is a communication situation quite unlike that of the West where the media are plentiful, the audience vast and the messages become more and more complex but, thanks to education and literacy, the field of common experience is at least adaptable.

Let us make a brief analysis of the PR requirements of a variety of organisations which will be found in most societies, developed or developing, and to some extent in underdeveloped ones.

INDUSTRY—MANUFACTURING COMPANIES

Whatever it makes, whether it be beer or motor-cars, soap or gramophone records, the publics of industry are basically those set out in the previous chapter. Each may be subdivided and extended. Staff may include management and executive, office, sales, factory, warehousing and transport, and some may have servicing staff. It will be necessary to communicate with people who live in the nearby community who need to be told what the company does. Community relations problems could include noise, dirt, pollution of the air or water, harm to the environment, labour disputes, vehicles which cause road hazards or congestion. The community may also be a source of labour. Internal or industrial relations will be vital, and this will be complementary to trade union relations and personnel management. For instance, a strike may be averted if management is frank with information. Personnel management may be aided by films and literature for the induction of new staff. Upward communication to management will be encouraged by 'speak up', suggestion boxes, incentive schemes and other techniques.

Externally, the company has to communicate with all those publics with whom it has to deal. Financial relations will range from the company's local bank to the share market and shareholders. Cash flow problems and credit, raising funds for development, business performance and dividends all involve special forms of PR. As we have seen in the section on marketing, many kinds of distributor may handle the goods. All of them need to understand the company's policy and goods, and how they satisfy customer needs. Then we come to the customers and their possible states of hostility, prejudice, apathy and ignorance. In addition, there are all those people — opinion-leaders — who have some influence on almost every aspect of the company's behaviour, image, performance and communications.

From this quick analysis it will be seen that the PR of a business organisation is much more complex than merely trying to create or maintain a favourable image. The 'favourable image' idea of the role of PR is an over-simplification which ignores the far wider field of PR requirement in business and trade.

SERVICING ORGANISATIONS

The servicing company such as a bank, insurance company, hotel, travel agency, bus company or airline has PR requirements similar to those of a manufacturer, producer or supplier, but it has one big difference which has great PR implications. The company is much closer to its customers, clients or patrons. A bank, for instance, operates in the high street like a retailer. Service industries depend on good-will and continual personal relationships. Unlike the manufacturer, the supplier of a service has a face-to-face relationship with its consumer public.

In Britain the Midland Bank has run an advertising campaign about the 'talking bank' which is pure PR expressed through advertising. The woodworm and dry rot division of Rentokil, which preserves timber in houses and other property, has claimed that 60 per cent of its business comes from recommendations. Again, this is pure PR. The world's airlines pay great attention to PR, training ticket agencies, ground staff, pilots and cabin crew to take good care of passengers. This is extended to corporate identity design as expressed by symbols, colour schemes and aircraft livery (the external decoration of aircraft), and the uniforms of air hostesses. The in-flight magazine is another service. Asian airlines are noted for their courtesy and hospitality.

PR or customer relations is therefore a major part of a servicing organisation's operation, for it will be judged by its behaviour. In some African countries one hears nationals criticising the behaviour of the air hostesses on their national airline, something which one would not hear elsewhere in the world. One also hears criticism of the servicing, administration or operation of some of these airways. The fault lies in poor training: the result is bad PR. One large African airline with an excellent fleet of aircraft, and an overwhelming demand both for its domestic and foreign flights, brought in one of the best European airlines to reorganise its administration.

RETAIL ORGANISATIONS

These are also servicing organisations, but since they have premises, and the one-to-one relationship is intensified, there are other PR aspects. This is true even in a supermarket where the personal service element is replaced by self-service. Shops, stores and supermarkets each have a character. Woolworth is different from Marks and Spencer, Kingsway from UTC, one Singapore plaza from another. Each gains the image or character it deserves, and it is a PR objective to achieve recognition of particular qualities. Gordon Selfridge, American pioneer of London's West End stores, set out 80 years ago to create a place where shopping was a pleasure.

The quality and reliability of the merchandise, fair prices, cash refunds or exchange of returned goods, a delivery service, careful packing of items purchased, free car-parking, facilities for children, and a restaurant contribute to the character of a store. So do attentive and helpful sales assistants, well-laid-out counters and displays, and easy access to floors by stairs, elevators or escalators.

Each shop will approach such things in different ways. PR is therefore inherent in the management philosophy of the retailer. Much of it may also depend on the advice and the techniques of the PR practitioner who can act as a transmitter of both management policies and feedback from customers.

CENTRAL GOVERNMENT

Government PR should not be confused with either propaganda on behalf of the Government of the day, or propaganda on behalf of the political party in power. It is essential to be clear about this distinction. It may not always be obvious or appreciated by the electorate, or by people overseas. The Government PRO or Information Officer may, of course, be responsible for advertising, PR and propaganda. In so doing he must be careful to understand which form of communication he is engaged in at any particular time, since each is very different from the other. Central Government PR will be of three kinds:

Internal staff PR

All government departments have staff with which ministers and heads of departments, as employers, have to maintain good relations. This is similar to the situation in a company. Ministries often have their own house journals and other media of employer–employee relations.

External PR

This will be a major activity aimed at explaining Government, or Government department, policy and services to the electorate. In developing countries this is extremely important since new services such as education, health, housing and advisory services to agriculture and industry have to be explained. If a census is being undertaken, a big PR task (sometimes overlooked, sometimes too dependent on advertising but well conducted in Malaysia and Singapore in 1980) is to explain *why* and *how* the head count is being conducted.

Overseas PR

International PR on behalf of Government policy is very important in order to aid trade and investment, and to promote tourism. People abroad are unfamiliar with the products and attractions of foreign countries, and 'educating the market' is essential PR. It will be conducted through embassies, tourist boards and in conjunction with national airlines, railways and shipping lines, and in co-operation with overseas travel agents. A country's postage stamps may contribute to this spread of knowledge and understanding.

In Britain the Central Office of Information handles international PR for the British Government, and also for British industries where their ideas and successes are of overseas interest and speak well for Britain. This helps in the export of British goods and in the creation and maintenance of good-will towards Britain. Other countries do the same thing, many of them operating trade and information centres in overseas cities like London, New York, Paris, Hamburg or Tokyo.

LOCAL GOVERNMENT

In Britain, local government is said to look after people from the cradle to the grave — from maternity clinics to cemeteries — with schools, housing, roads, hospitals, water, waste collection and so on in between birth and death. Local authorities — town, county, state or regional councils — may exist. Their work and services are provided for out of rates and taxes paid by the people (except in Macao where the casinos are taxed to provide the money!). The ratepayers are entitled to know how their money is being spent, and what services are being provided. The scope for PR activity is great. All the local popular media are invol-

ved, but so are more intimate activities such as talks to the members of
local societies and party visits to local authority undertakings such as
public buildings, waterworks, factory estates, housing developments
and so on.

The trading undertakings and special amenities of different authorities create various opportunities for PR work. Some towns may own
airports, ports, historic buildings, industrial estates, shopping centres,
sports centres, cultural or conference centres. All these will call for
special PR efforts to make these services and facilities known to their
respective public locally, nationally or internationally as the case may
be.

When these places are in the news, as when events are being held,
famous people are visiting them, or when other occasions merit media
coverage, there will be organisational and press relations work to attend
to. This may also call for the printing of posters, leaflets, programmes
and souvenir books; liaison with many services such as the police, transport, catering, car-parking, first aid, telephone, translation and so on as
may be necessary.

PUBLIC UTILITIES

Under this general title may be included undertakings, local, regional or
national, which are in public or part-public ownership for the provision
of public services. In some developing countries the term 'parastatal' is
used for organisations such as Indeco in Zambia which is a state-
controlled organisation involved in mining and other operations. In
Britain and other countries there are nationalised gas, electricity, coal,
railway, airway, postal, telecommunication, broadcasting, ports and
other services or industries.

They arise for one of two reasons: because they are initiated by the
state or because they are taken over from private industry (like much of
the French motor industry). They may be taken over for political reasons (public ownership of essential resources) or because they are losing
money but are vital to the economy. All these conditions create a host
of public relations requirements.

In Nigeria, NEPA has to inform the public how to conserve electricity and explain why there are inadequate supplies. A gas board may
have to teach users to use the fuel safely, and explain explosions. A
state airway may be in competition with private airlines (e.g. British

Airways and British Caledonian). In Saudi Arabia, the new King Abdul Aziz International Airport at Jeddah produced opportunities for the International Airports Projects to tell the world about its development. In Hong Kong the Mass Transit Railway required PR support right through the financing, building, opening and current operation.

RELIGIOUS FAITHS

It is one thing to propagate a religious belief, but a considerable PR task to achieve understanding, especially among non-believers. Some countries have different religions (or denominations of faiths) from others, but other countries may contain followers of more than one religion. There may be harmony, as in Singapore where religious tolerance is a national characteristic of great PR value, or disharmony, as in Northern Ireland, which is harmful to Britain's international image.

In a world where it becomes necessary to understand religious beliefs if hostility and prejudice are not to lead to intolerance and even war, the techniques of PR are the tools of tolerance.

Religious organisations publish educational literature, make films, contribute to community work and seek acceptance by those who never will join them. The Catholic Church advertises its publications, and so does the Society of Friends. Buddhists and Moslems place holy books in hotel bedrooms just as the Gideons distribute their Bibles. In Zambia the Catholic Church gave several thousand pounds so that a co-operative shop could be stocked by its disabled managers. Islam has become a powerful influence in some parts of the world, and people of other faiths and cultures must learn to respect its tenets. Moslems themselves have an important PR task to perform.

PR in this area can be difficult, as has been seen in the relations in Northern Ireland between Catholics and Protestants, in Israel between Jews and Arabs, in the Lebanon between Christians and Moslems, or in a complex multi-ethnic society like Nigeria. Religion can be intermingled with nationalist, language, racial, tribal and other differences. PR activities have to be distinguished from propagandist ones. Understanding is sought by PR, support by propaganda.

CHARITIES

Some charities are national or local, but many today are international and are involved in aiding the distressed during wars, famines, drought, floods, earthquakes and other disasters. There are charities which provide health, agricultural, education, training and other programmes for developing countries.

For most of these bodies, large or small, national or international, the following problems require PR attention:

1. In countries like Britain where there are many social services – a 'welfare state' – there may be a mistaken belief that charities are unnecessary or are state-financed.
2. In developing countries a foreign or international charity may be regarded with suspicion.
3. Money is constantly required. Emergency demands on funds may be constant.
4. Donors seldom understand that it costs money to promote and administer a charity. Not all the money can go to the needy, even though that is the giver's wish.
5. Repeated appeals for money can be irritating.
6. Some causes may be unattractive or hard to understand. Some foreign places, where a disaster has occurred, may be remote and unknown to potential donors. Few tragedies receive the publicity and sympathy of the Vietnamese boat people. A drought in Sahil is less easy to visualise. Certain diseases may be difficult to explain, and some people may tend to turn a blind eye to them.

One way in which many charities have succeeded in gaining financial support has been through the marketing of Christmas cards and products which have been purchased on merit and not only for charitable reasons.

PR will consist of news coverage, house journals, and coverage on radio and TV programmes where personalities associated with charities can contribute, an example being a lifeboat coxswain being interviewed on a Parkinson programme on the eve of a 'flag-day' street collection. It is also possible to get industrial and commercial firms to sponsor films about charities, or to contribute the proceeds from events to charity. For instance, the premières of new films are often in aid of charities, with considerable publicity in the media.

INSTITUTES AND SOCIETIES

The PR of voluntary bodies is often very similar to that of charities except that instead of being directed mainly to donors and prospective donors, and publics which need to be informed, the donors are replaced by members and potential members. The effort is often limited by lack of funds. Moreover, the body may represent a minority interest which may be of little concern to the mass media, and press coverage may be restricted to the trade, technical and professional press. This could be the case with a PR institute which would be of little news value to newspapers, and possibly not even to magazines devoted to advertising and marketing! Radio and TV might see the subject as only good for criticism.

There are, of course, some voluntary organisations which are of great news value because of their social, economic or political influence; the Confederation of British Industries is a good example in Britain while elsewhere in the world the United Nations organisations provide further examples. Here, the supporters are mainly industry and business, or governments. Chambers of Commerce and Trade, consumer organisations, sports associations and similar large organisations representing wide interest will command considerable media interest.

Some societies may win media interest because they represent unusual, topical or attractive interests such as Unidentified Flying Objects, Folk Dancing, Feminism, Real Ale, Noise Abatement, Anti-Blood Sports, Nuclear Disarmament, Consumer Protection, Environmental Protection or Ethnic Minorities. Here the society may be a pressure group whose activities will be well publicised. In fact, its articulate PR may well clash with the PR of organisations they are criticising.

POLITICAL PARTIES AND TRADE UNIONS

As with religious bodies, the distinction between propaganda and PR has to be made. Such organisations need to be understood as well as supported, and understood by non-supporters, often by people in other countries. Some names like Liberal and Social Democrat may mean different things in different countries.

There is a big educational job to be done here, and it requires all the techniques of PR. The aims and objects, the history, the social and political role, the place in the politico-economic structure, the internal election and policy-making procedures — all these need to be explained, otherwise reports of activities may well be misunderstood. These are often complicated matters which puzzle people. Antagonism can easily arise through lack of information, knowledge and understanding.

PR FOR INDIVIDUALS

We have spoken of PR for organisations but there are individuals who require PR and deserve to be understood.

Again, it is necessary to recognise the differences between PR and promotion or propaganda.

Famous people such as entertainers may employ press agents to gain publicity in the media, but that is not to be confused with PR.

In the USA we have had 'the making of the President' campaigns, and election campaigns in Britain for political leaders and their parties. These have been produced by advertising agencies such as J. Walter Thompson and Saatchi and Saatchi, not PR consultants. Political personalities have been promoted like products.

Nevertheless individuals do use PR consultants and press officers. This is true of business leaders. The White House, Downing Street, Buckingham Palace and Clarence House all have their professional press officers operating on behalf of their illustrious individuals.

27 The Public Relations Consultant

Consultant is a bad word for a person providing an outside PR service because he executes PR programmes as well as giving clients professional advice. Nor is he an agent, like an advertising agent, because his income does not come from commissions or discounts allowed him by the media but from professional fees based on time and expertise.

PR consultants differ from advertising agencies in three important ways, and they represent a very good reason why advertising agencies do not always combine PR and advertising services very well. In fact, when an advertising agency offers PR services it usually means press relations in support of advertising, that is, *product publicity*.

THREE DIFFERENCES BETWEEN PR CONSULTANCIES AND ADVERTISING AGENCIES

1. Agencies usually earn their income from commission on media purchases, discounts on purchase of materials and services, and added percentages on work farmed out, such as print. Consultancies are paid for their time and expertise by means of an hourly rate, and they recover monies spent on materials and expenses on which no percentage is charged. Of the two, the PR practitioner is the more professional because his fee is based on what he does and how well he does it — just like a lawyer, doctor or architect.
2. Except in very big PR consultancies there is not the division of labour found in advertising agencies (e.g. copywriter, visualiser, media buyer, production manager), and PR personnel tend to be jack-of-all-trades requiring many skills and much technical knowledge of subjects like photography and printing.

3. Whereas a company will appoint an advertising agency when its expenditure on advertising justifies this – and there is need for greater planning, creative and media buying skills – the opposite happens in PR. Consultancies are mostly engaged by companies which do not yet feel justified in setting up a PR department. However, large organisations with PR departments may also engage a PR consultancy for special services such as financial PR.

TYPES OF PR CONSULTANCY

Consultancies vary in size from the one-man unit to large and often international firms employing perhaps 200 people in a major city office in, say, London or New York. In Britain there are some 600 consultancies of which 100 do most of the business. A weakness with consultancies is that anyone can set up and call himself a PR consultant. It is not so easy to set up an advertising agency unless one has sufficient funds to provide the cash flow necessary to pay the media promptly (as required under recognition or accreditation agreements) while allowing clients credit.

PR consultancies may offer general services, but some specialise in certain areas such as consumer products, industrial and technical products, house journal production, corporate and financial PR and so on. In London some two dozen consultancies specialise in financial PR and are situated in the City of London close to the Stock Exchange, banks, insurance companies, stockbrokers and city (financial) editors of newspapers. In developing countries PR consultancies will tend to offer general services. Some will be local firms while others will be overseas offices of international PR consultancies set up to handle the business of foreign firms.

The main kinds of PR consultancies are:

PR department of advertising agency

This may seem convenient to the client who is using the agency services, but the PR service is likely to be limited. It will tend to play a supportive role to the advertising campaign rather than be a complete and separate PR programme for the total client organisation. It will be limited to the marketing activities of the client's business. Another problem is that advertising and PR can be very different forms of communication, and advertising people tend to misunderstand the role and techniques of PR.

For instance, because he is a writer the copywriter may think he can write news releases, but he may not understand that a news story must not advertise. However, in developing countries where agencies and consultancies may be small, advertising agencies may offer the only PR service available. Many well-known international advertising agencies (which may operate PR subsidiaries in the home country) may well offer an excellent PR service through overseas branches of their advertising agency.

PR subsidiary of advertising agency

This has been explained above. The subsidiary has its own name and operates like an independent PR consultancy except that: (*a*) it may serve clients of the parent advertising agency; and (*b*) it can enjoy creative and technical resources of the agency. But it may accept its own independent clients (including ones not involved in advertising, such as non-commercial organisations), and it will present its own propositions and charge its own fees. Typical examples are Lexington (J. Walter Thompson), Welbeck (Foote, Cone & Belding) while Charles Barker Lyons (Britain's largest PR consultancy) is part of the Charles Barker group of advertising agencies and PR consultancies.

Independent PR consultancy

Unattached to an advertising agency, the independent PR consultancy concentrates on PR and usually offers a very wide service covering all facets of PR for all types of organisation. Some, like Burson-Marsteller, may also offer some advertising services while being predominantly a PR consultancy.

Generally speaking, the independent PR consultancy would seem to offer the most experienced and professional service, but this is too broad a claim to be always true. The client needs to study the record, resources and personnel of the various PR services available before making an appointment. A guide could be whether the staff are professionally qualified, that is, being in membership of their professional Institute and holding qualifications such as the CAM Diploma. A journalist turned PR consultant overnight will have no training and no qualifications. To be a member of the Institute of Public Relations he has to have 5 years comprehensive experience, and journalism is not counted.

SERVICES PROVIDED BY CONSULTANTS

The service offered by the different kinds of consultancy will range from a simple press relations one to very sophisticated services covering all the communication needs of an organisation. Much will depend on the special experience of the principals. Some may offer very general experience while others may specialise in, say, technical, motoring, fashion, entertainments or finance.

Some idea of the variety of consultancy services is given by the following list:

1. Planning and executing a full PR programme.
2. Product publicity, distributing news about products and services.
3. Information bureaux services, handling media and public enquiries.
4. *Ad hoc* services such as organising one-off press events – receptions, works visits.
5. Educational PR – producing booklets and leaflets, supplying schools with wall-charts, video-cassettes, project packs.
6. Organising seminars and conferences.
7. Organising PR exhibitions, and PR support for participants in exhibitions.
8. Advising on or producing films, slide presentations, video-cassettes.
9. Organising photography.
10. Advising management on management–employee relations, including editing of employee newspapers.
11. Corporate and financial PR including production of annual reports, PR for share issues, informing City editors, and PR during take-over battles.
12. Corporate identity schemes.
13. Corporate image campaigns including corporate or advocacy advertising.
14. Commissioning opinion surveys, image studies and other research.

15. Distributor relations programmes including external house journals, works visits, dealer conferences.
16. Parliamentary liaison — advising clients of Parliamentary procedures and the progress of Parliamentary business as it affects clients, e.g. White Papers, readings of Bills, proposed legislation, Royal Commissions, and lobbying MPs with information.
17. Advising, organising, or PR in connection with sponsorships.

It is an imposing list and it indicates some of the areas where the consultant can offer special expertise to augment that of the in-house PRO.

PR CONSULTANCY COMPARED WITH PR DEPARTMENT

The one is not superior to or more efficient than the other. They are different, and it may be useful to have both an in-house PR department and an outside PR consultancy. They need not be regarded as rivals. It is easier for a consultant to deal with a professional colleague employed by the client.

The in-house PRO has the advantage of being intimately involved with the total communications of the whole organisation. This is important. On the other hand, the PR consultant has the advantage of being an outsider with wide experience gained from dealing with many clients and many communication problems. He may use more techniques, have contact with more media, and be familiar with more techniques than the staff PRO. His advisory role is valuable too. He can be paid to be frank, impartial and constructively critical, which may not be so easy for the inside man.

CONSULTANCY BUDGETING

Careful costing is essential so that the client knows what he is paying for, and so that the consultant is properly paid. Vague unspecified fees help neither side. Programmes must be fully budgeted. Many consultants have gone out of business because they charged too little and did too much.

Because the consultancy earns no commission its income comes from selling time and skill reckoned in man-hours which have to be recorded on time sheets. All expenses have to be accounted for, charged and recovered. It costs money merely to talk to the client. Table 27.1 is a brief example of a budget for a PR service. The hourly rate has to cover consultancy salaries, the overheads of running an office, and profit so that the fee represents the estimated number of hours work to carry out the programme.

TABLE 27.1. *PR consultancy budget for 12 months campaign*

	£/₦/$	£/₦/$
Twelve monthly client meetings	12 x Xhr x XX =	XXX.XX
Three press receptions	3 x Xhr x XX =	XXX.XX
Organising press facility visit	1 x Xhr x XX =	XXX.XX
Editing quarterly house journal	4 x Xhr x XX =	XXX.XX
Twelve news releases	12 x Xhr x XX =	XXX.XX
General advisory services	Xhr x XX =	XXX.XX
Writing Chairman's speeches	4 x Xhr x XX =	XXX.XX
Maintaining Information Service	hr x XX =	XXX.XX
TOTAL ANNUAL FEE		XX.XXX.XX
Estimated material cost		X.XXX.XX
Estimated expenses		X.XXX.XX
15% contingency fund		X.XXX.XX
TOTAL COST		XX.XXX.XX

Thus, if the hourly rate is 20 pounds, naira, dollars or whatever the currency may be, 12 monthly meetings of, say, 3 hours each would cost 720 pounds, naira or dollars. Estimates will be based on experience, but these costings can be flexible according to changing circumstances. The consultant's hourly rate may seem to be high, but he has to run his business and look for business, and his *earning time* may be 50 per cent or less of his *working time*.

PRCA CODE

The (British) Public Relations Consultants Association has a code of conduct which is similar to that of the Institute of Public Relations but it is more briefly worded and is specially related to consultancy practice. It is reproduced here as an example of the professional qualities of a consultancy.

CODE OF CONSULTANCY PRACTICE

Article 1. A member firm has a general duty of fair dealing towards its clients, past and present, fellow members and the public.

Article 2. A member firm shall not knowingly seek to displace another member firm's relationship with a client, other than in fair competition or at the behest of the client.

Article 3. A member firm shall cause all its clients to be listed in the Annual Register of the Public Relations Consultants Association.

Article 4. A member firm shall cause all its directors, executives and retained consultants who hold public office, are members of either House of Parliament, are members of local authorities or of any statutory organisation or body, to be recorded in the relevant sections of the Annual Register of the Public Relations Consultants Association.

Article 5. A member firm shall not offer or give nor cause a client to offer or give any inducement to such persons as described in Article 4 above who are not directors, executives or retained consultants with intent to further the interests of the member or of the client if such action is inconsistent with the public interest.

Article 6. A member firm shall not engage in any practice which tends to corrupt the integrity of channels of public communication or legislation.

Article 7. A member firm shall not negotiate, propose or agree to terms with a client or prospective client on the basis of fees being contingent upon specific achievements.

Article 8. A member firm shall not propose to clients any action which would constitute an improper influence on organs of government or legislation.

Article 9. A member firm shall not engage in any practice nor be seen to conduct itself in any manner detrimental to the reputation of the Public Relations Consultants Association or the reputation and the interests of public relations consultancy.

Article 10. A member shall not intentionally disseminate false or misleading information and is under an obligation to use reason-

able care to avoid dissemination of false or misleading information.

Article 11. A member firm shall not purport to serve an announced cause while actually serving an undisclosed special or
private interest.

Article 12. A member firm shall safeguard the confidences of
both present and former clients and shall not disclose or use these
confidences to the disadvantage or prejudice of such clients or to
the financial advantage of the member firm.

Article 13. A member firm shall only represent competing interests with the consent of all those concerned.

Article 14. A member firm shall not, without the client's consent,
accept fees or other valuable consideration from anyone other
than the client, in connection with services for that client.

Article 15. A member firm shall inform a client of any share-
holding or financial interest held by that firm in any company,
firm or person whose services it recommends.

28 Press Relations

In urbanised industrial societies where literacy is common the press is the predominant mass medium. It has not been superseded by television even though most householders own or rent a receiver. In Britain there are some 9000 daily, weekly, monthly, quarterly and yearly publications. There are national daily and Sunday newspapers, regional or local daily, Sunday and weekly newspapers, magazines and directories covering every possible interest. Some 100 daily newspapers are published outside London. Newspapers and magazines are delivered to thousands of homes every morning, they may also be bought from street vendors, and bookstalls and newsagents' shops display hundreds of publications.

Consequently, press relations plays a big part in British PR simply because it is easy to reach different publics with suitably written stories very quickly. A story of interest to readers of the national press — and there are newspapers which cater for different social grades — can be on the nation's breakfast table next day. This is because most people live in cities in a compact country well served by roads and railways. A newspaper printed in London at 10 o'clock at night can reach most parts of the country early in the morning, while Londoners receive the 4 a.m. edition.

This is different from the American system where, because of the size of the country, there are no national newspapers but large-circulation dailies are published in each city. In Britain people can buy a nationally published morning paper and a locally published evening paper, although there are a few regional dailies. Scotland, Wales and Northern Ireland have their own 'national' dailies in addition to the London papers.

British papers also have international circulations and *The Financial Times* is also printed in Germany. Many European cities have British papers by mid-morning, and London Sundays are on sale in Kano the same day.

The British press consists of:

National morning newspapers.
Regional morning newspapers.
London and regional evening newspapers.
Regional Sunday newspapers.
Regional weekly newspapers — series covering a county or counties.
Local weekly newspapers based on cities and towns.
Free sheet local weeklies delivered free to homes.
National consumer magazines — general interest, women's, etc.
National special-interest magazines — e.g. motoring, gardening, sports.
Regional magazines.
Chamber of Trade and Industry magazines — about 50 of them.
Give-away magazines — jobs, entertainments.
Trade journals — for distributors.
Technical magazines — for manufacturers, technicians.
Professional magazines — for professionals, e.g. doctors, teachers.
Local authority newspapers — issued to members of local communities.
Directories and yearbooks covering trades and professions.

It is an imposing list, and the papers may be bought from newsagents and newsvendors, or by postal subscription. Some, like *Marketing*, are supplied as part of an annual subscription to a professional body. Free sheets, with editorial of domestic interest and supported by generous advertising, have the merit of saturation coverage since every house in the circulation area gets a copy. Give-away magazines are usually distributed to passers-by in the street. Controlled-circulation magazines (mostly trade and technical) are mailed to a partly requested and partly selected readership. They have the merit of gaining good penetration of the particular market, and advertisement space is sold on the strength of this large guaranteed circulation.

The class breakdown of the British national press is interesting, (see Table 28.1) especially when the audited net sales are considered. Abroad, *The Times* is often mistakenly regarded as Britain's leading newspaper. Actually, it has a small and falling circulation. On the other hand *The Financial Times* may have a smaller circulation but it is very influential, and each copy is read by several readers, especially in offices. The political affinities of newspapers are fairly unimportant. Both *The Sun* and the *Daily Mirror* sell just under 4 million copies daily but the first is right-wing or Conservative and the second is left-wing or Labour in its political sympathies.

TABLE 28.1. *Class breakdown of London nationals*

(January–June 1981 Audit Bureau of Circulation figures — average daily sale)

Grade A (3%)	The Times	282,186
Upper middle class	The Financial Times	199,233
Grade B (13%)	Daily Telegraph	1,400,935
Middle class	The Guardian	393,729
Grade C1 (22%)	Daily Express	2,196,492
Lower middle class/white-collar	Daily Mail	1,963,054
Grade C2 (32%)		
Skilled working class/blue-collar	The Sun	3,622,720
Grade D (20%)	Daily Mirror	3,504,377
Semi-skilled/unskilled working class	Daily Star	1,336,116
Grade E (9%)		
Subsistence level/pensioners		
Total average daily sale of nationals		15,165,356

Outside the UK, newspapers do not usually reflect such sharp class distinctions (Table 28.2). Rather, they represent political, religious, language or ethnic distinctions. The one factor that does help to maintain large circulations in Britain, apart from literacy, is a single language. A problem overseas is that when newspapers have to be printed in a variety of languages the circulation of each will be restricted.

SPECIAL PROBLEMS AND CHARACTERISTICS OF NEWSPAPERS IN DEVELOPING COUNTRIES

As the circulation figures indicate, the press varies from country to

TABLE 28.2. *Some comparative circulation figures outside UK*
(based on figures published in *Benn's Press Directory*, 1981)

AUSTRALIA			
(Sydney)	*Daily Mirror*	361,520	
(Melbourne)	*Sun News-Pictorial*	637,332	
HONG KONG	*South China Morning Post*	53,179	
	The Star	4,850	(English)
		9,911	(Chinese)
INDIA			
(Delhi)	*Hindustan*	208,166	(Hindi)
	Hindustan Times	282,606	(English)
	Times of India	174,102	(English)
(Calcutta)	*Amritza Bazar Patrika*	118,128	(English)
		417,091	(Bengali)
JAMAICA	*Daily Gleaner*	46,227	
JAPAN	*Asahi Shimbun (Rising Sun)*	7,502,150	(all editions a.m)
		4,701,854	(all editions p.m.)
KENYA	*Daily Nation*	113,463	(English)
	Taifa Leo	55,668	(Swahili)
MALAYSIA	*New Straits Times*	183,654	(English)
	Nanyang Siang Pay Malaysia	109,061	(Chinese)
	Berita Harian	109,547	(Bahasa Malay printed in Rumi – Romanised Malay)
	Utusan Malaysia	143,824	(Rumi)
	Utusan Melayu	42,878	(Bahasa Malay printed in Jawi – Malay characters)

NIGERIA	*Daily Times*	400,000	(English)
	National Concord	250,000	(English)
	The Punch	230,000	(English)
	Daily Sketch	150,000	(English)
SINGAPORE	*Straits Times*	205,487	(English)
	Nanyang Siang Pau Singapore	84,267	(Chinese)
	Sin Chew Jit Poh Singapore	110,017	(Chinese)
TRINIDAD &	*Trinidad Express*	58,020	
TOBAGO	*Trinidad Guardian*	53,838	
ZAMBIA (Ndola)	*Times of Zambia*	57,119	
ZIMBABWE (Salisbury)	*The Herald*	82,331	

country. In Asia there will be newspapers in various langauges such as Chinese, Malay (with different written versions), Tamil, Hindi and Bengali. Most Nigerian newspapers are in English, but there are Hausa and Yoruba newspapers.

The Japanese *Asaki Shimbun* has a huge circulation and is published throughout the day. In Hong Kong there are upwards of 100 different Chinese newspapers. Large countries like Australia and India have fairly localised newspapers as in the USA. In Russia *Pravda* is printed in 40 cities. Not all newspapers submit to having their circulations audited. The Lagos *Daily Times* produced its first offset-litho issue with a full-colour picture on the front page in August 1980.

Special problems and characteristics are:

1. Circulations are limited to the percentage of the population which is literate. In African countries perhaps 80 per cent will be illiterate, but in Asian countries the proportion is usually smaller and in Indonesia it is only about 40 per cent.
2. Circulations are limited by the ability of people to buy copies. There are well-educated but unemployed Indians who cannot afford to buy a newspaper.
3. Long distances and poor roads make distribution difficult so that

daily newspapers may have to be produced by noon of the previous day, and may not arrive until the day after issue.

4. Import controls and exchange control problems may limit supply
   of paper and printing machinery. The high cost of paper imports
   have been a serious hardship to the Zambian press.

5. On the other hand, the growth of the press hand-in-hand with the
   growth of education and literacy has meant that newspapers have
   been created with modern web offset-litho machines so that
   newspaper production has, in some countries like Kenya, Malaysia and Trinidad, been in advance of traditional letterpress production, e.g. London's Fleet Street.

6. But progress sometimes has to be limited to avoid unemployment
   in countries where it can be economic to be labour-intensive. For
   instance, the editor of the *Daily Star* in Enugu told the author
   that while it was an advance to install a web offset-litho printing
   machine, it would be anti-social to install labour-saving machinery
   in other parts of the print shop which would dispense with workers in, say, the binding department, who worked by hand. The
   marvels of modern equipment can be seen in the composing room
   of *Al Ahram (Pyramids)* in Cairo, which has a specially designed
   computerised typesetting machine for setting Arabic characters, a
   feat of great ingenuity.

7. Because of limited circulations, newspapers are all things to all
   people and do not have the specialisation of the British daily
   press. This will be seen in a leading newspaper like the Nigerian
   Daily News but also in monster newspapers like the *Straits Times*.
   However, since installation of the civilian government in Nigeria
   we have seen the arrival of politically representative newspapers
   like the *National Concord* and *Sunday Concord*.

These and other considerations may affect the conduct of press relations. While, in Britain, there may be a great variety of publications
which rely on PR sources for a great deal of their information, and
frankly invite it, a different situation exists in the Third World. For
instance, more emphasis will be placed on government sources of
information, less on industrial and commercial. There may be editorial
scepticism, prejudice or hostility towards multi-nationals which may be
the main sources of business or product information.

The question of corruption arises. Journalists, in a poor country,
may regard private sector PR sources as being wealthy ones which can

afford bribes. Some multi-nationals nourish bribery by making the mistake of attaching banknotes to news releases. The 'envelope' system is well known in West Africa where journalists attending press receptions are given envelopes containing money. The 'taxi-fare' payment is another form of near-bribery. There is also the over-lavish press reception which can give the impression that the story is trivial if so much has to be spent on winning the journalist's favour.

But in countries where parties are a way of life it may be necessary for a press reception to take up more time than the couple of hours in London where journalists want a story, not lots of drinks, and are too busy to stay any longer than is necessary. Newspapers in the Third World may have so little revenue that they reject PR stories and tell organisations to buy advertisement space, and we see the irony of the paid-for space with the heading 'Press Release'. Such a thing would not be seen in the Western press.

In Nigeria it is possible to hold a press reception, get no press coverage, and have to buy space to print one's news release! This is turning PR on its head, although the fault could be that there was no news value in the event, and the news release merely served someone's vanity. In contrast to this it is interesting to see how the Trinidad press credits PROs as sources of information and even prints their pictures.

THE FUNCTIONS OF PRESS RELATIONS

There is a mistaken idea that the chief function of press relations is to obtain favourable mentions in the media. It is not, any more than the function of PR is to achieve a favourable image. PR would be much more widely accepted if this wretched word 'favourable' was forgotten because its use implies that anything unfavourable is suppressed. It also implies that PR is no better than propaganda. If it is to work, PR must be *credible*. Therefore, in the words of Ivy Ledbetter Lee who defined press relations so admirably, all material supplied to the media must be *'of interest and value'*. Its object is to create knowledge and understanding, even of the unfavourable. This could include an air crash, a mine disaster, even a political assassination.

Strictly speaking, press relations covers all the news media, but in this chapter we shall concentrate on the press. The main functions of press relations are:

Two-way Relations

At all times the press service (whether in-house PRO or outside PR consultancy) issues information and responds to requests for information. If for some special reason information cannot be given – because it would be undiplomatic, or legally *sub judice*, or because a policy decision has not been made – this should be explained. A PRO does not say 'no comment', which is banal and discourteous.

Of course there will be times when persistent demands for information may be a nuisance or embarrassing, but reporters have their jobs to do. Editors want stories in order to sell papers. The press is a business like any other.

It is therefore the duty of the PRO to be well-informed and to understand and anticipate what editors need in order to sell newspapers. It is not the job of the PRO to foist on the media stories which may interest his superiors but which are of no interest or value to readers or audiences. When the story is newsworthy, and is published or broadcast, this coverage should satisfy the PRO's superiors. But the accuracy of what is reported depends a lot on the good relations between the PRO and journalists, and the extent to which – in the past as well as when the story is released – the PRO has kept journalists well informed.

Issue of news releases

A regular task will be the issue of news releases. Later in this chapter the technique of writing a publishable release will be explained. The simplest way to learn how to write a news release is to *read* and *analyse* news reports in the press. Throughout the world, including Europe and America, editors complain about the rubbish they receive from PROs. It can only be assumed that the majority of PROs, whether trained originally as journalists or not, never read newspapers.

Supply of pictures

Very important in press relations is the supply of good, interesting pictures which help to make publications attractive. One of the skills of PR is to caption pictures properly, that is to fix to the back of the print a caption bearing the name, address and telephone number of the sender, and a description of the story behind the picture. The caption wording should say what the picture cannot say for itself. Captions must not be written on the backs of prints, nor included in the news release.

Negotiation of feature articles

If the PRO has a story which will make a good exclusive feature article, he can negotiate with an editor and write the number of words, with the treatment required, and supply by a given date as the editor may instruct.

Organising press conferences

When an urgent story breaks and it is necessary to communicate with the press quickly, a press conference may be called. This is a straight-forward occasion when a spokesman addresses the assembled reporters and answers questions. His message will be distributed as a news release. Hospitality will be simple and merely express courtesy to guests. Such an event may be organised quickly in the boardroom, press club, hotel room or perhaps in a VIP lounge at an airport if someone important is departing or arriving.

Organising press receptions

If the story is big enough to merit more than a news release, a press reception may be organised. This is more elaborate than a press con-ference and may need some time to plan and prepare. To really interest the press there should be a programme of activities and not a stand-around cocktail party. Ideally, there should be something to demon-strate, test, examine or sample such as a new product. This may be supported by a film, video-cassette or slide presentation. The latter can nowadays be very effective, especially with twin carousel cross-fade projection coupled with a synchronised or remote-control audio-tape recording. Invitations should set out a timetable of the programme.

Organising PR support for exhibitions

Public exhibitions and trade fairs offer many opportunities for media coverage, sometimes with the visiting foreign press. There may be a press room where releases and pictures can be displayed, a press day when journalists visit the show, or a press reception can be held on or associated with the stand or booth.

Organising press facility visits

These can include visits to the organisation (such as its factory, mill, hotel, airport or port), or to see what the organisation is doing or has done for a customer such as a construction job or the installation of equipment.

As will be seen from the above, the functions of press relations involve a great deal of planning and organising (including budgeting costs), and not just writing and being nice to journalists. All this calls for much more than journalistic ability or experience. The job specification for even a press officer, let alone a PRO, is very exacting. It needs to embrace understanding people, knowing how one's organisation is run, and being a person of the highest integrity who can be respected and trusted.

Now let's look at the techniques of press relations.

TECHNIQUES OF PRESS RELATIONS

In this section we shall deal with (1) how to write a news release; (2) how to present a news release; and (3) how to write a feature article. This advice is based on the more detailed recommendations contained in the author's *Planned Press and Public Relations* and *Effective Press Relations and House Journal Editing.*

How to write a news release

To be publishable a news release should be written in the same way that a journalist would write the story given the same information. Essentially, it has to be of 'interest and value' to the reader, not the sender.

The first thing to decide is the *subject,* which is usually what an organisation has done rather than the organisation itself. The subject must be in the first paragraph, and preferably in the first few words of the first sentence of the opening paragraph.

The opening paragraph is the all-important part of the release. The *essence* of the whole story should be contained in the first paragraph.

This will help the editor to judge the merits of the story at once. If space is scarce, and only this paragraph is printed, the message will have been published.

The report should be about something which has just happened. Too many releases report a future event, and editors dislike such stories in case the event fails to occur. Thus, one says a product is *now* available, *not* that it *will be* available next week or next month. Timing is important. There are exceptions to this when it will be useful to readers to know that, say, a new ferry will start operations on a certain date because that may affect their future plans. But generally the press like to report events, not make prophecies.

To demonstrate this, suppose an airline wishes to announce a new air service, the opening paragraph should not read:

(a) *Nigeria Airways announce that their new non-stop service to Japan will begin operations next month.*

(b) *We are proud to announce that Nigeria Airways will inaugurate a non-stop service to Japan next month.*

Both of these are bad. The first is bad because the writer thinks Nigeria Airways (being his organisation) is all-important. The second is bad because it uses the pronoun 'We' and the silly expression 'proud'. No journalist would write like that. No story would be printed like that. The subject is 'a new non-stop service to Japan'. So, this opening paragraph could be improved like this:

(c) *A new non-stop service to Japan will be inaugurated next month by Nigeria Airways.*

You will also notice that 'puffery' and superlatives are omitted. There is no advertising, merely information, and no self-praise such as 'the famous' Nigeria Airways. Just simple facts. The story could be made more specific by giving the date of the first flight instead of the vague 'next month', and even this may be stated later in the story. Try to squeeze as much vital information as possible into the first paragraph so that it succeeds as a complete story.

The following seven-point SOLAADS formula helps in the researching, writing and checking of a story. It provides a logical flow of information. The opening paragraph should include the *subject, organisation, location* and the highlight from the body of the story.

Seven-point formula for news releases

1. **S**ubject — what the story is about.
2. **O**rganisation — who it is about.
3. **L**ocation — where the story takes place.
4. **A**dvantages — what is new or different.
5. **A**pplications — how it can be used — the benefits.
6. **D**etails — specifications, prices, etc.
7. **S**ource — full name, address, telephone number of maker, supplier or organisation responsible.

With this formula in mind we can now improve the opening paragraph of the Nigeria Airways story like this:

> *A new non-stop service from Lagos to Tokyo will be inaugurated on December 1 by Nigeria Airways.*

Remembering that another rule of modern newspaper reporting is short paragraphs, short sentences and short words, and also that column widths are narrow so that long words are likely to be broken, how can this sentence be improved upon? Can we get rid of that ugly word 'inaugurated' which some people may not understand? 'Introduced' is also a long word. What about 'started' or better still 'start'?

The above is an exercise in writing a news release. You go on writing and re-writing, getting the message more and more precise, and paying special attention to the opening paragraph.

How to present a news release.

If you study newspapers carefully you will see that the press has its own special style which is often different from the way a secretary sets out a business letter. The following rules should be followed:

1. Use only one side of the paper.
2. Use double-space typing.
3. Provide a left-hand and a right-hand margin.
4. Use a simple release heading. Give plenty of space to the story.
5. Write a headline which identifies the story. Do not try to be clever. Editors write their own headlines.
6. Do not indent the first paragraph but indent all others, the

system used at the beginning of a chapter in this book.

7. Restrict capital letters to people's names, place names, other proper nouns like company and product names, and very important people like the President of a country but not the president, chairman or managing director of a company. Do not write whole words in caps.

8. Do not write full points between the initial letters of an organisation. Write NEPA, UK, IPR and not N.E.P.A, U.K., or I.P.R.

9. Write June 6, 1982 and *not* 6th June, 1982.

10. Write one, two, three, four, five, six, seven, eight, nine and then 10, 100, 1000 but use figures for all measurements, dates, prices or street numbers. Sentences should not begin with a figure, unless written in words. Thus: One ticket will cost ₦50 after December 25, but two tickets will cost only ₦80. They may be obtained from 121, Lagos Street. Luggage is limited to 20 kilos for each person, and no luggage should be more than 1m wide or 1m long.

11. Do not use *etc.* in a sentence.

12. Write among and while, *not* amongst and whilst.

13. Do not write 'for immediate release' or 'ends', which are unnecessary.

14. The embargo should be a privilege to an editor to allow him to read, say, a speech or report in advance. You cannot enforce an embargo, and it should be obvious that a request not to print a story before a certain day and time is sensible. An example might be that a speech has not yet been made, or because of a time differential between countries when it could be embarrassing if a story was published too early in one country.

15. Do not underline anything. This means set in italics. You should not tell editors what they should emphasise.

16. Do not use pronouns such as *you, we, our* or *us*.

17. Do not use adjectives or expressions like time-saving, money-saving, useful, beautiful, famous, leading, renowned or popular. Such things should be implied by *facts*. And do not use vague expressions such as 'tasty meals' or 'efficient service' — say why the meals are tasty or the service is efficient.

18. Restrict quotation marks (' ') to spoken speech. Never put quotation marks round brand names.

19. The percentage mark % is spelt out as per cent or percent.

20. Quotations may be used in a story if an authoritative person can

be quoted as saying something which is of value to the story.
But do not insert empty quotations such as 'This is an important breakthrough', says the marketing manager, Mr X.

21. Avoid clichés — hackneyed and boring expressions — such as
facilitates, a wide range, unique, exhaustive trials, this day and
age, top level, premium, official capacity, invalidates, last but
not least, paramount importance or considerable interest.

22. Number all pages, and write *more* in the bottom right-hand corner if there is a continuation. But try to keep a story on one
sheet of paper. Editors dislike long-winded releases.

23. At the end of the story write the author's name and telephone
number, and the date. If many releases are issued a serial number is useful.

WHAT EDITORS THINK ABOUT NEWS RELEASES

Throughout the world — north, south, east and west — editors are cynical about the material they receive from PROs. Most releases are so bad
they go in the waste bin after a quick glance. A London editor told the
author he had so many releases each morning that he had 'one second
flat' in which to decide whether a release was of interest.

The reasons why releases are rejected are mainly that the subject is
not apparent in the first few words; they are advertisements, not news
stories; they are unpublishable because they are not written and presented like newspaper reports; they are too long; they have been sent to
the wrong journal; and often they are too late. These faults are borne
out by the following summary of a report based on a survey of 16
English, Malay and Chinese newspapers published in Malaysia and Singapore. This significant study was conducted by Edward Sung Burongoh,
lecturer in public relations at the School of Mass Communication, Mara
Institute of Technology, Shah Alam, Malaysia. The worst senders of
'junkmail' were private companies and industries, whose offences were;

1. Eighty-six per cent reported that less than 50 per cent of the
press releases received met the newspapers' required style of
writing.

2. Fifty-seven per cent reported encountering releases with 'poor
journalistic writing' ALWAYS.

3. Seventy-one per cent reported that less than 50 per cent of press

releases met the accepted format for a release.

4. Eighty-six per cent felt that most press releases were ALWAYS more publicity-orientated.

5. Fifty-seven per cent felt most of the releases were ALWAYS written to please management of business organisations.

6. Seventy-one per cent reported encountering releases with 'unimportant information' SOMETIMES.

7. Eighty-six per cent reported that SOMETIMES there were attempts by press release senders to disguise advertising copy in the form of a press release.

8. Seventy-one per cent reported receiving calls from press release senders SOMETIMES demanding to know WHY their releases had not been published.

9. Eighty-six per cent reported that they SOMETIMES received calls from press release senders demanding to know WHEN their releases would be published.

10. Seventy-one per cent ranked 'too long' as the main weakness of press releases. (Seventy-one per cent also recommended a one-page maximum release.)

It is the author's experience that these criticisms are commonplace in all parts of the world. In Britain the rejection rate is about 70 per cent. A Chicago survey puts the figure at 80 per cent, a major fault being that stories are not localised to satisfy America's non-national daily press.

How to write a feature article

A feature article is not a long news release. It is a much more creative piece of writing in which the writer can use a more personalised style and a richer vocabulary. He can use anecdotes and experiences, quote interviews, be humorous perhaps. It has already been explained that the article should be discussed and agreed with an editor before anything is researched or written. It is also exclusive to one journal and not broadcast like a news release. While an editor has the right to re-write a news release because it is merely information, a well-written article should not need re-writing and should be published as written, like a book. Below is a useful seven-point plotting formula which can be applied to a great many articles, thus giving it an interesting narrative form.

The value of the PR article lies in its authoritative presentation, its occupation of more space, and the fact that it can be reprinted and used for many purposes such as give-away literature in showrooms, on exhibition stands or in correspondence. It may cost more in research time to produce than a news release, but it is likely to have a longer life than a news report.

Puffery should be avoided. The information should be factual and free of self-praise and plugs. The reader should feel he has learned something of real interest and value to him, and not merely read an account of how clever the organisation is.

Seven-point plotting formula for feature article
1. Opening paragraph.
2. Problem, or previous situation (which was different or inferior).
3. Search for a solution – what effort was made to find the solution?
4. The solution. This is the subject of the article. It could be a new appointment, a new building, a piece of equipment or a new service.
5. The results. What benefits have been gained?
6. Closing paragraph.
7. Check draft article with all those who were interviewed or provided information.

Points (2) to (6) are the ones which have to be researched, although the writer may be familiar with the solution. It is absolutely vital to check the draft with informants. They could have given wrong information unintentionally. The writer could have misunderstood what he was told. Figures and spellings must be checked. There are often alternative ways of spelling the same name. For instance it is astonishing how often the author is given the Welsh name Jenkins instead of the English name Jefkins. People can be very vain about correct spelling of their names! The writer has to keep faith with editor, readers and informants and be sure that what is published is correct.

The opening and closing paragraphs (1 and 6) should be written last, and ideas for them may spring from the heart of the article. But whereas the opening paragraph of the news release should 'blow' the story, that is, give the game away, the opposite is necessary for the article. Here, the opening paragraph should grasp the reader's attention, arouse his curiosity and interest and make him want to read on. A question may be posed, an astonishing statement may be made, a joke may be told or some other bait may be used to induce the reader to absorb the rest of the article.

The closing paragraph should bring the article to a satisfactory end, and it could be linked to the opening paragraph. For instance, the article could begin with words such as 'How long do you think it took to build the new East London tunnel'? and close with 'Using the new Smith drilling process, the East London tunnel took only nine months to bore.'

PRESS EVENTS

Press receptions in developing countries may differ from those held in industrial countries for the following reasons:

Industrial countries

1. In London, for instance, there may be more than 100 journals relevant to a story, and the attendance by journalists could be large. The host PRO may know few of them personally.
2. There is likely to be competition between receptions when dates clash, and journalists will have to choose between them or − if the venues are close by − they may spend a short time at more than one function.
3. Journalists are busy people and time is so precious to them that they will not attend unless there is promise of a good story. They will not expect the event to last more than about 2 hours, they may stay for only a short time, and they may arrive late.

It is therefore essential to offer a well-planned event, not just a cocktail party, and to set out the timetable on the invitation card. A typical programme might be *reception, address, demonstration, film, bar and buffet*. Drinking time will be limited to the beginning and end of the programme. Journalists do not come 'just for the beer'.

Developing countries

1. There will be few journals, and journalists and host PRO will probably know each other very well. Guests will be contacted easily by messenger or telephone.

2. There will be more emphasis on the social side since people like to enjoy themselves when they get together. The programme may extend to music, singing and dancing, which would be unknown in the West.
3. The event would not be hampered by pressure of time, and it could occupy more than 2 hours.
4. Whereas the bar is relatively unimportant in, say London, and is a courtesy, hospitality will be taken more seriously in a developing country. There will be more of a party atmosphere, and a large company (especially a foreign one!) will be expected to entertain well.

FACILITY VISITS

In a compact country like Britain, with motorways, fast inter-city trains, and frequent domestic air services, it is possible to convey a press party 100 miles or more and back in a day. Overnight accommodation would be rare unless the journey was to some very remote spot.

In developing countries distances may be greater, transport services may be less speedy and reliable, and weather conditions will be different. A press facility visit may be conducted more leisurely, and overnight accommodation and entertainment may be necessary.

29 Radio and Television as Public Relations Media

The two broadcast or electronic media, radio and TV have certain things in common but are generally very different. These two media also differ country by country. They both have *sound,* whether it be the human voice, music or noises of activity. They are both *transitory,* unlike the press which can be kept and read again. Nowadays it is possible to make a tape recording of a radio broadcast, and a video-tape of a TV programme. However, there are copyright limitations on the public or commercial use of such recordings.

RADIO

Radio has predominated in the developing world for decades, penetrating distances and reaching illiterates, this being helped by the fairly inexpensive little transistorised radio. But radio has gained new popularity in Britain as a result of the Sound Broadcasting Act, 1972. This Act permitted advertisements to be broadcast from a British radio station for the first time. Britain now has a nationalised network of local BBC and local commercial radio stations. More stations are to be set up. They are local in that they serve cities such as London, Manchester, Birmingham, Bristol, Plymouth, Glasgow and Portsmouth.

In developing countries local radio is more likely to cover larger regions than in Britain, and to be necessary because different languages are spoken there. This occurs in Nigeria where broadcasts in the north will be in Hausa and in the east they will be in Ibo, but throughout the country there will be English broadcasts. In Ghana radio commentators may speak in Ga, Ashanti and other languages as well as English.

Radio has existed in many countries since 1926. In the West Indies 1935 was a year of increased interest in cricket. New radio stations were established because of the upsurge of interest in cricket in British colonies such as British Guiana (now Guyana). In those days radio was not concerned with national development but with commercial interests such as advertising. During the 1940s radio in the West Indies tended to be influenced by programmes for the American Armed Forces, familiarising local listeners with the sounds of Benny Goodman, the Dorsey brothers and Glenn Miller.

Rediffusion has been a cheap means of bringing radio to many people. It came to Guyana and the Caribbean in 1950. 'Box' radio is widespread in Nigeria. Few homes in Singapore are without rediffusion sets, the cost being small. Rediffusion brings radio to public places such as cafés and bars.

Radio has certain advantages and disadvantages. Being an oral medium it is important that voices used should be attractive to the ear and clearly understood. Words may have to explain what cannot be seen. A disadvantage may be that the subject is of no interest to the listener. Some listeners may only want the company or background sound of radio, and music will be preferred. Two studies have tended to contradict the much-claimed mass appeal and penetration of radio.

How influential is radio?

A survey by Zambia Broadcasting Services showed that rural listeners were unaware of news about major political and international events that had been broadcast and that sets were often tuned in to foreign stations which played popular music. In contrast, the Farm Forum programme was popular because it helped farmers to improve their farming skills.

Dr Frank Ugboajah of the University of Lagos has produced his theory of mass media dysfunction in the African environment. He has shown that radio messages can fail to reach villagers because of the following factors:

1. Lack of receivers, lack of batteries because of cost, or sets which are not working.
2. Poor reception.
3. Irrelevant programme content. Local people are interested in local affairs, not national or international news.
4. Poor broadcasting staff.

5. Bad timing. Programmes may be inconvenient for people who work out-of-doors or go to bed early.
6. Wrong audience selection.
7. Lack of feedback to get audience reactions.

In Trinidad, Alfred Aguiton, of All Media Projects Ltd, told students on a course run by the author under the auspices of W. W. Mircon Ltd, that radio proceeds from language naturally as a pure medium, coming close to person-to-person contact. Radio can use idiomatic language and emphasis that would not be written. Local patois is more acceptable on radio than in the press. Precise language is necessary. A building should be described as a construction and not an erection. In the Caribbean, radio is a potent medium. People are great talkers and are impatient with print. Man is a talker. Language is first of all spoken. Writing comes later.

Radio as a PR medium

Radio can be the most effective medium for advertising, and this can also be true for public relations through news bulletins, taped and studio interviews. An interview can be taped wherever it may be convenient for interviewer and interviewee to meet – in the studio, at home, in the office, at a hotel.

The typical British or American *phone-in* programme is difficult to adopt in developing countries for two reasons: lack of or inefficiency of telephones, and the variety of languages. Phone-ins are restricted to urban dwellers speaking the same language. With the recent establishment of new telephone systems in Nigeria, phone-in programmes have possibilities in Nigerian cities which should not be overlooked by PROs. There is the opportunity to monitor listeners' opinions, and – provided this is not foolishly exploited – there is also the opportunity to phone in relevant information.

A primary strength of radio is its ability to supply instant news of interest and value to the public, and this advantage can often be used by public services, government departments, transport operators, the police and others. There have been extreme cases where wars and unrest have been averted by radio messages. King Hassan of Morocco reversed the onward march of half a million troops advancing on the Spanish Sahara by broadcasting to them in Arabic and French.

Ethnic groups and languages

Kenya contrasts with Nigeria in very interesting ways. It is a beautiful country which many of the 'white aristocracy' were loath to leave when it became independent in 1963. Since independence, Nairobi has been converted into a splendid modern city with a population close on a million, and it is quite the jewel of black Africa. The Kikuyu predominate in urban and political life, there are some 200,000 Asians, and the Masai are fine farmers with herds of British-bred livestock. Yet the total population is only 14 million with some tribes so remote that their only link with modern civilisation is the occasional aircraft passing over-head.

Whereas Nigeria has one principal language, English, major regional languages such as Hausa, Yoruba and Ibo and more than 60 lesser languages and dialects, Kenya has two principal languages, English (official) and Kiswahili (national). Among Kenya's 24 tribes there are at least a dozen languages which justify vernacular radio broadcasts. Kiswahili is fairly limited to the coast provinces and is badly spoken elsewhere.

Remote Kenyan tribes like the Turkana and even the Masai of the Rift Valley are cow and goat-keepers with no need for literacy, and lost literacy soon occurs when educated children work on the land. Ninety per cent of Kenyans are illiterate and 50 per cent of the population are under 15 years of age. While radio can reach them, they cannot always afford to buy receivers. In the north there are tribes based on a cow-herd economy (although not quite as delicately balanced as the old Fulani cattle societies in Nigeria) and a cash economy does not exist. It is not even as advanced as the use of cowrie shells in old Nigeria.

Inevitably, unless the radio stations are located in the tribal language area, as they are in different states in Nigeria and Ghana but only partially in Kenya, each language receives only a short period of broadcast time each day, and perhaps only each week. This was the case with the Zambia Farm Forum programme broadcast from Lusaka. When air-time is divided between different languages, other-language-speaking listeners are deprived of listening time. The value of a single national language is obvious.

Vernacular languages in Kenya are divided between the different stations of Voice of Kenya radio. The *central* station broadcasts in Kimasai, Kikuyu, Kikamba and Kimeru. The *north-eastern* station broadcasts in Kisomali, Kihorana, Kirendelle and Kiturkana. A third station in Ksumu broadcasts in Nyanza while the Western Province's broadcasts are in Kilulya, Kijalvo, Kikuria, Kiteso and Kikisii.

The prefix 'Ki', like the Malaysian Bahasa, means language; thus Kimasai: the language of the Masai. An interesting language problem in Hong Kong, where 96 per cent of the 5 million population are Chinese, is that the spoken but unwritten Chinese language is Cantonese, whereas written Chinese (including the characters on the umbrella-of-night-signs that adorn the streets) is Mandarin. The Singapore Government launched a sensible campaign in 1980 urging its largely Chinese population to use only Mandarin.

Radio versus the press

In countries which have wet and dry seasons, the distribution of newspapers may be affected by seasonal conditions. During heavy rainfall in Ghana it has been difficult to transport newspapers to the hinterland, whereas the country is well-equipped with broadcasting services. Moreover, the radio broadcasts in local languages but vernacular newspapers are not always available even if members of the largely farming community could read them. The situation is different in Nigeria where more cities, more publishing centres, more newspapers and comparatively better transportation help to offset seasonal hazards. The Nigerian press continues to become an important medium, especially with the growth of both general and adult literacy. Balance-of-payments problems restrict newsprint imports into Ghana, there are few newspapers and they have limited circulations so that radio scores in a big way.

Versatility of radio

Unlike any other medium, radio has remarkably varied characteristics such as:

1. Thanks to the transistor, the modern radio set is small and easily carried around so that programmes can be listened to anywhere.
2. Car radio is very popular.
3. Different audiences can be appealed to at different times of the day — families at breakfast, the car-driver going to and from work or during the day if he travels, the housewife working about the house, people at work, young people in their leisure time — espec-

ially in the evenings. People listen to radio when it is inconvenient to read newspapers or watch television.

4. It transcends frontiers. Foreign stations can be listened to. Foreign countries such as Britain, West Germany, the USA and Russia transmit foreign-language programmes overseas.
5. Very large audiences are reached by radio. They exceed newspaper circulation and readership figures, even in developed countries.
6. In developing countries radio satisfies the illiterate rural people whose world is one of sound, not of the visual symbols of urban and especially industrialised society. This is very true of India where 70 per cent of its 600 million people live in the countryside and only 23.7 per cent of rural dwellers are literate. More than half the Nigerian population, probably 65 per cent, can be reached by radio, which is important in a country of 356,700 square miles and 85 million people.

TELEVISION

Television in the Third World is not quite the elitist medium it used to be. It is fast becoming the main form of entertainment for the working-class family, just as it is in the West. While audiences may take some time to reach the 20 million often recorded for Britain's most popular programmes, it is true that in developing countries television is becoming far less of a luxury for the wealthy. There are interesting reasons for this, namely:

1. TV sets can be rented instead of purchased.
2. Community or viewing centres make public viewing possible. These may be in village community centres as in African countries or — as with tin mines in Malaysia — at remote work places. Viewing is mostly in the evening, and audiences tend to be chiefly male since women do not usually go out at night.
3. The old problem of 'no electricity' is being overcome as electrification proceeds.
4. In some countries special efforts have been made to provide TV as a national communication system. Indonesia is a country of 146 million people scattered over 30,000 islands comprising an area of 735,381 square miles as wide as the USA and having three

time zones. While there are some local languages, Bahasa Indonesia (a form of Malay) is the language of TV programmes, even though English is spoken by the educated and business community and 85 million of the people are in Java which includes the capital, Jakarta. Television is transmitted nationwide by means of a satellite and 96 stations.

5. The electricity problem has been overcome in South East Asia by the use of Japanese receivers run off 12-volt car batteries. However, it costs money to re-charge the batteries so viewers are very selective about what they watch, which encourages the producers, as in Indonesia, to take pains over their productions.

The opportunities for contributing PR material to TV programmes can be greater than on radio because of the greater variety of programmes such as news bulletins, interviews and magazines. This is not to be confused with the sponsoring of TV programmes which is purely advertising. Where equipment is available, outside broadcasts are also possible such as PR coverage of an event or activity.

TV VERSUS RADIO AND PRESS

TV has its own characteristics which are worth analysing.

1. Just as radio in the Caribbean was stimulated by the interest in cricket more than 40 years ago so, in Britain, interest in TV was stimulated by the Coronation in 1951, and video-cassettes gained popularity with the Royal Wedding in 1981.
2. It is a visual medium requiring attractive visual material whether it be faces, costume or other subject material. This also means that viewers will be critical of anything unattractive on the screen. They are not aware of appearances in the radio station, but the cameras bring the TV studio view right into the home.
3. Most developing countries have colour TV, an expensive accident since the manufacturers convinced many people including the Nigerians that black-and-white sets were obsolete. Actually the world demand, especially in the West, for the less expensive black-and-white sets has obliged the manufacturers to continue production. A lot of people still cannot afford colour TV, and most portables are black-and-white.

Colour can be an important factor in PR. It enables the corporate identity to come across as with the livery of an airline. If a programme is about holidays and tourism it is more realistic in colour. Realism is therefore a big advantage of the medium.

4. There is also movement so that physical demonstration is possible — something which is impossible with press and radio.

5. But unlike the press and the radio, TV is immobile — that is, until we have miniaturised sets to wear on our wrists or carry in our pockets! Normally, we have to sit down and concentrate on the screen.

6. For most people, TV can be watched only at certain times of the day, mainly in the evening. Viewing time is therefore limited, hence the expression 'prime viewing time' which is the time between arriving home from work and going to bed.

7. As with radio, the message is fleeting although the overall impact is greater.

8. Whereas the press is fairly standardised, from the training of journalists to methods of typesetting and printing, TV depends on costly programme material — costly to produce and buy. Not all TV companies can afford good material, and audiences may be disappointed at the quality of programmes. Poor programmes may consist of very old British or American films (often black and white), too many static studio interviews because of the lack of outside broadcast facilities, rather inexperienced native actors and performers, and limited sports coverage because of dependence on commercial sponsors. When British audiences complain about too many 'repeats', one can imagine the situation in the Third World where costs are even more critical.

On the Trinidad course mentioned earlier in this chapter, another speaker was Jai Parasram of Trinidad and Tobago Television. To summarise his remarks, he pointed out that TV was important in development support communications. Through TV it was possible to change lifestyles and overcome traditions, by influencing group leaders. It was an intimate medium, addressing a small domestic audience. It was unlike addressing a theatre audience. There was a curious paradox of a mass medium actually addressing numerous small family audiences. Among its disadvantages were breaks in transmission due to interference, lack of person-to-person communication, lack of feedback and inability to check unfamiliar words. When reading one can go back and re-read or check what is unfamiliar.

Another problem with TV is time. Whereas a news story can be edited, set and printed fairly quickly, and radio can be instantaneous, TV takes time. For instance, one of the most popular British TV programmes is ITN's *News At Ten*. It takes all day to produce, beginning at about 8 a.m. Research, rehearsal, shooting, processing (if it is film) and editing all take time. Availability of equipment such as cameras and studios, and of production crews has also to be considered.

But TV does have some special advantages. It can, pictorially, familiarise people with the unfamiliar. Many people in developing countries have never seen the wildlife in their own countries, yet these creatures are familiar from childhood to people in London, Paris or New York. Not many Africans have ever seen the creatures that adorn their postage stamps. But TV can educate them about their own country, in itself a Government PR task. Thus, TV has the special merit of speeding up the process of communications, knowledge and understanding.

30 Documentary Films and Visual Aids

Visual aids convey messages in some graphic form with or without written or spoken language. The pictorial, and sometimes movement, elements help to achieve understanding quickly when there are communication problems of illiteracy or different languages. For example, a road sign bearing a picture of an elephant is readily understood by a European motorist more familiar with a similar sign depicting a cow. Films for world distribution can be made with no spoken commentary, yet the message is made understandable by the scenes themselves, miming by characters, and music which sets the mood. The creative PRO has the choice of the following visual aids.

Documentary, industrial or sponsored films

These are private non-fiction films. 'Industrial' is used in the same sense as 'industrial' editor for house journal editor. It does not mean that such films are confined to industrial or technical subjects; rather that they are made on behalf of industries which might be consumer or industrial. Films are, in fact, one of the most important private media used by *any* organisation engaged in PR. Governments, the police, tourist boards, state enterprises and parastatals, charities and so on all make PR films.

Films are unlikely to be replaced by video-tapes because 16 mm film projectors are universally available whereas video-cassette recorders are not and they require transmission through a TV set. However, film can be converted to tape, and vice versa.

Although the initial cost of a film may be high its life may be 5 years or more, and it can be shown repeatedly to numerous audiences according to the number of prints available.

With its blend of movement, colour and sound the film has realism coupled with entertainment value.

When making a film three things should be considered:

1. *Purpose.* What PR job has the film got to do? Inform, educate, convince, train? A film should not be made for the sake of vanity or because it seems a nice idea.
2. *Audience.* A film should be made for a particular audience – businessmen, schoolchildren, doctors, tourists, for instance – and not vaguely for a general audience. It should be a choice of media and method to reach specific publics in order to achieve a PR objective, and budgeted accordingly.
3. *Distribution.* When made, how will the chosen audience be reached – by invitation to film shows, at press receptions, on exhibition stands, in the showroom, at staff induction sessions, on training courses, or to customers and prospective customers? There is no point in putting the can in a drawer and hoping some-one will ask to borrow it. It may be necessary to send out letters offering the film to schools, clubs and societies, or to advertise its availability in appropriate journals.

In developing countries there are usually organisations – commercial or Government – which organise mobile film units which tour the villages, and documentaries are shown.

The content of the film should match the needs of the audience. A tourist film shown to Western audiences could run for 20 to 30 minutes and use sophisticated techniques to present a panorama of topics. But a film made for villagers needs to be shorter, maybe 8 to 10 minutes, if it is to retain concentration. The subject should be presented simply, the message should be repetitive, and the images presented should not be unfamiliar to the audience, otherwise interest will be lost.

Some European and American films have failed when shown to African rural audiences because they have been too long, too compli-cated, and too full of puzzling, unknown sights. White characters, cold wintry scenes, congested city streets, women scantily clothed, air travel, the sea and ships, birds such as swans or seagulls, and so on, could be bewildering to a village audience. People in Europe, thanks to Holly-wood films and TV, are so used to scenes in New York and San Francisco they feel they have been there, but an African villager may have no idea what his own capital city looks like. In making films for such audiences the message must not be defeated by mental confusion.

Video-tapes

These have the same impact as films except that being seen on a television screen the audience will be smaller and more intimate. Tapes are less expensive and easier to make than film. Tapes do not have to be processed, although editing is necessary. In the West, large companies have their own video studios and produce perhaps 20 to 40 programmes a year for PR, employee relations and training purposes.

Video-disc

Rivalling the video-tape is the video-disc, which has the merits of being cheap to mass-produce, less bulky to store, and so light and thin it can be posted in an envelope. Here are two examples which demonstrate the possibilities of the video-disc. Ford have put all their servicing instructions on a library of video-discs. Sears Roebuck, whose vast printed mail-order catalogue is bigger than a telephone directory, have put their new catalogue on to video-disc. The only problem is that a special recorder is necessary for playback through a television receiver.

Slides

The most inexpensive photographic visual aid is the 35 mm slide, and projectors are likewise inexpensive although for frequent use it pays to use a Kodak carousel. Slides can be taken on a normal camera and are easily replaced so that a presentation can be improved or up-dated. They can be shown singly, and controlled by a remote control hand-switch.

An audio-tape can be used in conjunction with slides. Something closely resembling a film effect can be achieved by using a pair of projectors with cross-fade so that there is no gap on the screen between slides. To this can be synchronised an audio-tape with vocal commentary, music and, sound effects. To avoid monotony it pays to have two commentators with contrasting voices, male and female being ideal.

Models

Few things can demonstrate a subject better than a scale model. The world knows what Concorde looks like because of models in travel agency and airline windows. The Federal Palace Hotel development in

Lagos has been demonstrated for several years with a scale model displayed in the entrance to the original hotel. Oil exploration companies make use of scale model oil rigs. Shipping companies have long been famous for their scale models. They can be used in company premises and showrooms, in sales offices, on exhibition stands, as portable displays, and are an excellent way of explaining large subjects.

Printed aids

For various display purposes printed visual aids can convey information effectively. A good example is the detailed pictorial poster. It can explain a subject such as the growing of cotton, coffee, tea or rubber; or how to identify flowers, trees, birds or animals; or the operation of an industry like oil, coal, gas or electricity. Being educational, these poster wall charts are popular in schools. Young people can be an important public. They can teach their elders, and they are tomorrow's citizens, workers and customers.

Pictorial maps can provide tourist information; safety-first posters can protect staff or the public; pest-control posters can help farmers protect crops and livestock. Illustrations can be cartoon drawings, and simple effects such as a straight-line mouth and a curved mouth can indicate good and bad, pleasant and unpleasant.

31 Internal and External House Journals

House journals are a popular PR medium throughout the world, which is not surprising since they are one of the oldest forms of PR communication. One of the first was published by the Singer sewing machine company in the USA in 1865. This was an external for customers. For the past 30 years Caltex Pacifica Indonesia have published a daily staff journal which contains world news items monitored from the radio. This is welcomed by oil workers in remote places.

Great changes have been taking place in the editing and production of house journals. Many today are printed by web-offset in tabloid newspaper style, replacing the former letterpress-printed magazine style. Extravagantly produced prestige journals have given way to externals which have to work hard as PR educational and informative publications. The content of employee newspapers has changed from sermons by management to an expression of worker democracy with readers' letters and even critical comments from the staff. This is part of the general move towards upward communication in employee–employer relations.

We have mentioned two kinds of journal: internal and external. The mistake should not be made of trying to make one journal do both jobs. They are quite different, the readers are different, and therefore the content must be of interest and value to the particular readership.

An *internal* should be distributed to people employed by the organisation, the only outside circulation going to pensioners, share-holders and certain specially interested people. An *external* should not be circulated generally but should be aimed at a specific readership such as customers, dealers, users, specifiers, franchise-holders or agents according to the nature of the business.

However, in some developing countries where magazines are scarce a good external house journal may even be sold on bookstalls. *Enter-*

prise, the ZIMCO house journal, is sold like this in Zambia.

This is a big subject so in this chapter we will concentrate on the considerations facing an editor when planning a new house journal. Here is a 15-point check-list:

1. *Readership.* For whom is the journal intended? All the staff or certain staff such as management and executives; office workers; factory workers; salesmen; or external readers such as agents and brokers; shopkeepers; technical buyers; consumers? The contents must satisfy the readers, otherwise the journal will be a disaster.

2. *Editorial policy.* This must be agreed with management so that disputes do not occur between the editor and management later on. The journal must be seen to have a clear policy, and not vary from issue to issue. This will cover the type of material published, the general design and character, and other matters which will be discussed as we proceed.

3. *Format.* What will the journal look like? An A4 magazine, a pocket magazine, a newsletter or a tabloid newspaper?

4. *The title.* Again, this is something which should not change so its choice right at the beginning is vital. Is it to be an invented title, an attractive word, or something resembling a newspaper title? Clever titles should be avoided, and one used by many other organisations is not very original. A simple title like *Ford Times* is good, but *Habit* is a very appropriate title for a magazine issued to investors in the Abbey National Building Society.

5. *The frequency.* Will it be published daily, weekly, fortnightly, monthly, every 2 months or quarterly? Less than quarterly is undesirable because reader interest will be lost by the lack of continuity. Much depends on the urgency of the contents. This decision will depend on two things: the budget and the reader's need for the information. A building constructor published a daily journal for every major building project because it was necessary to have a progress report for financiers, suppliers, sub-contractors and the owners. However, monthly and quarterly journals are the most common.

   There should be a definite publishing date. This is important to contributors, the editor, the printer and the readers.

6. *Number of pages.* This will be controlled by a number of fac-

tors, these being the budget, the frequency, the page size or
format, cost factors such as the number of illustrations and whether it is to be printed in black and white, have a second colour,
or be in full colour. You may be able to have twice as many
pages if it is printed in black and white instead of full colour, or
if it is quarterly instead of monthly.

7. *Picture content.* Is it to contain mainly editorial with the
occasional picture, or are lots of pictures to be a main feature?
Employees like seeing their picture in the paper, and offset printing means that pictures can be reproduced more cheaply and
with better quality than when letterpress is used.

8. *Black and white or colour.* Apart from the considerations
mentioned above, there may be good reasons why black and
white is adequate for an employee newspaper while full colour
may be essential for a hotel, airline or tourist board journal.

9. *Paper.* What quality and weight of paper is to be used? A big
mistake is often made in printing house journals on too shiny or
too heavy a paper. It may look prestigious but it can destroy the
appearance of a genuine magazine. It is better to use paper similar to that used by commercial publications of the same sort. A
newspaper format house journal on glossy paper looks absurd.

10. *Printing process.* Shall it be letterpress or offset-litho? This
decision may depend on the printing facilities available. Nowadays, offset-litho is popular but on the other hand there is
some dreadful offset-litho printing in some parts of the Third
World. A lot depends on the kind, age and production quality of
the machine! Before accepting a printer's quotation it is wise to
see samples of his work.

11. *Obtaining editorial material.* A good editor does not send out
general invitations to people to write for the magazine, or hope
that contributions will be volunteered. He plans two or three
issues ahead, knows what he wants to print, and tells people
what he wants them to write and supply by a certain date. He
may have to write everything himself.

In large organisations it is a good plan to have appointed
correspondents who are responsible for collecting and supplying
news and pictures, these correspondents being known to the
staff. These correspondents can cover local factories or branch
offices and shops, so that the editor has a network of reliable
contributors. They are also people the editor can contact for

local information, or instruct on the coverage of a local story.

12. *Method of distribution.*   How the journal will reach readers is vital to its ability to be read. If copies are handed out at the place of work they may be put on one side and discarded or forgotten. Different methods will be practical in particular situations. The ideal method, which does involve the cost of envelope or wrapper plus postage, is to post copies to home addresses.

13. *Free or cover price.*   Some readers may object to paying for a company magazine, yet if the journal is of real interest and value they may be prepared to pay for it. The biggest-circulation house journals in Britain are sold.

14. *Advertisements.*   Should there be advertisements, either ones from outside firms, on behalf of the sponsor's products, or reader advertisements for sales and wants? Some editors find that advertisements make the publication look more like a 'real' magazine, while reader advertisements have been found to add to the reader interest. Outside advertisements should not be charitable ones: the journal must have sufficient circulation to be a worthwhile medium for the advertiser.

15. *Feedback.*   What methods will be used to test what readers think of the journal, what they like and what they dislike? Readers' letters are one form of response. Questionnaires can be issued from time to time, or readers can be asked to place regular features in order of preference so that the editor can learn which are the most and the least popular items.

House journals are one of the most important features in most PR campaigns. Even though there is competition from the video-tape, the permanent and portable printed journal is likely to prosper for a long time, especially in the Third World where television sets are not in everyone's home.

32 Photography

Good photography is the hallmark of the good PRO. Unfortunately, much of PR photography is bad. Yet a picture may tell a story better than words, and words may sometimes be useless in a developing country which is multi-lingual and largely illiterate. The picture is therefore even more important to the Third World PRO.

There are two reasons why so many PR pictures are bad, quite apart from technical problems over printing and developing. First, it has not been decided what message the picture is to convey. Second, the photographer has not been properly instructed on what he is to photograph. Never leave it to the photographer to take what he fancies. He has no idea what message his client is trying to transmit, nor which are the particularly interesting aspects of the subject he is photographing. Only the PRO can tell him these things.

Here is a check-list of the important things to consider when taking PR pictures:

1. *Avoid taking straightforward record shots.* Try to make the picture interesting. It may be simply a product picture, but it may look more interesting if it is taken at an angle, or if someone is using the product naturally. Even a hotel looks more interesting if someone is walking in the door, or eating at a table. A can of paint looks better on top of a step-ladder or in someone's hand. A picture may be improved if only part of it is shown. Close-ups are more dramatic than distance shots.

2. *Take care with the lighting.* Many pictures are poor because they were badly lit, have unwanted shadows, or have halo shadows, behind heads when flash is used indoors.

3. *When supplying portraits* to the press or printing them in house journals, crop or trim the picture to just below the knot of a tie

or the Adam's apple of the throat. Never send or print a portrait with the head perched on half a torso like an orange on a pumpkin. The original negative can include half the body, but when prints are ordered the photographer should be instructed to print only the portion described above.

4. *Avoid 'busy' pictures,* that is pictures with unnecessary details which conflict with the subject. The PRO should always try to accompany a photographer, and it is his job to see that the scene is clear of things that will spoil a picture. For instance, it is better that a portrait is taken against a plain wall. It may be necessary to drape a white sheet or a sheet of white paper behind a subject to obscure an unwanted background, as when photographing machinery in a factory.

5. *Don't take flat one-dimensional pictures.* Depth or a three-dimensional effect can be obtained by shooting at an angle or turning an object (or a face) to get a more interesting composition. To understand this, experiment with a box of matches. Taken face on, only the label side is visible. But turn the box and look down on it so that three sides are visible and a more satisfying picture becomes possible. This sort of composition skill produces publishable pictures.

6. *Don't have blatant name displays.* PR pictures should not be advertisements, yet if only two or three letters of a name are visible the rest is obvious. If a picture of an airliner just showed the letters *NIG* it would be obvious that it was a Nigeria Airways plane.

7. *Try to humanise pictures.* Human interest can be an asset in PR pictures, but make sure the people used are right for the picture and are correctly dressed. If it is a building site make sure that safety helmets are worn, if it is a holiday picture choose a normal family rather than a beautiful girl. People should look genuinely part of the scene. Have people doing things, not grinning at the camera.

8. *'A little can tell all'* is a thought worth remembering. If everything is photographed the picture will have to be taken at a distance so that the subject may seem smaller than it really is. A building is a good example. But take only part of it and the size of the building will become more apparent.

9. *Demonstrating size* may be important. Small objects will look small, large objects will look large, if related to something of

known size, as when a battery is held in the hand or a person stands against an earth-mover.

10. *Make sure you have permission* to take pictures which are to be published publicly.

Two further important questions arise. Make sure that the copyright of the picture is owned by the organisation, that is, taken by the PRO himself or commissioned by the PRO or some member of the organisation. Editors print PR pictures free-of-fee on the understanding that the copyright is owned by the sender. Otherwise a reproduction fee will be due to the owner of the copyright, and editors will not want to pay this.

Make sure that every picture sent out bears a caption on the back. Do not write on the back of a print but attach a caption stating the name, address and telephone number of the sender, and describing what the picture cannot say for itself. Do not use as a caption the opening paragraph of an accompanying news release, and do not refer to the picture or include the caption in the release. After the close of the story a note can be added that pictures are available, or that one accompanies the release. The picture must be complete in itself. It could be kept in a picture library long after the release has been used or even thrown away.

33 Dealer Relations

This is an area of PR which is sometimes overlooked, and yet it is essential to efficient distribution, and eventually or indirectly to good customer relations. Looked at the other way round, customers may judge the manufacturer by the dealer's opinion of him! Or by his knowledge of the product and his ability to give advice. The helpful dealer can create credibility and confidence in the product and the manufacturer.

PR methods can be applied to help achieve good dealer relations, and subsequently good customer relations, in the following ways:

1. *Works visits* bring the dealer closer to the manufacturer and enable him to understand how a product is made, and the efforts which are made to conduct quality control.
2. *Staff training* is important for the dealer's staff, whether he is selling cosmetics, sewing-machines, electronic products or motorcars. Some manufacturers issue certificates of competence which can be displayed on the dealer's premises.
3. *Dealer magazines* are external house journals addressed to the dealer to tell him about the company and about products with perhaps advice on shop displays, demonstrations and business management generally.
4. *Visual aids,* such as counter-top units for slide presentations, or video-cassettes and replay equipment, may be supplied, so that dealers can either learn about the product or demonstrate it visually to customers.
5. *Dealer conferences* can be organised to brief dealers on new products and advertising support for them. These may be on a national or regional basis.
6. *News in the trade press* and PR stories in other publications can

keep the dealer aware of what the company is doing, and the publicity may support retail sales.

7. *Advice* can be sent to dealers, telling them that the product is to be the subject of editorial coverage, or is to be the subject of a radio or TV programme, so that they can make an effort to read, see or watch the coverage.

8. *Dealer contests can be organised* with prizes for, say, the best window display, dealers submitting photographs of their arrangement.

9. *Dealers can be invited to exhibitions,* hospitality being provided on the manufacturer's stand, and admission tickets being provided. In some cases, parties of dealers may be taken to the exhibition.

From the above suggestions it will be seen that dealer relations is a valuable part of PR activity which needs to be built into the overall PR programme. It calls for close co-operation with the marketing, sales and advertising departments and with the advertising agency. It is also an example of the need to plan PR programmes over a long period such as a year so that the PR activity is not isolated but is an integral part of a company's communications.

Here is a simple example of the importance of educating the dealer. The sales manager of Rentokil wondered why orders for cans of woodworm killer were mostly for the smallest size. A visit was made to some stockists and it was observed that when a customer came in and asked for something to get rid of woodworm the shop assistant handed her the smallest and cheapest can. It was the easiest way to secure a sale. But the company had been receiving complaints from customers who said the insecticide had not worked. The reason was that the salesman in the shop did not ask the customer what was attacked by woodworm and what was the extent of the damage.

Rentokil therefore produced a stand with shelves. The top shelf carried the biggest can, and each shelf carried a different size can down to the smallest size on the bottom shelf. At the side of each shelf was fixed a metal plate which stated 'Enough for a roof void', 'Enough for a floor', 'Enough for a set of chairs' and so on. When the customer came in all the sales assistant had to do was ask 'where have you got the woodworm?' and then sell the correct size.

The result was that the customer was satisfied, the dealer sold more products, and the company sold the full range and made a bigger sale.

Here, PR and marketing worked together.

The value of works visits can be shown when the customer asks the dealer's advice and is told 'I know this is a good one. I've seen it made.'

When Berger first introduced one-coat non-drip paint, and it was advertised in Britain, the product did not sell at first because the dealers did not believe you could paint properly without first putting on an undercoat. It took a PR programme of dealer education to reverse that attitude and get the dealers to sell the product.

Ideally, when introducing a new product the retail trade should be made thoroughly familiar with the product before it is advertised.

34 Market Education

Market education is an essential part of the marketing strategy, although sadly it is not always carried out, with costly results as we saw with the example of Berger paints in the previous chapter, a whole selling and advertising campaign being wasted. Disaster occurred with the launch of a new smoking mixture (NSM) as a substitute for tobacco. The public refused to buy cigarettes made with NSM, and they had to be withdrawn from the market in spite of a fortune having been spent on advertising.

The moral of this is that although advertising is a splendid means of reaching potential customers they will not buy if they have no faith in the product, or perhaps in its maker. This can be very important in developing countries where new products are strange and may conflict with long-held traditions.

Airlines, for instance, have had the problem of convincing people who have never flown that it is safe to fly. This was a PR problem experienced by Pakistan International Airlines some years ago, while Nigeria Airways suffered loss of confidence when one of their aircraft crashed. In New Zealand, an exhibition was toured round village schools to encourage farmers to make visits to Britain, children seeing the exhibition during the day and their parents during the evening.

Sophisticated new products such as computers, which cost a lot of money to buy or lease and operate, have been the subject of extensive customer education programmes. Very often it has been necessary to educate the man who signs the cheque as well as the data-processing staff. Five-day courses for managing directors have been run by IBM.

Educating the market may be a continuous process, or it may be necessary to organise a market education programme for 12 to 18 months before the product is advertised.

Gas and electricity companies can be blamed for accidents so they find it sensible to mount extensive educational programmes on how to use the fuels, equipment and appliances correctly, including simple things like how to wire a plug. A lot of this is done through schools, for the market is always growing up and children can often educate parents. But it can also be done through newspaper articles, talks on the radio, publicly displayed posters, and leaflets distributed to households.

The market is not necessarily a commercial one. It may be necessary to educate parents to send their children to school, or explain to them why it is necessary to give correct information to an enumerator during a census. The latter was done very intelligently in Singapore in 1980 when educational features were published in the *Straits Times* and elsewhere, explaining the purpose of a census and how it would be conducted.

The role of public relations in informing and educating is very clear in these examples, and when it leads to knowledge and understanding PR has performed its function.

An educated market means a co-operative one. If the public do not understand why there are flight delays, breakdowns on the railway, hold-ups in postal deliveries, power cuts or failures in the gas and water supplies, they are left in that negative PR state of ignorance which quickly creates ill-will. It is not a case of apologising – PR is not in the apology business – but of explaining. When people know they are more likely to understand and make efforts to avoid putting more strain on the system or at least to tolerate breakdowns.

The expectations of people in developing countries may be higher than it is possible to achieve. In the West, recession has meant in recent years that people have had to give up many of the expectations they might have achieved in the 1960s. In the Third World, these expectations are growing all the time. The PROs of many commercial and non-commercial undertakings can help to lessen feelings of frustration and disappointment if they conduct frank and practical educational programmes.

A particularly good example is that of NEPA in Nigeria. Few organisations in the Third World have aroused such antagonism as the Nigerian electricity authority. Since the country found oil, the economy has been boosted, and people have demanded all manner of electrical goods such as air-conditioners, colour TV, cookers, refrigerators and so on. The demand has been out of all proportion to the supply estimated before the oil bonanza. It takes many years to build and put into operation new power stations. But the public is impatient, the system gets overloaded, and there are power cuts. Consequently, NEPA has a monstrous PR problem in educating users to ration usage and understand the reasons for the shortage of supply.

The means of educating the market have been explained in earlier chapters but to summarise they may include:

1. All forms of press relations, but especially the feature article.
2. External house journals.
3. Documentary films, slide presentations and video-cassettes.
4. Works visits for customers.
5. Exhibitions — whether participating in public ones, touring private shows or having permanent exhibits on the premises.
6. Educational literature ranging from leaflets to sponsored books.
7. Short training courses.
8. In-store demonstrations which are educational as well as selling exercises.
9. School programmes such as talks, literature, films, kits for projects.
10. Educating dealers so that they can inform customers.

From the above list it will be seen that some PR programmes could be mainly ones of market education.

35 Planning Public Relations Programmes

Now let us put together what this part of the book has been all about. Previous chapters have described the breadth of PR services and activities and the media and techniques which can be used by the PR practitioner, whether he be working for an organisation or a consultancy. The planning in either case is identical. The financing is similar, except that the consultancy has to make a profit. The task of PR is largely problem-solving in order to create knowledge and understanding. We are engaged in neither 'free' advertising nor propaganda. We shall be content if our publics understand our message, not that they have a favourable impression, fair or false. Moreover, we are concerned with public relations which achieves precise objectives.

A PR programme, like that for production, recruitment, marketing, sales or advertising, has to be prepared in advance. We do not operate from the seat of our pants on a day-to-day haphazard basis. So, if the programme is for the year beginning January 1 we shall probably start planning about August or September. It depends on the nature of the organisation, perhaps on when management or the treasury department has to have budgets. We have to be familiar with the forward plans and forecasts of the organisation. This requires access to top management and collaboration with all departmental heads.

The framework of PR programme planning is as follows:

Six point PR planning model
1. Appreciation of the situation.
2. Definition of objectives.
3. Definition of publics.
4. Choice of media and techniques.
5. Budget.
6. Evaluation of results.

Let us elaborate on each of these in turn, recalling what has been said on some of these topics in previous chapters.

APPRECIATION OF THE SITUATION

Before attempting to plan anything we have to know why a plan is necessary. There is no point in suddenly deciding to send out news releases, make a documentary film or launch a house journal. Why, if at all, are these needed? What purpose must they serve? It is too simple to merely say that we want to create a favourable climate of opinion, which is a pretty meaningless statement although a lot of slap-happy PR programmes are based on no more than that.

The important thing is to find out where we are now, what people know or don't know, what misconceptions exist, what attitudes are held — in other words what is the *current image* of the organisation, its people, policies, products or services.

This is best discovered by means of an opinion poll or an image study. But we can also study published opinions such as press reports. We can examine the annual report and accounts and current sales figures. We can also talk to people who have contact with our publics. One thing is certain: nothing must be taken for granted, and we must beware of the *mirror* image which is held by people inside the organisation.

DEFINITION OF OBJECTIVES

Numerous objectives may be listed after talks with management and department heads. They may concern community, employee, corporate, supplier, financial, dealer, user and consumer relations. There could be a list as long as your arm.

Although the model is an orderly list several items will have to be considered simultaneously. A process of constraint will have to be applied. PR activities are limited by the time, money and resources which are available. If we attempt to do everything we finish up doing nothing well. So, as we plan we have to determine priorities. What is feasible within the limits of manpower (represented by salaries or consultancy fees), money for other costs, and the availability of resources such as office space, typewriters, cameras, projectors, vehicles or whatever we may need?

Another reason for defining objectives is that if we have objectives *we can measure results.* Either we achieve those results or we do not, or we achieve them to some recognisable or measurable extent. PR does not have to be intangible. If it is intangible it is usually a waste of money.

DEFINITION OF PUBLICS

In order to achieve objectives — such as educating the market for a new product, recruiting the right calibre of staff, succeeding with a new share issue, satisfying the demands of conservationists or improving employee-employer relations — we need to define the many groups of people (publics) with whom we have to communicate. Publics were discussed in Chapter 25.

CHOICE OF MEDIA AND TECHNIQUES

How do we reach those publics? Can we use existing media such as press, radio and TV, or do we have to create media such as house journals, documentary films, video-tapes? Do we have to take a mobile cinema van or a puppet show round the villages?

BUDGET

We may be given a set sum of money or we may have to produce an estimate of what it will cost to achieve our objectives. Either way, budgeting is important for the following reasons:

1. It will show management that we are responsible people who understand how to manage our affairs in a businesslike way. Some management and marketing people think that PROs know only how to spend expense accounts and run up bills for lavish hospitality. PR is no longer in the gin-and-tonic business. We are accountable.
2. It will help us in the planning and execution of the PR pro-

gramme because costs represent jobs that have to be done, at the right price and on schedule. The budget is thus related to the timetable of activities.

The budget should include everything that has to be expended such as:

Salaries of PR staff.
Overheads, e.g. office, heating/air-conditioning, lighting, cleaning.
Car and travel expenses.
Stationery.
Postage, telephone, Telex.
Photography, production of films, slides, video-tapes.
Printing.
Equipment (purchase or hire), e.g. typewriters, copying machines,
    cameras, projectors, vehicles.
Catering and hire of rooms for PR functions.
Hospitality for journalists and other guests.

EVALUATION OF RESULTS

If we began with an opinion poll or an image study it will be sensible to organise another in order to measure any change in attitudes or understanding. It may have happened that the original survey showed that only 10 per cent of the sample interviewed had ever heard of the organisation. An objective may be to increase awareness or recognition to 40 per cent. At the end of the year a further survey will demonstrate whether this or a different result has been achieved.

But it all depends on the objectives: some may be self-evident by observation or known results. The market may have been so well educated that when the product was advertised there was an immediate good response. There could be a marked improvement in the calibre of staff recruited. The new shares were fully taken up, perhaps oversubscribed, when placed on the stock market. Articulate demonstrations by conservationists may have ceased. A new understanding may have developed in employee-employer relations and perhaps a strike has been averted. And if the organisation had been subject to a hostile press perhaps the press is now more sympathetic. Results can be both quantitative and qualitative.

To conclude, now let us look at some examples of PR in action. The reader will be able to judge to what extent the 'six-point model' principles were followed. Costings are not included but these examples do highlight some of the special communication problems which may handicap PR operations in developing countries. But they also emphasise the importance of PR in the Third World.

NAIROBI SCHOOL BUS SERVICE

A problem in Nairobi was that school children were finding it difficult to get on public service vehicles. (In Britain we have the opposite problem!) The Nairobi City Council arranged for the provision of extra buses exclusively for school children. The PR programme included:

1. The Council informed the public through the press, and there is a good press in Nairobi.
2. Researchers checked areas which needed more buses.
3. Parents were asked to complete questionnaires.
4. A route timetable was issued.
5. Street posters carried wording such as TRANSPORT NOW AVAILABLE FOR THE SCHOOL CHILDREN – AVOID YOUR CHILDREN BEING SQUASHED BY ADULTS. Parents were asked to fill in forms and send them back before a certain date.
6. Priority was given to the subject on radio news bulletins.
7. On TV, children were shown enjoying comfortable rides to and from school, and how relaxed they were when they began their lessons.

FIRST BANK OF NIGERIA

Here is an example of how a change of name, and the PR programme associated with it, helped to enhance the fortunes of a long-established Nigerian bank.

In 1977 the Federal Government directed that all foreign enterprises should obey a decree on indigenisation. Because of the general antipathy towards multi-nationals it was therefore decided to also change the name of the Standard Bank to one that did not look foreign to Nigerians. This fitted in with gaining credibility for the fact that to comply with the indigenisation decree 60 per cent of the bank's shares were sold.

It was believed that a new name would be welcomed by Nigerians because they responded well to change. Moreover, the Standard Bank had gone through three previous changes of name: British Bank of West Africa, Bank of West Africa and Standard Bank of Nigeria. It would also help if the new name pleased the aspirations of the people.

The management of the bank did not object to this idea, and before the 1979 annual general meeting the Standard Bank had sold 44.8 per cent of its shares to the Federal Government of Nigeria, 19.2 per cent to the public and 38 per cent were retained by Standard Chartered Bank, the bank's overseas associates.

At the 1979 annual general meeting of the Standard Bank it was un-animously agreed that the name should be changed. The name First Bank of Nigeria Limited was believed to be most suitable since it was literally the first bank to be established in Nigeria — in 1894 — and also it was now a fully Nigerian bank.

The PR department was then instructed to mount a campaign to educate the public about the new name, and to create new designs for a corporate image and a corporate identity.

The 1979 annual general meeting thus became a launch-pad for a sound PR campaign. Since the new name was already accepted by the shareholders it was believed that public acceptance would not be too difficult. The advertising and PR department, headed by Brian Adeyemi and assisted by O. O. Omole, began work on the assignment.

While Mr Adeyemi was busy planning the new logo, Mr Omole headed a section which prepared the press for a spontaneous spotlight on the bank. A news release was written describing the objectives of the bank, the number of branches and its staff strength, and announcing the new name.

Spaces were bought in four national dailies, and advertisements announced the change of name.

A press facility visit for press, radio and TV was organised, this being a full-day programme of visits to all the key branches of the bank in Lagos. Hitherto, the media had been hostile to the bank. Now they became convinced of the bank's efficient operation. The name change gave the media a chance to take an inside look.

The new name, First Bank of Nigeria Limited, proved to be good marketing strategy for the bank gained new popularity with the people, and attracted new customers.

The employees were not overlooked. The authorised share capital was not fully subscribed and was sold to members of staff.

The PR department stepped up the changing of all the neon signs to coincide with the change of name and the corporate outdoor advertising on poster sites. All the bank's vehicles were repainted in the new livery which incorporated the new logo. The bank's stationery was quickly replaced.

Today, the First Bank of Nigeria prospers with 166 branches throughout the country, employing 7000 staff.

MAURITIUS SUGAR INDUSTRY

After 158 years of British rule, a good sports tradition is established in Mauritius. Soccer is the national game but volley-ball, athletics, basket-ball, badminton and tennis are also popular. Daily newspapers give much coverage to local sporting events, and there is a specialist weekly sports paper.

Workers in the sugar industry are provided with sports facilities which are among the best in the 720 square mile island. Mauritius has a multi-racial population of nearly a million, and sugar and its by-product molasses account for about 85 per cent of the island's visible exports. Sugar-cane covers 45 per cent of the area, and the industry is the largest employer. It employs some 70,000 people or 30 per cent of the gain-fully employed population. With these numbers, the importance of sport can be appreciated.

The responsibility for promoting sports among the sugar workers is that of the PRO attached to the sugar estate. The work of the estate PROs is co-ordinated by the Public Relations Office of the Sugar Industry (PROSI), and the PROs also belong to the Sugar Industry Public Relations Officers' Team (SIPROT). Public relations is therefore very well organised in the Mauritian sugar industry, PROSI dealing largely with external affairs and SIPROT dealing with internal affairs such as sports. PROSI was set up following the island's independence in 1968.

Playgrounds, club houses and sporting equipment are provided by the sugar companies, and employees and their families are encouraged to make full use of them. Sport has been a PR instrument for bringing together workers of different status and social background. They have been able to meet outside their site of work and share their talent. There have been two objectives: recreation and the establishment of better understanding and team spirit.

Sports have gained respect for the sugar industry because they have brought about multi-racial teams in a country where race or religion have tended to govern groupings in sports clubs.

The industry inter-estate tournaments have been popular for many years with high-quality games and an atmosphere of friendship.

PR is a continuous and changing process, and the attitudes and behaviour of people have been changing rapidly in recent years. This has been felt even on an island in the Indian Ocean, seemingly far away from the strife in other parts of the world. Perhaps the instant communication of TV has had its effect. Today the Mauritian estate PROs are facing up to new problems.

Just as we have football hooliganism in Britain so the rather cosy and paternalistic sports contests are becoming less idealistic in Mauritius. The attitude of spectators has changed and disrespectful remarks are made towards members of staff (as distinct from workers) who are playing in soccer teams. Industrial democracy seems to be creeping into Mauritius, no doubt encouraged by the Socialist Government which dislikes the autocratic and capitalist estate companies.

Some sugar estates complain about excessive outbidding from rival estates. To be a good footballer or athlete is an important factor when applying for a job. Some estates have bigger sports budgets than others. Prestige is at stake and there is competition fever. 'Winning by all means' has replaced 'participation for the pleasure it gives', but this is true of sport the world over. So, the Mauritian estate PROs are caught up in the dilemma of change. It is of course evidence of the swing from management paternalism (or downward communication) to the modern trend towards worker participation (or upward communication). Refusal to accept this has been at the heart of Britain's economic crisis of the 1980's let alone the problems of Mauritius.

ELECTIONS IN UGANDA

In a volatile situation such as the Uganda general elections of 1980, a pre-election information programme existed side by side with the propaganda efforts of the contesting political parties and their candidates.

Returning officers appeared – familiar in Western democracies but less familiar dignitaries in Uganda after a period of dictatorial rule. Electoral Commission officials used commercial air-time to tell viewers and listeners about dates and places for registration as voters. This was repeated in the Government press and in commercial weeklies. Posters were displayed. Throughout, the *credibility* of the elections was sought by emphasising the impartiality, freedom and fairness of the officials, the secrecy of the vote, and the duty of everyone to vote. Events showed what a difficult task this proved to be.

HEALTH CAMPAIGN IN KENYA

The Central Government Information Service conducted a campaign in 1980 to combat the spread of cholera. It did so through:

1. Announcements on national radio.
2. Press coverage, e.g. *Daily Nation, Standard,* Kiswahili press.
3. TV programmes.
4. Mobile cinemas in the rural areas.
5. Films shown at static cinemas.
6. Meetings at community centres when visiting speakers gave educational talks.
7. Poster displays.
8. Small hand-out booklets.

With this well-integrated campaign using all available media, Kenyans were encouraged to maintain high standards of hygiene in all public places and in the home. Insect control was explained. Wherever possible, pictures were used to clarify the message, thus overcoming problems of different language and illiteracy.

NIGERIAN DRIVING CHANGE-OVER

A major PR problem occurs when a country decides to change over from left-hand to right-hand driving. The Swedish campaign of some years ago is often taken as a model. Although the Nigerian exercise took place a few years ago it is well worth recounting here. The significance of such a programme is that the change has to take place *on one day,* and hazardous chaos would occur if the operation failed. To do this in a vast country like Nigeria with a population of more than 80 million and some cities a 1000 miles apart was not easy.

In effecting the change-over of traffic in Nigeria the Federal Govern-

ment information service, with the co-operation of the state information service, undertook a big task which was successful. Nigeria has
long been PR-conscious and the network of official information services
was a big asset.

The Federal Government, in trying to inform the people about the
new system, made use of demonstrations by traffic policemen, documentary films, posters, booklets, mobile film units, radio, TV, static
cinema and, of course, the extensive press which covers the country.

Just over a year before the actual change-over the Federal Government decided to bring about the change, and this was announced to all
the mass media which gave the story generous coverage.

Then during the second phase, a poster campaign was launched
through wall posters and hoardings. Posters were pasted near schools,
markets and on large poster sites beside main highways. Also, there was
a miniature poster campaign reproduced in the newspapers with a
slogan reiterating the date of the change-over.

About a year to the 'D' day, demonstrations were given by the
traffic police department of the Nigerian police. There were also conferences, debates and lectures to discuss the advantages and disadvantages
of this new system of driving. A radio campaign used a jingle which
advised both drivers and pedestrians about their roles in the change-
over. Most local radio stations also made versions of the jingle in the
local language and in the form which was most effective in the area.

The TV campaign used the poster theme, and a voice was dubbed in
explaining how everything would work and what every road-user was
expected to do to contribute to a smooth change-over.

During this run-up period the Federal and state ministries of information launched these campaigns while the Federal film units were used
to complement the activities of the local state film units which went
into the villages to educate the country folk. There were translated
versions of the films.

The film units used documentary films based on the posters, radio
and TV programmes, thus integrating the whole campaign. Posters were
also produced for the villages, picturing local characters as drivers and
pedestrians. Audio-visual aids were used to educate the illiterates.

In the cities, the media of TV, radio and cinema were complemented
by posters, and by the state information service lecturing market
women on pedestrian crossing in the new traffic change-over. In
Nigerian cities there are hundreds of market women with their stalls,
and thousands of people shopping in the street markets.

Use was also made of booklets printed by the ministries of information and by private individuals engaged in the transportation business. For example, driver-training schools printed a booklet showing the differences between the old and the new systems, and explaining the road sign changes. Large quantities of descriptive leaflets were also distributed. There was also a special postage stamp.

All the campaign efforts culminated in the successful launching of the new system on 'D-day'. Calmly, Nigeria — in spite of its well-known traffic jams in Lagos and elsewhere and dangerous highways between cities — adopted right-hand driving with little difficulty. The only accidents reported were of the normal types, and no major casualities resulted from the change-over.

This is a very good example of a well-planned PR programme, prepared well in advance and sustained over a sufficient length of time and with sufficient intensity and penetration to achieve the desired objective. This was tangible PR.

Sample Examination Paper - Public Relations

HIGHER STAGE

THE LONDON CHAMBER OF COMMERCE AND INDUSTRY

SPRING EXAMINATION 1981

WEDNESDAY 13 MAY—6 to 9 p.m..

PUBLIC RELATIONS

INSTRUCTIONS TO CANDIDATES
- *(a)* **First,** *read through* **all** *the questions and do not attempt to answer any until you understand the scope and limitations of the questions you have selected.*
- *(b)* *Question 1 is compulsory.* **Four** *other questions may be answered.*
- *(c)* *All questions carry equal marks.*
- *(d)* *Questions need not be answered in numerical order, but all five answers must be clearly and correctly numbered.*

1.   COMPULSORY QUESTION
You are writing *both* a news release for newspapers and a feature article for a magazine. Choose your own subject, and demonstrate the different techniques required for opening a news release and a feature article by writing a suitable short opening paragraph for each.

2.   The definition known as 'The Mexican Statement' reads as follows: 'PUBLIC RELATIONS PRACTICE is the art and social science of analysing trends, predicting their consequences, counselling organisation leaders, and implementing planned pro-

grammes of action which will serve both the organisation's and the public interest.'

What is especially important about this definition, and how does it differ from any other with which you are familiar?

3.   Why is it necessary to brief a photographer on exactly what to photograph? Give an example, real or imaginary, of what could go wrong if you failed to work closely with the photographer, giving him precise instructions.

4.   In spite of frequent editorial criticism of PR, why does the press in practice find PR sources of information genuinely useful?

5.   Many employee newspapers are nowadays printed by offset-litho—sometimes by web-offset-litho—instead of by letterpress. How do you account for this change, and what advantages does the offset-litho process offer to the editor and designer of an employee newspaper?

6.   Public relations consultancy services may be provided by:
(a)   an advertising agency with a PR department;
(b)   a PR consultancy which is a subsidiary of an advertising agency;
(c)   an independent PR consultancy.
What are the advantages and disadvantages of each to you as a client, assuming that you require only a PR service?

7.   If you were responsible for PR for a voluntary organisation or charity with limited funds for your PR programme, how could you increase your PR activities through sponsorship by commercial companies or by joint PR schemes with other organisations of various kinds?

8.   Throughout the world national PR institutes and associations have introduced codes of professional practice. Allowing for special national requirements, what principles are common to most codes of PR practice?

9.   Describe some of the special communication problems which exist in developing countries, but which do not exist in Western countries.

10. How can the BBC External Services assist the PR practitioner, and how do they differ from the overseas radio services of the Central Office of Information?

11. Documentary films, various kinds of slide presentation, and video cassettes are visual aids which provide valuable PR media. Describe the special characteristics, advantages, disadvantages and PR uses of these three kinds of visual aid.

12. Give brief explanations of each of the following:

(a)	Wire service	*(f)*	OB
(b)	Embargo	*(g)*	IRN
(c)	Special correspondent	*(h)*	CERP
(d)	Features Editor	*(i)*	PA
(e)	Lobby correspondent	*(j)*	AP

13. If you were planning to take a party of journalists on a visit to a factory about 100 miles away from the starting point, what additional arrangements and expenses would be involved compared with those for holding a press reception at a hotel which was easily accessible to invited journalists?

14. What research techniques can be used to
(a) appreciate the situation before planning a PR programme and
(b) test the progress and results of a PR programme?

Further Reading

Advertising Law, R. C. Lawson, Macdonald & Evans, Plymouth, 1978.

Advertising Made Simple, (Third Edition), Frank Jefkins, Heinemann Made Simple Books, London, 1982.

Assessing the Effectiveness of Advertising, Jack Potter and Mark Lovell, Business Books, London, 1975.

Business Analysis for Marketing Managers, L. A. Rogers, Heinemann, London, 1981.

Effective Press Relations and House Journal Editing, (Second Edition), Frank Jefkins, Frank Jefkins School of Public Relations, Croydon, 1980.

Fundamentals and Practice of Marketing, The, John Wilmshurst, Heinemann, London, 1980.

Introduction to Marketing, John Frain, Macdonald & Evans, Plymouth, 1981.

Management Guide to Market Research, James M. Livingstone, Macmillan, London, 1977.

Marketing: An Introductory Text, (Third Edition), Michael J. Baker, Macmillan, London, 1981.

Marketing Made Simple, B. Howard Elvy, Heinemann Made Simple Books, London, 1980.

Marketing Research, Tony Proctor and Marilyn A. Stone, Macdonald & Evans, Plymouth, 1978.

Marketing Theory & Practice, Ed. Michael J. Baker, Macmillan, London, 1979.

Marketing Today, (Second Edition), R. V. Chapman, Intertext Books, Glasgow, 1973.

Planned Press and Public Relations, Frank Jefkins, Intertext, Glasgow, 1977.

Practice of Public Relations, The, Ed. Wilfred Howard, Heinemann, London, 1982.

Printing Reproduction Pocket Pal, (Fourth Edition), The Advertising Agency Production Association, London, 1979.

Public Relations, Frank Jefkins, Macdonald & Evans, Plymouth, 1980.

Public Relations for Marketing Management, Frank Jefkins, Macmillan, London, 1978.

Public Relations Made Simple, Frank Jefkins, Heinemann Made Simple Books, London, 1982.

Index